RESPONSIBLE BUREAUCRACY

RESPONSIBLE BUREAUCRACY
A Study of the Swiss Civil Service

BY

CARL JOACHIM FRIEDRICH

and

TAYLOR COLE

ASSOCIATE PROFESSOR OF GOVERNMENT AT LOUISIANA STATE UNIVERSITY;
SOMETIME TUTOR IN HISTORY, GOVERNMENT, AND
ECONOMICS AT HARVARD UNIVERSITY

NEW YORK / RUSSELL & RUSSELL

TO

A. N. HOLCOMBE

PREFACE TO THE FIRST STUDY

This study would have been impossible without the loyal coöperation of the Swiss Federal Personnel Office and its Director, Dr. J. Oetiker, who furnished an admirable collection of unprinted material. Professor William Rappard of the University of Geneva also lent his help in this connection. Valuable assistance was also received from Professor Brooks of Swarthmore College, from Professors Elliott, Wright and Emerson of Harvard University and from Professor Bryan of Louisiana State University who kindly read parts of the manuscript and offered critical suggestions.

In any coöperative enterprise it is always difficult to attribute any particular part to one of the co-authors. Yet it may be worth pointing out that Mr. Cole has been concerned primarily with the detailed analysis of the material furnished by the Federal Personnel Office, while Mr. Friedrich has undertaken the general analysis. The Introduction, Chapters I and II and the Conclusion are for that reason primarily Mr. Friedrich's work, while Chapters III–V are primarily Mr. Cole's. Mr. Cole also prepared the bibliography and the index.

Two persons cannot become one, and a certain unevenness is therefore inevitable in a book written by two people. We are prepared, however, to bear together the responsibility for each other's shortcomings.

C. J. F.
T. C.

TABLE OF CONTENTS

14090

ABBREVIATIONS

PUBLICATIONS

A.S., *Amtliche Sammlung der Bundesgesetze und Verordnungen der schweizerischen Eidgenossenschaft.*

R.O., *Recueil officiel des lois.*

A.B. St., *Amtliches stenographisches Bulletin der Bundesversammlung.*

V.E.R., *Bundesgesetz über das Dienstverhältnis der Bundesbeamten, Verhandlungen der eidgen. Räte* (1927).

R.S., *Revue syndicale Suisse.*

ASSOCIATIONS OF PERSONNEL

V.S.Z.B., Verband schweizerischer Zollbeamten.

A.S.F.T.T., Association suisse des fonctionnaires des télégraphes et téléphones.

S.S.M.C., Société suisse des mécaniciens des chemins de fer.

S.S.F.P., Société suisse des fonctionnaires postaux.

U.F.P.F., Union fédérative du personnel fédéral et des entreprises publiques de transport.

S.E.V., Fédération suisse des cheminots.

S.B.P., Société suisse des buralistes postaux.

G.C.V., Fédération chrétienne du personnel des entreprises publiques de transport de la Suisse.

S.G., Schweizerischer Gewerkschaftsbund.

F.S.E.D., Fédération suisse des employés des douanes.

RESPONSIBLE BUREAUCRACY

INTRODUCTION

The man in the street is an enemy of the political scientist, but the politician and the political propagandist are far worse. It is an almost hopeless task to cleanse words, which are essential for our work, of the layers of surface associations which deft orators have heaped upon them. Bureaucracy is one of those words. "Bureaucracy is the term usually applied to a system of government the control of which is so completely in the hand of officials that their power jeopardizes the liberty of ordinary citizens," writes Harold Laski in an able article on this subject, without ever using the word again in that sense.[1] And indeed bureaucracy has never been and probably never will be a system of government, whatever that may mean. Nor is the emphasis so much upon the officials, as it is upon the impersonal bureau, which has led Frenchmen to coin the poignant expression *M. le Bureau* when they wish to emphasize the lack of human reactions which characterizes men when they become engulfed by the fixed rules and established routine of a public function. In its reference to the rule of the bureau lies the value of this word, so misshapen from a linguistic point of view.

We are here confronted with a basic and natural trend inherent in social activities of man. Wherever it becomes necessary to organize large numbers of people for the accomplishment of a common purpose, success depends upon the extent to which each member of the organization can be brought to subordinate his other objectives to the objective of the organization. Just as we criticize a friend for being late for dinner because we do not feel any profound sympathy for the thoughts or activity which delayed him, as we would not do if we felt such sympathy and therefore appreciated the urgency of these thoughts or activities, so also we condemn as bureaucratic the delay and lack of response from the representative of a large organization, whether public or private, because we do not sympathize with or do not understand at all the ultimate objective or combination of objectives which this organization is supposed to realize. In such stituations the word bureaucracy is widely used to decry acts of officials which, while required for the sake of "efficiency," are cumbersome and irritating to the person subjected to them. This simply means that often the objectives of an organization clash with those of an individual or other

[1] *Encyclopedia of the Social Sciences,* Vol. III (1930), p. 70.

organization dealing with it. To defy the action of the offending official as bureaucratic, even though it be not only justified but desirable from the point of view of his office, is a most common occurrence. A simple example will illustrate this point. If you wish to collect the money which has been sent to you through a postal money order of the United States Post Office, you are supposed to establish your identity to the teller before the official is to give you your money. If, upon request, you produce a letter addressed to yourself, you will at many post offices receive your money. From the point of view of the post office, the official should reject this evidence. In fact, he should reject every variety of evidence which you may have found, together with the postal money order itself. But insistence upon this point by a postal official would produce violent charges of "bureaucratic inefficiency," as I have myself heard them made by otherwise quite sensible people. All of us have encountered such situations, and all of us have had similar reactions when encountering them. It is upon this vast body of common grievances that the popular orator can draw when he sets out to decry the "evils of bureaucracy." And since the government is by far the largest single organization of this variety, the cumulative effect of such experiences has in the mind of most people prevented any realization of the fact that a church, a trade union or a business corporation tends to show the same characteristics.[2] In connection with the party, the problem has begun to be studied in considerable detail by Charles E. Merriam and others.[3] The American people with their genius for suggestive imagery have introduced the phrase "party machine." This imagery tends, however, to obscure the similarity of the growth of party "machines" and the vast organizations which "absolute" monarchs in continental Europe built up during the seventeenth and eighteenth centuries. It tends even more to let people forget the analogy which these developments represent to the organized bureaucracy which the popes forged out of the shattered

[2] See for the church the brilliant essay of Carl Schmitt, *Katholozismus und politische Form.* The bureaucratic tendencies of modern parties, whether authoritarian or anti-authoritarian in their platforms, have been set forth with striking persuasiveness by Robert Michels in *Political Parties—A Sociological Study of the Oligarchical Tendencies of Modern Democracy* (Transl. by Eden & Cedar Paul, 1915). His point of view is developed more broadly in his new *Corso di Sociologia Politica* (1927).

[3] See his *New Aspects of Politics* (1925) and Harold F. Gosnell's able case study, *Boss Platt and his New York Machine* (1924).

remnants of the Roman Empire, thus giving to European civilization its first fully developed bureaucratic hierarchy.[4] But the objections which are nowadays popularized under the epithet "bureaucracy" were then attacked as tyranny. Tyranny suggests power without authority; and since all authority was held to be from God, it is not surprising that the first successful effort in this direction should have been undertaken by him who could claim, although not without being continually challenged in the conclusions he drew from it, to be the representative of God on earth. And though the Holy Roman Emperors were unsuccessful in putting through their opposing counter-claims,[5] the independent city-states, as well as the territorial princes, one by one, undertook the organization of such hierarchies within their more limited domain. This is not the place for tracing the long history of this eventful struggle, even in outline.[6] But what deserves to be pointed out here is the fact itself that the great modern bureaucracies were developed by the monarchs of the seventeenth and eighteenth centuries. As a result, the fierce struggle waged against these monarchs over the control of these bureaucracies partly fed upon arousing popular indignation against the bureaucracy itself, although nobody who in this fashion attacked the hierarchies has ever been known to suggest any substitute for them. This natural tendency of all those engaged in the fight for the victory of democracy to decry the bureaucrats as servants of the prince (which they were in the eighteenth and nineteenth centuries in an ever more limited degree,[7]) has led to constructing a specious antithesis between democracy and bureaucracy and a

[4] See J. Haller, *Papsttum und Kirchenreform* (1903), I, 26 and elsewhere. Furthermore Albert Hauck, *Kirchengeschichte Deutschlands*, IV. The legal aspects of this problem are well discussed in Carl Schmitt, *Die Diktatur—Von den Anfängen des modernen Souveränitätsgedankens bis zum proletarischen Klassenkampf* (1928), pp. 43 ff. where Haller and Hauck are cited.

[5] Considerable beginnings, like the *Reichskammergericht* (1495), cannot alter the general conclusion.

[6] The literature is very extensive, though somewhat scattered, and digested only by countries. See, however, the bibliographies contained in *The Civil Service in the Modern State* (1930) and, for interpretation, the suggestive survey by L. D. White introducing this collection of documents, as well as C. J. Friedrich's introductory essay to "The German and Prussian Civil Service" in the same volume.

[7] Note Frederick the Great's famous dictum: "I am the first servant of the state."

widespread belief that bureaucracy was necessarily "irresponsible" and therefore undemocratic.[8] But inasmuch as the social and economic forces of modern industrial civilization depend for their smooth functioning upon an ever-increasing "public business," able and far-sighted politicians, wishing to stress the positive value of such activities have found a more sympathetic substitute for the many-eyed monster, bureaucracy, in calling it the civil service. Civil service! A nice word, the pleasant associations of which facilitate the maintenance of all that is essential in a bureaucracy[9] without stressing its dubious past. But as often happens, the considerations which recommend this word for practical politics render its use for systematic and analytical purposes questionable. In the first place, it refers distinctly to a specific legal order (England, the United States). In the second place, it is limited in its application to the governmental bureaucracies. In the third place, it applies only to a late phase of governmental bureaucracy, namely, the democratic phase.[10] Therefore we have to maintain, on account of a clear terminology, that the civil service is only one form of bureaucracy; but we have to maintain also that it is indeed some form of bureaucracy.

Obviously, it will be our contention, then, that no necessary antithesis exists between bureaucracy and responsible government. It may be well to say a few words here concerning responsibility. Because of the peculiar conditions under which the English government developed, there is a widespread belief in English-speaking countries to the effect that a clear line of distinction can be drawn and must be drawn between political responsibility of the government enforceable through cabinet responsibility or general elections on the one hand, and personal responsibility of the agents of the government, the civil servant (or servants of the crown), enforceable through the courts.[11] Such a distinction, which historically speaking is a feudal heritage, is totally

[8] Two books by Ramsay Muir, *Peers and Bureaucrats* (1910) and *How Britain is Governed—A Critical Analysis of Modern Developments in the British System of Government* (1930), present this essentially superficial view most ably and persuasively, in the tradition of political pamphleteering.

[9] The corresponding German catchword is *Beamstentum*, while the French use *service public* and *fonctionnaire*.

[10] For greater elaboration of this point see below, particularly Chap. i.

[11] A matter of extensive discussion, it will be recalled. The most interesting recent book on this matter concerning England is W. A. Robson, *Justice and Administrative Law* (1928).

inadmissible under modern conditions. The modern legalized government can be made responsible to the courts for the acts of every member of its organization. It is a minor problem whether this function is exercised by the regular courts or by specialized "administrative" courts; and the solution of the problem depends upon technical expediency, historical tradition and the organization of the courts of the particular government. As compared to this instrument for bringing about responsibility of a given bureaucracy, the advisory committee which Laski[12] advocates, though useful in itself, is of very minor importance. As has often been remarked, this responsibility of the government (the state) as a corporate whole has also a very wholesome effect upon the personnel of the service, for it increases their efficiency and initiative, if they do not need to tremble at every moment concerning their personal fortune when taking action under equivocal legal provisions.

But there is another problem of considerable importance which deserves consideration in the light of historical facts. It may well be urged that a responsible bureaucracy has usually been the result of superimposing responsibility through the establishment of parliamentary government, *after* the hierarchy had been built up by unlimited autocracy. That certainly has been the course of events in most European countries, at least on the Continent.[13] Some notable exceptions, like Italy, are reaping the harvest of having placed the cart of parliamentary government before the horse of a well-developed bureaucracy in the form of a dictatorial régime which promises to remedy this deficiency by a radical reorganization of the entire government, whose outstanding characteristic is the emphasis upon hierarchical structure.[14] Is it impossible, then, to develop a bureaucratic structure within a responsible government? Must a state pass through the smithy of dictatorial government in order to acquire the basic structure? This, it seems, is one of the most anxious questions which the

[12] *Loc. cit.* Such advisory committees have existed on the continent of Europe for centuries, for example in commerce; the French *Conseil National Economique* is an outgrowth of such an advisory committee, established under Henry IV.

[13] The development of the Interstate Commerce Commission in its relation to the great railroad corporations in the United States and England can be viewed from the same angle when considered with regard to their bureaucracy.

[14] See J. Marschak, "Der Korporative und der hierarchische Gedanke im Faschismus" in *Archiv für Sozialwissenschaft und Sozialpolitik*, 52, 695 ff. and Robert Michels, *Sozialismus und Fascismus in Italien*, Vol. II.

political scientist may be called upon to answer at the present time. And it is this question which in part led us to the investigation of the Swiss civil service. For here we are told is a full-fledged responsible bureaucracy, grown in the womb of distinctly responsible government. Is it true? And if it is true, how is this bureaucracy organized? An answer to these questions will be attempted in the following pages.

But there is another question of hardly lesser urgency. Can a fully organized bureaucracy flourish under responsible government? Or must it necessarily deteriorate, as many observers of French and German developments are inclined to believe? The onslaught of powerful groups of citizens, held together by a community of interests, economic, professional and otherwise, challenges the superiority of the government in claiming the allegiance of its members.[15] In recent years, this development has been given a very novel turn by the formation of associations among the civil servants themselves; in other words among the very people upon whom the government rests.[16] Is this development bound to lead to a dissolution of the government? Or are there possible ways of re-integrating these disintegrating forces? Switzerland has a vigorous and influential trade-union movement among its bureaucrats. It will be our task to examine the relation which it bears to the government and to indicate the trend of its future development.

But before a fruitful inquiry into the facts can be undertaken, a more detailed analysis of the concept of bureaucracy is essential, if we

---

[15] See the ever-increasing literature on pluralism, so-called, in its many forms, ranging from Duguit through Laski to Cole. The economic council movement represents an attempt to realign these groups with the government, and, from our point of view, to integrate their bureaucracies with that of the government.

[16] This trend has received particular attention in modern France. Maxime Leroy, *Les transformations de la puissance public* (1907), Georges Cahen, *Les fonctionnaires* (1911) and Alexandre Lefas, *L'État et les fonctionnaires* (1913) did, among others, the pioneer work in setting forth the sociological and political facts, while Léon Duguit and Maurice Hauriou attempted in their well-known comprehensive treatises on public law to interpret these developments from a legal standpoint. These trends are ably summarized and their acceleration since the war is set forth by Walter R. Sharp, ''The Political Bureaucracy of France since the War'' in *The American Political Science Review*, XII, 301 ff. (1928). A special study of ''Trade-Unionism among Civil Servants in France'' (with special reference to the postal service) was made by Professor J. A. Burdine under my direction, and, although this essay has remained unpublished, I desire to make acknowledgment to it here, because it greatly enriched my comprehension of detailed facts and particular problems.

are going to reach at least a certain measure of systematic clarity and some precision in our conclusions. This analysis will necessarily have a certain pragmatic hue, because the final and basic categories upon which the analysis proceeds are only rather dimly perceived. But that is perhaps an unavoidable shortcoming in a field which is new and relatively unexplored. Certain facetious persons, who are fond of telling us that the philosopher is like a blind man looking in the dark for a hat which is not there, only prove that they have assumed the rôle of the magician of old by trying to persuade us that the hat is not there, simply because they have not found it. For it may in truth be said that the lover of knowledge is indeed like a blind man looking in a dark room for a hat that *may or may not* be there. And whether you call him a philosopher, as the Greeks did, or a scientist, as we do, matters little. For after an ardent search for understanding, no matter how striking its results, he will still feel as Thomas of Aquinas did after constructing his gigantic system of knowledge, by concluding: *Ignoramus, Ignorabimus.*

CHAPTER I

THE SYSTEMATIC CONCEPT OF BUREAUCRACY

The much quoted epigram of Pope, "for forms of government let fools contest, whate'er is best administer'd is best," is happily adapted to after-dinner speeches because it leaves us at sea. It assumes that there is a standard for evaluating administration, but it does not tell us what it is. No doubt its duplicity and evasiveness have contributed a good deal to the popularity of this apothegm. It still reflects the attitude of multitudes of people toward government, particularly business people, and it probably always will. Perhaps this is due to the fact that, beneath its apparent indistinctness, there is hidden a suggestion concerning a fundamental antithesis of political outlook. There are those who tend to emphasize the structure or form of organization, and there are others who emphasize the men who conduct it. Nobody of much importance has ever probably interpreted political events completely in terms of one of these alternatives and entirely excluded the other, but the distinction is there and the shift of emphasis is marked in different writers. And the varying interpretation of what is has led to varying assertions as to what ought to be, just as much as varying hunches and preferences for what ought to be have led to varying interpretations of what is. All this is well known enough and hardly deserves being repeated here, if it were not for the fact that many writers have tended to separate writers, thinkers and talkers with reference to this distinction, although in reality it would be hard to find people who came even near one or the other of these extremes, when examined thoroughly and without any urgent desire to classify them.

But the distinction is valuable in focusing attention upon the fact that we are more likely to reach a real understanding of the facts before us, if we get away as far as possible from any considerations of what should be done. In considering bureaucracy, to be specific, let us get away from trying to *decide* whether we want one, or whether we like one, and turn to the question of why and under what circumstances people have wanted one and of what its characteristics consist.

We noted already that political science with other social sciences suffers from the fact that its subject matter forms part and parcel of the talk of men in the street. Consequently, all its basic categories are tainted by the value judgments which are associated with them in the minds of men for the purposes of action. Therefore, writers of profundity and knowledge have demanded that we throw out discussions of value.[1] But discussions of value cannot be thrown out of political science, because the processes with the interpretation of which we are concerned are shot through with value judgments; and it is essential for us to comprehend the meaning of these value judgments. But it is one thing to discuss values as to what they are and what they mean, and another to assert their validity. This point is so obvious that it needs constant emphasizing (for obvious points are usually neglected by acute, profound and sophisticated thinkers). However, the question which we put at the outset, "What constitutes a good administration?", shows that the various processes which are directed toward the realization of values are themselves subject to value judgments in terms of their own intrinsic excellence. This observation suggests that a distinction deserves to be drawn between final and intermediate values and standards of value. Political and social theory are constantly advancing value judgments of this intermediate variety, because the very statement of how a certain kind of activity is conditioned amounts to a judgment as to when it will work well and when it will not do so. The fruitfulness of this distinction seems to me considerable for political science. It palliates, if it does not eliminate, the acrimonious discussions about the problem whether or not values form a part of political science. The answer here suggested is that they do, but that final values constitute a marginal problem of political theory and that they indicate one of the points where political science, like every other science, rests upon speculative philosophy.[2] The ultimate solution lies, in my opinion, in the direction suggested by Whitehead's metaphysics which gives to values universal significance. That "value is . . . the intrinsic reality of an event" and that "value arises because there is now a real togetherness of the ideal aspects, as in thought, with the actual aspects, as in process of occurrence"[3] are

[1] Many writers of the so-called pragmatic school, too numerous to mention, in this country. Furthermore, Max Weber and Vilfredo Pareto.

[2] It seems to me the major contribution of Mr. W. Y. Elliott's *The Pragmatic Revolt in Politics* (1928) lies in its emphasis upon this connection by tracing out various problems which are rooted in this twilight zone between clearly intermediate and clearly final values.

[3] *Science and the Modern World* (1925), pp. 136 and 154 *et. seq.* Max Scheler's searching critical study of Kantian Ethics, *Der Formalismus in der Ethik und die*

propositions which point in the right direction. This is nowhere as apparent as it is political science.

What interests us here, then, is first of all that certain people tend to emphasize the structure and form of organization because they attach considerable "value" to certain forms and certain structural devices, while others tend to emphasize the human beings involved because they attach considerable "value" to them.[4] Both are, of course, important. But it is the task of the scientist to try to find out under which conditions each of these determinants operates, and to formulate working hypotheses which seem plausible in the light of the available facts. It would seem possible, logically, then to evaluate a government both in terms of its structure and in terms of its personnel. It would, furthermore, be possible to investigate the extent to which a given national group has tended to evaluate its government in those terms. All these are important and valuable topics for political science. But it is my belief that they are too big for the mouth of the political scientist, who seems to be just about growing his second-year molar. The problem has been indicated in its magnitude, in order to set the stage for the discussion of a more limited aspect of it. For the problem of bureaucracy, and particularly that of administrative personnel, must itself be treated in terms of this antithesis. As the organization increases in size, the problem of securing and maintaining high-grade personnel can only be solved in terms of well-defined standards of norms, which involve the recognition of recurrent, normal situations.

It should be stated at once, however, that the problem of bureaucracy is not identical with that of the administrative personnel, in the legal sense of the word "administrative." The antithesis which

---

materiale Wertethik, expresses a similar point of view in the strictly ethical realm.

[4] It may be remarked in passing that an emphasis upon structure and form in turn depends upon stressing those elements in a series of events which they have in common, while an emphasis upon the individual human beings involves stressing those aspects of an event which render it singular and unique. The formulation of Grotius, *De Jure Belli ac Pacis*, I, 8 is striking: " . . . causae cur populus jus totum imperandi a se abdicet, aliique tradat, puta quia in periculum vitae adductus alia lege qui se defendat reperire non potest; . . ." All claims of "absolutism" were put upon some such grounds. At this point the inescapable intertwining of value judgments and the interpretation of facts, the moment you venture upon being "practical," is quite apparent.

political agitators have constructed between the body of legislators and the body of administrators, a distinction drawn for very specific political purposes, must under no circumstances be considered absolutely relevant. For the problem here in hand, this distinction is not relevant. A bureaucracy may exist and has existed in legislative bodies,[5] for the object with the realization of which a certain group is occupied has no direct relation to its bureaucratization.

The much used distinction between legislation and administration, although adequate for the analysis of certain problems, is quite misleading with regard to others. As it is commonly used when people talk of the legislative and the executive power, it covers two distinctions which need to be treated separately. On the one hand there is the distinction between legislative and administrative functions, and on the other there is the distinction between legislative and administrative agencies (or authorities).[6] Reflection suggests that the essential notion for distinguishing legislative from administrative *functions* may be found in the theoretical distinction between general and specific decisions, i.e., between setting norms and taking measures, a distinction which has been developed with particular nicety by Adolf Merkl[7] in his attempt to lay a foundation for a theory of administration. M. Hauriou's notion of an administrative measure (*mesure administrative*) is very similar, particularly when taken together with his notion of an official action (*action d'office*)[8] which is not clearly distinguishable from it. Hauriou seems to base this distinction upon his antecedent distinction between an administrative function and an administrative power. But this seems itself not very well-defined. When contrasting an administrative power with an administrative function[9] he seems to think of the latter in terms of normal situations; while, when he comes to the discussion of an administrative function by itself, he includes under it even the reëstablishment of public order.[10]

---

[5] Note as an example the English parliament in the eighteenth century.

[6] If these two distinctions could not be separated, a discussion like that contained in J. P. Comer's *Legislative Functions of National Administrative Authorities* (1927), which deals with delegated legislation in the United States, would be meaningless. That it is not, an examination of it will show.

[7] In his *Allgemeine Verwaltungslehre* (1927).

[8] *Précis de Droit Administratif et de Droit Public* (x. ed., 1921), pp. 19 ff.

[9] *Ibid.*, p. 16.

[10] *Ibid.*, p. 21.

It seems that Hauriou is trying to introduce this distinction in order to escape from the otherwise inescapable conclusion that, (theoretically) in facing clearly the technicality of a given measure exclusively in terms of its objective, you are obliged to admit its kinship to dictatorship.[11] This may be serviceable for practical (legal) purposes, but for scientific explanation it will not do. The theoretical interpretation of legislative and administrative functions in terms of general and specific decisions will, on the other hand, hardly ever do for practical (legal) purposes, because the two are two aspects of the same process of deciding in group life, as in the life of the individual human being.[12]

After this distinction has been made, the distinction between legislative and administrative agencies (or authorities) becomes a matter of convenience, based upon so-called "pure" matter of fact. If we find two agencies or sets of agencies, *primarily* engaged respectively in legislative functions and in administrative functions, as just interpreted, we *may* call them legislative and administrative agencies respectively. But it is a matter of convenience which of course includes tradition. Since no body of men ever has been in fact limited to either of our two functions, nor to any other one function as defined by various writers, there is at present no apparent reason why we should assume that such a body of men will ever come into existence. Since no criterion has ever been given thus far beyond the criterion used for distinguishing legislative and administrative functions,[13] we may just as well avoid falling into the vicious circle characteristic of all legal "definitions" running on the following model: "Legislation is

[11] To have pointed this out with great lucidity is the merit of Carl Schmitt's epochal *Die Diktatur* (1928). A discussion of some of the problems which it raised will appear elsewhere. See in the meanwhile the brief remarks toward the end of my article, "Dictatorship in Germany?" in *Foreign Affairs*, October, 1930.

[12] This point will be developed more fully in a forthcoming article, "The Restatement of the Doctrine of the Separation of Powers," by C. J. Friedrich.

[13] There has been in recent years an increasing literature on this subject, particularly in this country, where lawyers have attempted more or less successfully to grapple with the legal implications of such organizations as the Interstate Commerce Commission. Acute observations on the effect of the doctrine of separation of powers in the United States are offered by John Dickinson in *Administrative Justice and the Supremacy of Law* (1927), pp. 33 ff. and elsewhere. Dickinson points out the very necessary distinction between the doctrine of separation of *powers* and a theory of administrative and judicial *functions*. See, for a recent comprehensive discussion of the entire complex of questions, Carl Schmitt, *Verfassungslehre* (1928), pp. 126 ff. and 182 ff.

what the Legislative Power does—The Legislative Power is that power which legislates"—and so forth and so on.[14] If an attempt is to be made to distinguish between the body of men called the legislative power and the body of men called the executive power, the problem to which we would have to address ourselves is the problem whether these two functions, viz., the making of general decisions and the making of specific decisions, do through their own nature tend to impose a particular type of organization upon any body of men who are there to make primarily one kind of such decisions. I believe that even a cursory examination will show that this is so, and that the making of general decisions tends to produce an assembly form of organization, while the making of specific decisions tends to produce an hierarchical form. But this is not meant to say that an hierarchically organized body of men may not make any number of general decisions, nor that an associationally organized body of men may not make any number of specific decisions.[15] But it does indicate why one is justified in choosing a body of men primarily concerned with administrative functions in a study of bureaucracy.

We have referred already to the hostile attitude toward bureaucracy which the public has inherited from the past because of the historical fact that a large bureaucracy was built up by the great "absolute" monarchs in continental Europe. But the permanence of this hostility is also, in part, due to the fact the general public comes into very frequent contact with the administrative agents of the government. The cumulative displeasure which is felt by all about the inevitable instances of interference coalesces into a resentment which finds ready expression in several distinct stereotypes,[16] of which bureaucracy is perhaps the most potent and fully developed. This is shown by the vast mass of *satirical* and humorous folk-lore on this subject,[17] no less than by the strong tendency of all popular govern-

[14] Felix Frankfurter's otherwise suggestive little book, *The Public and Its Government* (1930), is marred by this variety of confusion.

[15] For a more elaborate statement and illustration of this point, see the article referred to in footnote (6) on p. 3 above.

[16] See Walter Lippman, *Public Opinion* (1929), Parts I and III, and the suggestive application by Stuart A. Rice, *Quantitative Methods in Politics* (1928), Chap. v, which, unfortunately, does not include a bureaucrat.

[17] France and Germany, for obvious reasons, are particularly rich in it. "Der Bureaukrat tut seine Pflicht von neun bis eins, mehr tut er nicht" ("The bureaucrat fulfills his duty from nine till one, but never more") is just one of the

ments to keep the salaries of government employees low. The concept bureaucracy has the advantage of implying clearly this antagonism. It emphasizes that any large body of men organized for common action will tend to act in a way which will appear arbitrary and therefore irrational to the outsider, although the particular act may be completely rational when looked at from within. This is of course as true of other organizations as it is of the government and its agents, the officials.[18]

But there is a distinction. It is the essence of *governmental* bureaucracy to be *neutral* with regard to the interests and opinions which divide the community. This is not to say that every or even any bureaucrat is in fact neutral, but it is their tendency to be that. Naturally, public services are composed of human beings with opinions and prejudices of their own (although some writers have at times forgot that), yet the neutrality of the whole remains of central significance. This conclusion is not altered by the observation that the public services participate in the making of legislation by drafting most of the statutes. For this activity is, for technical reasons, best carried on by a group of persons whose experiences with governmental activity in the various fields predestine them to be counselors in regard to proposed changes in these activities.

It was keen insight into the actual workings of the modern state that made the defenders of the constitutional monarchy in continental Europe insist that a modern public service, an organized bureaucracy, depends for its working efficiency and integrity upon the existence of a neutral "power,"[19] although as usual the attempt of using the concept of a neutral power for immediate political purposes prevented its accurate formulation as a limiting concept. But for our present purpose this rather rudimentary idea of the monarch as a neutral

---

more or less sarcastic utterances which the busy professional and business man indulges in, when thinking of his more leisurely brother. The immortal satire of Georges Courteline, *Messieurs les Ronds-du-cuir*, is the apogee of French wit on the same subject.

[18] See above, pp. 2 ff. C. J. Friedrich has indicated a few aspects of this important parallel in an article entitled ''Das Berufsbeamtentum in den Vereinigten Staaten'' in *Beamtenjahrbuch*, XVI, 3 (1930), in so far as business corporations in this country are concerned.

[19] See particularly Benjamin Constant, *Reflexions sur les constitutions et les garanties* (1814).

power will suffice. For once ultimate and complete control was taken from the monarch and divided between him and a popularly elected parliament, such a system resulted in a neutral sphere occupied by the king between the executive power of his cabinet and the legislative power of the popularly elected chambers. This neutral sphere stimulated the growth of a fully organized public service considerably in German states no less than in France. In all these countries great difficulties have been encountered since the dualism of kings and parliaments has been swept away and a unified parliamentary control has been substituted. It deserves notice that the shortcomings of many parliamentary democracies in this respect are analogous to those of an absolute monarchy. In both cases an excessive integration of political power exists. Such accumulation of final control is valuable in periods of stress and emergency, but it tends to be abused in periods of relative stability.[20] In France since the establishment of the Third Republic, in Germany, Prussia, Austria and other states which have adopted new constitutions the problem of how to create the necessary neutral sphere required for the maintenance of a fully organized governmental bureaucracy has been a matter of grave concern. To some extent the public opinion of these countries has provided such a neutral sphere, and how powerful a factor it may be is shown by the developments in Switzerland during the last fifty years, the result of which is discussed in the subsequent chapters.[21] But the effectiveness of public opinion in regard to technical matters is limited to small communities. The example of France shows that the effectiveness of public opinion gradually wears off as the public becomes "sophisticated" in the face of inefficiency, of abuse and even corruption. The question then naturally arises whether a neutral sphere can be organized either legally or constitutionally. The American Civil Service Commissions represent efforts in this direction. It is, however, well-known that the independence of these commissions is not sufficient at the present time. Probably the focus of their competences is too narrow also. The German presidential office, modeled on the lines of the position of the constitutional monarch, is another attempt. To be sure, the German president cannot act without the counter-signature of

[20] This is often just as true of democracies with a rigid system of "separation of powers."

[21] This point is brought out with striking emphasis by Robert C. Brooks, *Civic Training in Switzerland* (1930).

the responsible minister. But neither can he be forced to act contrary to his convictions. The comparatively long term of office and the high age at which men are likely to be elected (which makes a second term rather immaterial to them) are favorable circumstances for the development and maintenance of a neutrality above party, creed and interest. The very fact that such a president has to work with cabinets of different party affiliation will render him neutral and detached. Now the Swiss Federal Council as a whole has acquired a somewhat similar position, as the custom of long tenure and virtual independence from the legislative chambers has developed. Naturally, such institutional safeguards of a "neutral" sphere are never more than approximations. But as such they are significant.

There is, however, another form of securing independence of the bureaucracy, namely, permanent tenure of the individual office-holder. It is well-known that this method has been employed in all modern states to a very considerable extent,[22] whatever their constitutional structure.[23] But there has been a tendency, for various reasons, to overemphasize the advantages of such an arrangement which is easily made subservient to the inherent tendency of the incumbents of such offices to "privatize" their positions, to insist upon having the emoluments of their office treated as private property rights. Any constitutional recognition of a legal "right" to an office or its emoluments contains the germs of destruction of a fully organized bureaucracy and may lead back to feudal conditions. The provisions of the German Constitution in this respect must be looked upon with considerable apprehension.[24]

We shall now proceed to give a general and abstract description of a fully developed, organized bureaucracy. Such a general description serves as a measuring rod or standard for evaluating a particular organization in terms of its bureaucratization. Without such a standard it would be impossible to compare a given organization with

[22] One extensive and fairly early application of this idea in England was the Act of Settlement (1701) in so far as it applied to the English Judiciary.

[23] Concerning Switzerland, see below, pp. 36 ff.

[24] See Article 129. Note particularly the phrase: ". . . The duly acquired rights of civil servants are inviolable. . . ." From the point of view of our problem here, it is significant, however, that a special tax was placed upon salaried persons when the recent economic crisis seemed to demand urgently a downward revision of the salaries and pensions.

other similar organizations. But it should always be remembered that, throughout this analysis, we do not wish to imply that we attach any praise or blame to an organization by evaluating it in terms of its bureaucratization. We do not pretend to be able to contribute, through this inquiry, toward a decision which would involve either opposition to or support of this process of bureaucratization. All that we are concerned with is to note that such a process does take place, and furthermore to suggest what are its essential characteristics. This will necessarily involve the statement of propositions which would be of value to anyone who either wanted to oppose or to support this process in some organization or other. But we do not propose to derive the justification of our inquiry from this variety of usefulness, but exclusively from the contribution which those tentative conclusions we may offer have for gaining an *understanding* of this process. Without wishing to commit ourselves as to whether the stars might be deflected from their course or not, if a wrathful god should be inclined to attempt it, we remain satisfied with ascertaining what the path of these stars is and what rules it seems to follow. If any divine being (like his Majesty, the American people) should be tempted to aim at them, let it follow its own counsel concerning the best way of hitting them.

It will be found that our general description[25] develops three characteristics. Each of these could of course be expanded by exploring the implications of each of the terms used in the description. We would then get further characteristics. But, for the present purpose, these three characteristics or criteria afford a satisfactory starting point[26] at present.

[25] It is with purpose that we speak of description and not of definition. Reality is not defined but described. If our description is to cover many individual objects or events, it must be general and abstract.

[26] Later improvements are hoped for, and critical discussion is most sincerely solicited. The following analysis is founded upon Max Weber's valuable discussion of bureaucracy in *Wirtschaft und Gesellschaft* (1924), First Part, Chap. III, §§3-5 and Third Part, Chap. VI, to which the authors are heavily indebted. The reading of these sections of Weber's work is highly recommended to anyone who wishes to go further than this brief sketch of a general description attempts to go. It will, however, be noted that the simplifications are not just abbreviations. But this is not the place to elaborate the meaning and significance of this divergence which centers around two basic positions of Max Weber: his concept of value and his emphasis upon coercion in dealing with *Herrschaft* (power?). These

There is found, first of all, a determinate distribution of offices or functions among the members of the organization. These are often called competences or jurisdictions. There is found, secondly, a determinate distribution of the powers of control and coercion attached to these offices. This is called the heirarchy. There are, thirdly, determinate qualifications required for the fulfillment of those several functions. Their development goes hand in hand with the rationalized distribution of functions, and since such requirements presuppose rather elaborate preparation of the prospective candidate, they depend upon a fixed salary, secure tenure, regular promotion in anticipation of which the candidate undertakes to secure the necessary training. This process may be called professionalization.

If we speak of a distribution of offices or functions among the members of the organization, the proposition will be obvious enough as long as we deal with individuals who are on the same level in the organization, so to speak; where, in other words, no subordination or hierarchy is involved. It is evident that much is gained by entrusting each activity to one and only one person, or, if several persons have to be used for carrying on the same activity, by circumscribing as carefully as possible the sphere within which each person is to be confined. Such a rule belongs in the ABC of management. But the rule is more easily prescribed than put into effect, and in reality we can never expect more than approximations to this standard. It is, moreover, important to remember that when we pass from one level of offices or activity in a large organization to the next higher one, the rule applies again between the individuals on that level; but each person's sphere is larger and comprises as a rule the spheres of activity of several individuals on the lower level within itself. Therefore the rule does not in all strictness apply to the relations of persons on different levels; these are described by the second criterion, the hierarchy. Any investigation of modern governments will show that their bureaucracies tend to approximate the standard suggested by this criterion to an ever-increasing degree.

It should be mentioned here in passing that there exist considerable limitations, apart from the inherent difficulty of drawing practicable distinctions. There is a tendency within all organizations to expand

---

problems will be considered in *The State as Organized Community*, as yet unpublished.

under certain conditions. What these conditions are must await more careful investigation. ''The inherent tendency of bureaucracy to expand'' upon which popular writers are prone to dwell is certainly an over-statement; for, under certain conditions, a bureaucracy shows no such tendency at all (post-war France, on the whole, for example). But whenever an organization within a government, like a certain ministry, does show this tendency to expand, it will usually employ the broad indistinctness of such words as commerce or labor to put forward claims for functions which theoretically could doubtlessly be brought under either of these terms.[27] Under any scheme of government such claims of competing organizations are likely to be partly crowned by success. The result is inefficiency.

A federal structure greatly increases the chances for such limitations of a full-fledged development of bureaucracy, as measured by this first criterion. Hoepker-Aschoff, the present Prussian Minister of Finance, is quoted as saying that about half of the time of the higher officials in Prussia is consumed by controversies over their sphere of competence with officials of the government of the Reich.[28] Such extensive controversies at the top are paralleled in the lower cadres by a flat refusal to coöperate. What is true of the state with federational structure is often equally true of the decentralized unitary state with strongly developed local self-government.[29] We are, therefore, at this point able to discern that a state with a federational structure has a distribution of power which involves an antithesis to the distribution of power required for a fully organized bureaucracy. This proposi-

[27] The American Federal Administration is full of instances like these, and Mr. Hoover's experiences as Secretary of Commerce have led him to organize an interdepartmental board of coördination. See for other good illustrations L. D. White, *Principles of Public Administration* (1926), pp. 69-73 and elsewhere.

[28] See concerning this problem *Verfassungsausschuss der Länderkonferenz Beratungsunterlagen* (1928), particularly the report by Hans Simons, pp. 333 ff. The corresponding situation in this country is too well known to require elaboration. Only as an example I shall mention the continuous efforts of the Interstate Commerce Commission to eliminate some of the duplication of work by encouraging voluntary coöperation; see the *Reports* of the Commission. The German governments have developed voluntary administrative associations (*Verwaltungsgemeinschaften*) along similar lines. See the *Beratungsunterlagen*, pp. 70 ff.

[29] All this is not said for the purpose of arguing either against or for a federal or decentralized state, but in order to indicate what effect they produce upon an organized bureaucracy.

tion becomes immediately more evident, when we turn to our second criterion, the hierarchy.

The hierarchy is a concomitant of the rational distribution of functions, because as soon as an organization grows to any size, the large number of individuals who exercise functions which directly impinge upon individuals outside the organization stands in constant need of integration.[30] This seems obvious enough, and yet the implications of this proposition have received wholly inadequate attention. For on the one hand, the detailed and specific functions need constant re-interpretation in terms of the larger objectives which they presumably serve; on the other hand, the obstacles and difficulties encountered in the exercise of these detailed and specific functions require consideration with a view to possible improvement or alteration of these objectives. It is the emphasis upon the first aspect which finds expression in the prevalent practice of the United States (and certain other countries) to entrust the integration of all specific and detailed functions to the legislature, in accordance with the famous proposition that thus may be secured a government of laws and not of men. This is another aspect of the separation of powers doctrine which is vital to our present purpose, an aspect which was given little or no consideration by those who formulated the doctrine.

The gradual rise of an industrial civilization, however, has forced governmental agencies entrusted with various technical functions to attempt to exercise these functions in the light of the obstacles and difficulties encountered in the exercise of these detailed and specific functions, and to attempt to develop gradually an impact of administrative experience upon legislation.[31] Where even this did not suffice, the technical realms of rule-making have been entrusted to expert bodies like the Interstate Commerce Commission which themselves were at the same time entrusted with the administration of these rules.[32] Besides, certain considerable bodies of so-called moral legis-

[30] The importance of the problem of integration for an understanding of political phenomena has recently been emphasized by Rudolf Smend in *Verfassung und Verfassungsrecht* (1928), pp. 27 ff., whose critical observations concerning Max Weber's overemphasis upon technical rationality point, I believe, in the right direction.

[31] Note the more and more common practice of "recommendations to Congress" by commissions, boards and other predominantly administrative agencies.

[32] These commissions tend toward developing into more or less independent hierarchies which are not integrated with each other. Conflicts of competence between themselves, the "departments" and the "courts" are the order of the day.

lation, enacted without reference to the physiological and psychological predispositions of the community, have given rise to a considerable tendency on the part of administrative officials to nullify such legislation by not enforcing it.[33] This tendency is a result of neglecting the hierarchical aspects of the governmental bureaucracy in the United States.

The determinate distribution of the powers of control and coercion connected with the offices or functions suggests a single individual (or bureau) having ultimate control and powers of coercion.[34] Max Weber suggests calling such a structure monocratic, and he believes that a fully organized bureaucracy is of this type.[35] Moreover, such an individual would have to be part of the hierarchical structure himself; he must be an integral part of it. The Prime Minister in a unitary parliamentary government would be such an individual, perhaps, as long as he is in power. In a federal state, however, there exist several such hierarchies alongside each other. These are integrated by a constitution, or perhaps, as in the case of Imperial Germany, by a corporate body consisting of the heads of the constituent hierarchies.[36] In the latter case the elimination of conflicting competences is facilitated, but in either case the delays involved in bringing about coordination (through court decision or constitutional amendment) produce in fact a certain, comparatively high and probably fairly constant amount of duplication of governmental activity.[37] Not only does the existence of a federal organization, but that of any multiple hierarchy in a given sphere of activity has the same effect. The existence of two telegraph companies like the Western Union and the Postal Telegraph Company represents a violation of the second criterion of organized bureaucracy through the inevitable duplication of

[33] See the valuable article by S. Wallace, "Nullification, a Process of Government," in *Political Science Quarterly* (1930).

[34] Max Weber speaks in this connection of "a monopoly of legitimate employment of physical force," when dealing with the governmental bureaucracy, but his use of the concept of legitimacy is purely pragmatic, to be sure, (*loc. cit.* p. 19), and does not play any important part in his later analysis of bureaucracy.

[35] *Loc. cit.*, pp. 126, 650 and elsewhere.

[36] This is the dominant aspect of the Federal Council (*Bundesrat*) which makes it difficult to compare it with a body like the Senate of the United States.

[37] As one activity becomes coördinated and integrated, another activity arises in various parts of the federational structure. This is not only true of the administrative but of the legislative realm as well, of course.

functions.[38] If such parallel hierarchies are brought under effective unified control, it may and often does result in a rationalization of the distribution of functions and consequently may be considered a step in the direction of more fully developed bureaucracy. Governmental coördinating agencies may accomplish a good deal in this direction, both through enforcing uniform standards and through stimulating the better coöperation of "private" enterprises as a protection against governmental interference. This aspect of the activity of bodies like the American Interstate Commerce Commission has been appreciated very little indeed.[39] It indicates that the distinction between private and public activities, so important from a legal point of view, is only of rather limited application in systematic political science, in general, and in connection with bureaucracy in particular. We may and do speak of a governmental bureaucracy, but it is easier to overestimate than to underestimate the difference between such governmental bureaucracy and the church bureaucracy, the party bureaucracy, or the bureaucracy of the business corporations. Much depends upon the circumstances of time and place.

If the tendency toward monocratic structure is implicit in the hierarchical aspect of bureaucracy, it would nevertheless be undesirable from a systematic point of view to interpret hierarchical structure as meaning monocratic structure necessarily. It seems preferable to use the word hierarchy for the purpose of describing more generally a determinate system of distributing the powers of control and coercion by subordinating individuals performing very specific and tangible

[38] This aspect of "free competition" has only recently received a certain amount of attention from economists, because it depends upon the development of large-scale organizations. See particularly J. M. Clark, *Studies in the Economics of Overhead Costs* (1926).

[39] This is due, I believe, to the fact that in business the economic aspects have received almost exclusive attention, although the institutionalists have attempted to tackle other aspects. As far as I can see, the institutionalists "feel" the problem, without succeeding in formulating it clearly. Certainly the mere fact that business life in reality cannot be "understood" in all its aspects in terms of economics does not warrant our casting aside the highly developed conceptual apparatus of classical economics. The fact that certain uncritical people have freely predicted the course of actual events after analyzing only the economic aspects of it does in no wise justify us in discarding the tools used in the analysis. It does, however, justify us in inquiring into the problem of what these other aspects are. Not economic theory, but the philosophical systems erected upon it deserve to be discarded.

functions to other individuals, who supervise a determinate number of these individuals, who in turn may be supervised by a still more limited number of individuals. But the subordination may also take the form of subordinating groups of individuals acting together to groups of individuals acting together in turn, or subordinating several individuals operating individually to a group of individuals acting together. This is the structure of the judicial system in Anglo-Saxon countries as well as in continental Europe, and it is perhaps significant that there exists no administrative counterpart to the expression ''stages of appeal'' which applies to court procedure, while on the continent of Europe an expression has developed which signifies the sequel of subordinations for the administrative as well as for the judicial bureaucracy. But what is evident for the judiciary is equally important for strict service bureaucracies, whether governmental or otherwise, namely, that the exercise of the powers of control and coercion is ordinarily and normally limited by and directed towards the realization of the purposes for which the hierarchy exists. But at this point a most serious problem arises, namely, the problem: who determines whether the particular command issued in the exercise of the power of control and coercion is in line with the purpose which it is supposed to realize? The hierarchical idea seems to imply strict subordination. The extent to which a given hierarchy conforms to the idea is indicated by its rules of discipline.

Some rudimentary discipline is implicit in any organized bureaucracy but its strictness supplies us with another criterion for determining the development of such a bureaucracy, subject however to one very important qualification. The rigour of the discipline must be considered in relation to the nature of the purpose of the organization. More specifically, a purpose which is likely to be defeated by delay in execution will produce a more rigorous discipline, other things being equal. The army and business enterprises afford good examples. In the modern world, the comparatively static condition of most governmental activities during peace time, on the other hand, has made it possible to subject all disciplinary action to fairly elaborate judicial procedure.[40] The

---

[40] About this important matter see more below, p. 44. It is sometimes not clearly realized that codes of disciplinary regulations, far from indicating a disadvantage of governmental as compared with non-governmental functionaries, are in fact a most valuable protection of the functionaries against arbitrary action on the part of their superiors.

connection which such disciplinary problems has with the permanence of office, salary and pension, leads us to our third criterion, the determinate qualifications required for the fulfillment of the several functions, and the emoluments of office which accompany such "expertise".

Much has been written on this score in recent years. In fact, the organization of a "civil service" in the United States has revolved around the problem of how to secure personnel with adequate qualifications, and special civil service commissions have been created for the purpose of determining what these qualifications should be and how they should be ascertained. All this is obvious enough. But what is often overlooked is that these commissions represent attempts to overcome at least some of the difficulties which the lack of integration between the educational system and the public "functions" has necessarily produced. When looked at from this angle, it becomes very apparent that the system of public schools characteristic of continental European countries has its root to some extent at least in the necessities of the community for trained public servants.[41] The purely individualistic arguments advanced against this system by Americans neglect the historical need which alone accounts for the growth of modern education. Speaking abstractly and analytically, a public school and university system fulfills the function of integrating the educational agencies with the hierarchy of functions through an elaborate system of standardized examinations. If such integration is effective, it becomes possible to consider the degrees from such educational institutions as constituting at least in part satisfactory evidence that the person holding such a degree is qualified for a certain function in the hierarchy. This is the profound significance of the systems of state education on the continent of Europe from the point of view of our discussion here. Through its control over the educational preparation of prospective office-holders (and in a sense even the "free" professions constitute a part of the public service), the government and through it the community are in a position to secure well-qualified personnel which will render satisfactory service. And even if party pressure will interfere with the promotion of individual members of the service, the minimum standard of performance will be sufficiently high to safeguard the public interest.

[41] The history of higher education is most instructive in this respect. Many of the high schools (*gymnasia* or *collegia*) and universities were founded by princes and cities who felt the need for trained public servants.

Civil service commissions are a poor substitute for a system of public education, at least from the point of view of a fully developed bureaucracy. The resentment which is felt by superior officers at being deprived of the necessary choice among applicants, which frequently turns upon imponderable elements of personality and similar considerations, corresponds to the lack of incentive on the part of inferior officers to fit themselves into the hierarchy which is thus weakened. Moreover, the examinations given by such a commission are either in line with the preliminary training of the applicants in which case there might just as well be substituted a certificate testifying to this preliminary training; or, the examinations are not in line with the preliminary training, in which case it would be more rational either to have the preliminary training amended in terms of the examination, or to have the examination altered to suit the training. This seems too obvious to need further elaboration, and yet a great many writers dealing with the civil service have neglected this aspect of the problem. This tendency toward more and more specific and detailed requirements of training and preparation goes parallel with an ever more elaborate and determinate system of emoluments of office. The increasing expenditure (investment of capital), which such training and preparation necessitates, will not and cannot be undertaken unless there are increasingly determinate prospects of a return in terms of a rising salary (career) combined with reasonable security of tenure of office and, at a still more advanced stage, provision for disability, old age and dependents. Here, again, it may be pointed out that the assumption often made that governmental agencies are singular in these respects is utterly false. In the early stages of European civilization the church carried this principle further than any secular power, and the investiture struggle between pope and emperor is significant in showing that the church was ahead of secular communities in the process of bureaucratization. But business organizations or trade unions, no less than universities in America, seem to develop according to this tendency as their staffs grow in size. And this standardization of the emoluments of office tends in turn to carry with it the idea that the incumbent of such an office is not permitted to engage in other gainful activities.

These observations may suffice as a preliminary and general discussion of each of the three main criteria of an organized bureaucracy. But there is one aspect common to them all which deserves some further attention. This is the aspect of determinateness. In itself perfectly clear, such determinateness, insuring equality of treatment under equal conditions to all members of a given organization, is never apparent unless full publicity enables any reasonably intelligent and interested person to judge for himself. As a result, a fully developed bureaucracy, whether governmental or otherwise, will be characterized by full publicity about its arrangements concerning each of the three characteristics and their various concomitant circumstances. The absence of such publicity marks a large part of the unintegrated bits of non-governmental bureaucracy as "not fully organized." But even the governmental services do not fulfill this requirement completely. On the continent of Europe the gradual transformation from a feudal tenant to a royal servant and finally to a civil servant is paralleled by a gradual evolution of "publicity." This has given rise to the idea that such publicity is entirely forced upon the bureaucracy from the outside for purposes of control and supervision. But leaving the question of historical causation aside, it would seem that publicity is of the essence of a fully developed bureaucracy, and that consequently the demands of the outsiders (the public) for publicity have merely accelerated a process which lay implicit in the tendency toward full rationalization.

In order to appreciate the full historical significance of these observations, it may be well to conclude this general analysis by sketching certain historical aspects of the evolution of governmental bureaucracies in Europe. At all stages of this gradual transformation, there has been a tendency on the part of the servants themselves to "privatize" public functions, to convert the emoluments of their office into private property. In fact, the considerable success of royal servants during the Middle Ages in this direction is the essence of feudalism from our point of view.[42] Consequently, the development from feudal tenant to civil servant was not straight and uninterrupted. It had its ups and downs. A strong king would succeed in superimposing a royal public service, which under his weaker successors would disintegrate again into a more or less feudal proprietary relationship. Many examples from Charles the Great downward could be given for every kingdom of Christendom, and England, France, Spain, Austria, Prussia and all the others are similar in this respect. The earliest evolution

[42] The fact incidentally obliges us to reject any absolute antithesis between the Middle Ages and later periods, or between feudalism and later forms of organizing public functions.

of a distinctly public service, however, took place within the great city-states of Italy, the Netherlands, Germany and Switzerland. And this development is linked to another of hardly lesser importance for our topic. The increasing success of such city-states leagued together in large federations to oppose the territorial princes is often the result of their use of large bodies of infantry drafted from among the body of citizens. The early struggle for independence of the Swiss Federation is only one among many similar, though frequently less successful efforts. And wherever the wealth of the city and its citizens allowed it, this compulsory military service was converted into payments for the purpose of hiring substitutes.[43] Emperors, kings and smaller princes followed the lead intermittently, and as the financial burdens involved permitted it. But what is quite apparent is that the development of large armies stimulated the growth of a royal public service immensely. Sombart has gone so far as to say that the development of the modern state and of the modern army are identical with each.[44] If we disregard the paradoxical overemphasis of this statement, we may yet admit that it stresses rightly the very close parallel which the development of modern military organization and the modern state exhibit. Schmoller has rendered a great service in stressing the extent to which the financial needs of these vast military establishments have furthered the growth not only of a considerable revenue collecting bureaucracy but of an industrial system the increasing complexities of which in turn require continually new extensions of governmental administrative activity.[45] In other words, the modern industrial system and the modern bureaucratic state are phenomena which are interrelated in their development, and any proposition, according to which one or the other came first and was the cause, should be rejected. This policy of the government to push the industrial development of the country ahead remained a tradition in Continental Europe, no less than the policy of claiming governmental supervision, control and eventually operation wherever monopolistic tendencies seemed to be in the public interest. At this point it becomes apparent that the progress of the socialization of the industrial system depends upon the existence, maintenance and development of an organized bureaucracy.

[43] See H. Delbrück, *Geschichte der Kriegskunst*, Vols. III and IV.

[44] Werner Sombart, *Der Moderne Kapitalismus* (1902), Vol. I, p. 242. This work is of the greatest value in showing the interrelation of military, political and economic development.

[45] Compare here *ibid.*, Vols. II and III.

But this industrial progress resulted also in a rapid increase of the population accompanied by an ever greater urbanization of these industrialized nations.[46] It is well-known that this urbanization is one of the essential conditions of the growth of democracy. If, then, a fully organized bureaucracy is essential for an industrial system, and if, on the other hand, an industrial system produces a large urban population which is democratically organized, the maintenance of such a bureaucracy within a democracy is of paramount importance for the maintenance of modern European society. Not only must we reject the idea that democracy is opposed to bureaucracy, but we must recognize that the future of democracy depends upon its ability to maintain a fully organized bureaucracy. For the industrial system which demands it is with us for better or worse since the life of millions of human beings depends upon it. If a popular government is incapable of maintaining a bureaucratic hierarchy, it is bound to give way to a form of government which will accomplish that, whether it be the dictatorship of an individual or of a small group in the name of the nation, the people, or the proletariat.

[46] See concerning these problems Alfred Weber, *Theory of the Location of Industry* (English edition with notes by C. J. Friedrich, 1929). The sociological aspects of this evolution are suggestively developed by Alfred Weber, *Ideen zur Staats- und Kultursoziologie* (1927), pp. 81 ff.

CHAPTER II

THE FUNCTIONS OF THE SWISS CIVIL SERVICE

It will be recalled that we suggested as the first characteristic of an organized bureaucracy a determinate distribution of offices or functions. Now of course there exists in Switzerland an elaborate system of competences, as in every modern state, both in the Federal hierarchy and in the cantonal jurisdictions. And yet, even a casual glance at the figures for 1920 of the numerical distribution of employees among the federal services will show that the postal service, the telegraph and railroads take up about 85% of the entire service.

Central Administration	Customs	Posts	Telegraphs and Telephones	Railways	Total
7,935	3,052	16,961	7,040	39,410	74,398

And further inquiry will reveal that, in a sense, modern bureaucracy has come into existence in Switzerland only in connection with these services.[1] No emperor or king stood at the cradle of the Swiss civil service goose-stepping it into the manyfold activities of the modern state alongside with army and navy. To be sure before the times of the *Sonderbund* and the making of the constitution of 1848,[2] the old families had carried on the limited functions of government in canton and federation in a thoroughly patriarchal and traditional fashion.[3] But such administration could hardly become the nucleus for any fully organized bureaucracy. After 1848, on the other hand, the pressure of economic and industrial necessities soon led to the establishment of one after another of these large economic services. As a consequence we can hardly say that the bureaucracy in Switzerland expanded into these fields of economic activity; we are obliged to admit that the bureaucracy was born when the Federation undertook these activities.[4] Our later discussion will

---

[1] See, for a general discussion of the economic and social aspects of this development, A. N. Holcombe, *The Public Ownership of Telephones on the Continent of Europe* (1911), Chaps. XII-XIV.

[2] See the concise summary of these events in R. C. Brooks, *Government and Politics in Switzerland* (1921), Chap. II.

[3] Max Weber suggests the expression *Honoratiorenverwaltung* for this type of arrangement, but I despair of finding an English equivalent. ''Administration by notables'' is the literal translation.

[4] See E. Fueter, *Die Schweiz seit 1848*, pp. 65 ff., 166 ff. and elsewhere.

indicate to what extent this has been of determining significance in shaping the present status of the Swiss civil service in all its aspects.

But while the usual distribution of functions is found when one looks at the structure from the outside, Switzerland is notable for its hesitancy in openly recognizing this inherently monocratic trend of a fully organized bureaucracy. The famous dictum of Napoleon, "Agir est le fait d'un seul," has not been frankly admitted in Switzerland. To be sure, one member of the Federal Council stands at the head of each of the administrative departments, but their relation to each other is collegial and not monocratically integrated. The collegial organization of the Swiss chief executive, government by commission, is too well known to require detailed analysis here.[5] By the constitution the Federal Council is enjoined to act collectively; but, in fact, it rarely does.[6] The same is true, although perhaps to a lesser extent, of the cantonal councils. But the idea is carried further; a great many commissions are organized for the purpose of advising the various administrative officials in canton and federation. Even though these advisory commissions have no direct administrative responsibility, they weaken the administrative responsibility of the officer in charge whenever they result in a conflict of competences.

The unique historical background of the Swiss bureaucracy has had the further effect of restricting it much more decidedly to the administrative functions. The vast powers which fall to the bureaucracies of France, Germany and other continental European countries with a monarchical past in connection with the drafting of legislation are more restricted in Switzerland, although the increasing technicality of certain types of legislation has resulted in a continual increase in this type of activity in the several departments into which the central administrative activities of the Federation are divided. These divisions differ little, if at all, from the usual organization of central ministeries. Since the year 1914 the following seven departments have existed:

The Political Department
The Department of the Interior
The Department of Justice and Police
The Military Department
The Department of Finance and Customs

[5] See Brooks, *op. cit.*, Chap. v. A monographic study of actual performance is greatly needed, however, and has been started.

[6] See Fritz Fleiner, *Schweizerisches Bundesstaatsrecht* (1923), 190 ff.

The Department of National Economy
The Department of Posts and Railroads.[7]

No careful analysis of the actual political relation of these departments to the legislative chambers in Switzerland is available at present,[8] although there are hints in the concluding paragraph of Fleiner's work to the effect that in Switzerland the administrative authorities participate to a very considerable extent in determining the content of legislation. He adds that in the Federation the great majority of all statutes originate in the Federal Council.[9]—"Members of the Federal Council enjoy a great influence over the legislature partly because of their prestige as party leaders, partly because of the experience and special knowledge which they are able to gain through their official position."[10]

Besides the function of legislative drafting, the function of making ordinances (carefully divided between the various bureaus according to the subject matter concerned) deserves to be mentioned as an important function of the Swiss bureaucracy. Ordinances containing a general legal rule can only be issued by administrative authorities, when and if authorized by the constitution or a statute. The value of such ordinances, from an administrative point of view, lies in the fact that they are not subject to the optional referendum.[11] Federal statutes have granted such ordinance-making power to the departments under the Federal Council quite frequently. The most extensive grant occurred in connection with the food stuff legislation of 1905,[12] which left the most important matters to the Federal Council. But since, legally speaking, any law-making ordinance (*Rechtsverordnung*)[13] is liable

[7] Federal Law Concerning the Organization of the Federal Administration of March 26, 1914, *AS* 30, 292.

[8] The analysis of Swiss legislation in Fritz Fleiner's *Schweizerisches Bundesstaatsrecht*, pp. 399 ff., is intentionally limited to certain controversial legal aspects of this process.

[9] *Ibid.*, p. 763.

[10] Brooks, *op. cit.*, p. 113. This is also the opinion of leading Swiss writers.

[11] Fleiner, *op. cit.*, pp. 411 ff. It would, however, be possible to assail any such ordinance by optional referendum, if such ordinance were issued within ninety days, by subjecting the enabling clause of the statute to referendum.

[12] Federal Law concerning the Trade with Food Stuffs, etc. (Dec. 8, 1905), *AS* 22, 337; according to Fleiner, *op. cit.*, p. 415.

[13] Such law-making ordinances have to be distinguished clearly from administrative ordinances (*Verwaltungsverordnung*) which are discussed below p. 33. While

to be declared null and void by the courts if, in the opinion of the court, it transcends the authorization of the law which it supplements, the Swiss bureaucracy during the World War was enabled to revert to the ancient device of emergency ordinances under an enabling act of August 3, 1914 (since the constitution had neglected to provide for such emergencies).[14] This comprehensive competence for the issuance of emergency ordinances was in typical fashion created for the purpose of maintaining the security, integrity and neutrality of Switzerland, of safeguarding the credit of the country, and of safeguarding the food supply. This is not the place to discuss the difficult legal problems which arise in connection with the exercise of this emergency power. Suffice it is to say that under this emergency power even provisions of the constitution may be altered or suspended, and that the Federal Court has refused to review the authority of the Federal Council in issuing such ordinances. A broad grant of powers![15] However, since 1919, such ordinances are subject to the subsequent approval of the legislative chambers. Still the emergency ordinance is a typical path-maker for a fully organized bureaucracy. It represents, in the sphere of activities affecting the entire state, an application of the basic idea of the administrative function, the taking of measures[16] which characterizes the functioning of a bureaucracy in all spheres. The establishment of this power in Switzerland is therefore at once a striking illustration of the all-engulfing technicality of the conditions of modern industrial civilization and of the inexorable forward march of fully developed monocratic bureaucracy as the type of organization of human beings best adapted to its technical necessities. An appeal to these necessities will assist in all efforts for expanding the competences or functions of the bureaucracy in Switzerland as in other countries.

---

the law-making ordinance creates a legal rule, an administrative ordinance contains commands dealing with the internal relations of the governmental services, particularly instructions to civil servants. See Fleiner, *op. cit.*, pp. 412 ff.

[14] See Robert Hoerni, *De l'Etat de nécessité en droit public fédéral suisse* (1917), a dissertation which Fleiner rightly praises, *op. cit.*, p. 416. However, Fleiner's own discussion *ibid.*, pp. 416 ff. and 217 summarizes the situation very well. The enabling act itself is to be found in *AS* 30, 347.

[15] The collection of these ordinances by F. Baer, *Die schweizerischen Kriegsverordnungen* (3 vols., 1916-18), gives a good idea of the extent of the use made of this grant during the war.

[16] See above Chap. I.

But in more limited fields of application, such taking of measures is peculiar to all administrative activity. It is the specific tool of the *police*. It always is directed towards a particular situation with which it proposes to deal. If a health officer gives an order to kill a cow, he takes a measure in the typical sense.[17] From these measures must be distinguished the administrative ordinance which contains a general rule, but one which applies within the administrative organization itself. Every administrative authority, every sector of the hierarchy which is charged with administering a certain law, may issue such ordinances.[18] Although the majority of such ordinances are issued in the name of the Federal Council, in accordance with Article 102, pars. 2 and 5 of the Constitution, many of them are in fact the work of the heads of the departments. Naturally, since these administrative ordinances apply within the hierarchy, there is no appeal against them except through the administrative hierarchy itself. Since many of these ordinances do impinge upon the interests of outsiders, or raise controversies concerning competences, the Federal Council was bound to find itself swamped with an ever increasing mass of quasi-judicial activity, as the Federal hierarchy grew. Out of the inevitable inadequacy of this situation arose a demand for an administrative tribunal, independent of the administrative hierarchy itself and solely occupied with these adjudications, before which redress could be sought against such ordinances as well as against other measures of the officials. Such an administrative court has recently been organized.[19] This development is of the greatest importance for maintaining a fully organized bureaucracy in Switzerland. It has been recognized for some

[17] Fleiner suggests the term *Verfügung* as *terminus technicus* for such acts. In English the word ''order'' would happily correspond to that term, were it not for the ''order in council'' in England which almost always contains a general rule.

[18] Fleiner and other scholars use the term *Verwaltungsverordnung* for designating this type of ordinance, to distinguish it from the *Rechtsverordnung* on the one hand and from the *Verfügung* on the other. But of course the statutes and court decisions use several other expressions interchangeably, like *Vorschrift, Reglement, Instruktion*, etc.

[19] By the Federal Law on Administrative and Disciplinary Jurisdiction of June 11, 1928, the size of the Federal Court was increased to twenty-eight members with nine alternates, and a limited jurisdiction over administrative cases was conferred upon that body. *R.O.*, 1928, 837 ff. Most of the cases come before the Section of Public and Administrative Law, but certain types of questions may be adjudicated by the Civil Law Sections. Matters affecting the service relationship of federal officials now fall within the competence of a specially created Chamber

time that the situation had become very threatening.[20] As long as the
Federation possessed only small competences, the Federal Council was
able to examine such controversies concerning actions of the members
of the administrative hierarchy carefully and thoroughly. But the competences and therefore the administrative tasks of the Federation grew
so rapidly after 1874 that the Federal Council became totally unable to
judge judicially even the most important administrative controversies. Yet, the majority of the members of the Federal Council and a
considerable part of the higher bureaucracy were greatly opposed to
the establishment of the administrative court which the constitutional
amendment, embodied in article 114 *bis* of the constitution (1914), had
made possible.

The strongly authoritarian attitude of the Swiss official has often
been noted.[21] The very fact that the tenure of his office depends upon
the choice of the people makes him jealous in the maintenance of the
prerogative of his office while he occupies it. As a consequence he is
loath to have the dignity of an administrative decision lessened by a
judicial decision. But this reasoning is essentially false. The citizen
who seeks redress against the decision of an administrative official is
rarely satisfied when the only appeal lies to the superiors of this official. He is inclined to suspect that justice has been denied to him.
When such appeal can be presented before an independent administrative court, on the other hand, the weight of the decision is increased
and the moral position of the government in the community is strength-
ened. Moreover, such an administrative court can render its decisions
with greater speed and more thorough consideration of precedent.
''The authority of the government cannot be maintained by multiplying
competences. It must be based upon the conviction of the citizens that
all power of the government is kept within limits by the law.''[22]

of Claims of Civil Servants (*Chambre des contentieux des fonctionnaires*), Arts.
1-3; see Chap. III. The jurisdiction of the Federal Court is limited almost exclusively to questions of a financial nature, both when acting as a court of original
jurisdiction and as a court of appellate jurisdiction. Arts. 4-6, 17-18. That a broad
jurisdiction in administrative matters was retained by the Federal Council may
be seen by a review of Arts. 22-23.

[20] See for this statement and what follows Fleiner, *op. cit.*, pp. 222 ff. and the
literature cited there.

[21] See for example Fritz Fleiner, *Schweizerische und Deutsche Staatsauffassung*,
p. 15.

[22] Fleiner, *Schweizerisches Bundesstaatsrecht*, p. 224.

What is true of the man in the street is equally true of the man in the hierarchy. The official who is being punished by a superior will feel the sting much more lastingly if his appeal against such punishment may be considered by a judicial tribunal than if it will finally be decided by superiors in the hierarchy whom he may suspect of the same personal animus or party bias against himself which animated the immediate superior in punishing him. This consideration is of the greatest importance in a democracy where the members of the hierarchy may belong and very probably do belong to different political parties and thus have serious clashes of opinion based upon subjectively genuine disagreement as to the desirable course of action to pursue. This problem is particularly pressing in European communities at the present time, when the question arises as to how to deal with extremely radical elements of the population. When it is a matter of how to handle a communist meeting, it will make a vital difference whether the police commissioner is a Socialist or a social reactionary, and the same will be true of other functionaries concerned with the situation. If an independent judicial tribunal watches over the exercise and the distribution of functions, it will be in a better position to eliminate friction and controversies which are otherwise inescapable under popular government.

CHAPTER III

THE SWISS HIERARCHY

The typical form of administrative organization in modern states is the hierarchical one. Strictly speaking an hierarchical organization involves the power of one official to suspend, annul or interfere with the acts committed by another.[1] There is consequently necessitated a clear distinction between the official who has the power of interference and the official whose acts are subject to modification or annulment. As a result one becomes the superior agent and the other the inferior. Between the ultimate superior and the lowest subordinate there range various gradations, while underlying the whole relationship there stands the principle of authority; in fact, the result is an organized system of authority.[2] This authority which the superior possesses over the inferior depends ultimately on the legal provisions upon which the system is based. In Switzerland these superior officials (*gouvernants*) consist of the Federal Council, the Federal Court and the Federal Insurance Court.[3]

Beneath the superior officials there stand the various classes of subordinate officials of the confederation. According to the Federal Law on Civil Servants of June 30, 1927, a civil servant is any person "appointed as such by the Federal Council, by a department subordinate to it, by the Federal Court, or by the Federal Insurance Court."[4] The act is thus considered applicable only to the service relationship (*rapports de service*) which exists between the state and the subordinate

---

[1] Gaston Jèze, *Les principes généraux du droit administratif* (1904), 47.

[2] René Hugot-Derville, *Le principe hiérarchique* (1913), 25 ff.; Max Gilbert, *La discipline des fonctions publiques* (1912), 43 ff. Since Switzerland combines legislative centralization with administrative decentralization, cantonal officials are frequently responsible for carrying out federal laws. The government of the confederation acts over these civil servants by way of supervision and advice. As we are concerned, however, only with the officials of the confederation, a discussion of the cantonal officials except for the purposes of numerical comparison has been omitted.

[3] The Federal Council and the Federal Court have been treated in various commentaries. The Federal Insurance Court is a special tribunal created in 1917 for hearing appeals involving the insurance laws of the confederation. It was originally composed of seven judges named by the Federal Assembly, and its jurisdiction is both original and appellate. *R.O.*, 1917, 535 ff.

[4] L. D. White, "Federal Law on Civil Servants," *The Civil Service in the Modern State*, Art. I, 362.

officials of the Federal Council, the Federal Court and the Federal Insurance Court. Members of these specified bodies and the Chancellor whose service relationships are governed by special laws are thus excluded.[5] No person who is the holder of an office not subjected to the disciplinary power of the confederation is included. Consequently members of the Federal Assembly, of parliamentary commissions, of administrative councils and of other federal bodies are eliminated. It is also necessary, in accordance with the provisions of the law, that the activities of the officers be in the federal services. Members of autonomous establishments and international bureaus are thus omitted.[6] In addition to the civil servants, legally speaking, there are the employees, a class which includes the auxiliary personnel of the departments, agents of bureaus engaged by the month, the rural mail carriers, the personnel employed temporarily in the transport services and other groups.[7] The workers (*ouvriers*) are those persons who are employed and paid by the hour and day. They are temporary officials only, and it does not matter whether or not their work for the Confederation is their only employment. A fourth class of officials, which does not fall properly under the other three groups, includes the diplomatic representatives in foreign countries and the members of the Federal Polytechnic School.[8]

Down to 1921 the numerical growth of these subordinate officials

[5] *Message* . . . *d'un projet de loi sur le statut des fonctionnaires fédéraux* (1924), 41.

[6] *Ibid.*, 42.

[7] *Message* . . . *concernant l'état des fonctions dont les titulaires ont qualité de fonctionnaires* (1930), 3.

[8] Before 1927 the conditions of employment did not permit a grouping according to the juridical nature of the service relationship. This fact accounts for the following classification of the federal personnel made by the Federal Council in 1924:

1. The civil servants or permanent employees who are selected for the administrative period of three years, who receive an annual salary, and who are held to a strictly personal service during the period.
2. The personnel of the legations and consulates.
3. The members of the teaching corps of the Polytechnic School.
4. Employees working by the day or hour.
5. Holders of third class postal, telephone, railway, etc., positions.
6. The auxiliary personnel.
7. Personnel employed "according to the rules of public law." *Message*, 1924, II; *ibid.*, 1930, 3.

was a regular and steady one. With the centralization in its hands in 1848 of the postal, customs, and coinage services, the Confederation was employing in 1849 approximately 2,830 officials. Due chiefly to the development of the postal service, the number had increased to 3,608 in 1852. The total in 1875 stood at 7,781, a figure which included 1,061 telegraph and telephone officials.[9]

The statistics of the various public services will indicate the numerical development on from 1875. For example, the total personnel employed on all railroads grew from 15,787 in 1885 (twelve years before the nationalization of all the important lines) to 26,066 in 1895 and to 47,974 in 1915.[10] The following table will serve to indicate the growth from 1875 to 1920:

PERSONNEL OF THE CONFEDERATION[11]

Year	Central Administration	Customs	Posts	Telegraph and Telephone	Railways	Total
1875	807	755	5,148	1,061		7,871
1900	4,216	1,742	10,157	3,762		19,877
1910	4,908	2,340	15,136	4,454	34,984	61,822
1913	5,799	2,398	16,758	4,230	37,683	66,868
1920	7,935	3,052	16,961	7,040	39,410	74,398

If the demands of the war period thus caused the total number of personnel to exceed 74,000 in 1920, the necessities of the post-war period led to a gradual reduction after 1921. This decrease was brought about largely by the failure to fill vacancies caused by death or retirement.[12] By the end of 1929 the total federal personnel consisted of 45,817 civil servants, 9,768 employees, 7,945 workers, and 770 auxiliaries, or a total of 64,300. From 1920 to 1929, the number had thus decreased over 10,000 units, two-thirds of the reduction having taken place between 1920 and 1923. Despite this fact, the number of officials classed as civil servants has increased by 2,050 over the figure for

[9] Ernst Kupper, *Die Besoldungspolitik des Bundes seit 1848* (1929), 11-14.

[10] *Annuaire statistique de la Suisse*, 1927, 223.

[11] Kupper, *op. cit.*, 20. The statistics for the railroad personnel in 1900 are not available.

[12] *Rapport du conseil fédéral sur sa gestion*, 1922, 514; *Rapport de l'office du personnel*, 1930, 1.

1923. A total of 46,000 officials are now classed as civil servants in which are included 59% of the total personnel engaged in the general administrative services and 82% in the railway administration.

Although it is generally taken for granted that a large majority of the public officials in Switzerland are in the cantonal and municipal services, the most recent figures available will hardly support this view. The comparative sizes of the respective groups may be ascertained from the following chart for the year 1920:

Field of Activity	Services of Confederation		Services of Cantons and Municipalities		Total
	Number	Per cent	Number	Per cent	
Central Administration	7,940	10.5	16,607	21.4	24,547
Traffic Institutions	60,073	79.4	3,093	4.0	63,166
Educational Institutions	289	0.4	27,683	35.6	27,972
Metal and Machine Industries	6,084	8.0	289	0.4	6,373
Public Construction	518	0.7	9,494	12.2	10,012
Water, Gas and Power Plants...	42	0.1	7,872	10.1	7,914
Trade and Banking Services....	99	0.1	3,134	4.0	3,233
Land and Forest Economy	25	0.03	6,496	8.4	6,521
Public Health.....	49	0.1	2,043	2.6	2,092
Miscellaneous	495	0.7	1,004	1.3	1,499
TOTAL	75,614	100.0	77,715	100.0	153,329[13]

It is thus evident that in 1920 there were roughly only about 2,000 more public officials employed by the cantons and municipalities than by the Confederation. It is also worthy of notice that 79.4% of the personnel of the Confederation were engaged in the so-called traffic services, and that 35.6% of the personnel of the cantons and municipalities were engaged in educational activities. These 153,329 public officials constitute 8.3% of the 1,852,053 persons gainfully employed in Switzerland; they represent approximately 4% of the total population.

[13] We are indebted to the Federal Personnel Office for having compiled and transmitted these statistics in a personal communication of May 12, 1930.

When one attempts to explain the causes of the growth in size of this body of public officials, he immediately enters the realm of the problematical. The desire to create offices for political purposes and defective administrative organizations which partially explain the number of public officials in other states, however, do not seem to have obtained in Switzerland to any marked degree. When it is remembered that 53,975 out of a total of 63,977 individuals in 1927 were engaged in the railroad, telegraph and telephone, and postal services, one is constrained to suggest that the normal expansion of these services largely accounts for the accretion in numbers since 1900. Nevertheless "civil-servant determinism" has played its rôle. Strong pressure has continuously been brought to bear by certain of the organizations of personnel to include as many categories as possible within the civil servant class. Naturally the desire is to secure for them the superior financial advantages and greater security of tenure which inclusion would entail. The Federative Union made such demands when the project of the Federal Law was under discussion.[14] Since 1927 especial efforts have been expended looking toward the inclusion of the rural mail carriers and the workers in the workshops.[15] The reduction in the number of offices after 1921 took place in the face of the opposition of the personnel which desired that the places be retained for purposes of promotion.[16] These facts indicate that in Switzerland as elsewhere the bureaucracy is generally expansionistic.

As has already been pointed out these officials of the Confederation, superior and subordinate, are grouped into seven administrative departments; that is, all except those which are included in the Federal Chancellerie and those which fall under the jurisdiction of the Federal Courts. At the head of each is to be found a federal councillor and below him the various direct agents of the government (*agents directs des gouvernements*) in the form of the chiefs of divisions, the chiefs of sections, the chiefs of services and the inferior chiefs of various categories. A description of the present structure of the railroad organization, while not typical, will indicate the nature of the gradations. By the Federal Law of February 1, 1923, "for the simplifica-

[14] *Message*, 1924, 44.
[15] *Ibid.*, 1930, 8.
[16] *Rapport de l'office du personnel du 15 Avril 1930*, 1.

tion of the administration of the railroads,''[17] the ultimate control is rested in the hands of the Federal Council.[18] The Federal Council selects an Administrative Council[19] and, upon the recommendation of this body, appoints the members of the General Directorate of the Railroads.[20] Administrative divisions are provided for under the control of the General Directorate, the heads of which are, however, appointed by the Administrative Council.[21] The entire country is divided into three territorial divisions or *arrondissements,* each of which is headed by a director selected by the Federal Council upon the recommendation of the Administrative Council.[22] In addition there are *arrondissement* Councils.[23] The type of organization which is more typical may be found in the postal service.[24] General control is vested in the hands of the Federal Council, and regulations regarding the posts emanate from it. Subordinate to the Federal Council stand the head of the Department of Posts and Railways and the General Directorate of Posts, each of which is charged with certain duties. The General Directorate is headed by a Director General. Territorially the country is divided into eleven *arrondissements,* each of which is supervised by a director.

For purposes of classifying the functions, the administration has been divided into five groups:[25]

1. The departments and the Federal Chancellerie.
2. The Federal Courts.
3. The administration of customs.
4. The administration of posts and telegraphs.
5. The administration of federal railways.

The functions are then grouped according to their nature, indicating

[17] *R.O.,* 1923, 227 ff.

[18] *Ibid.,* Arts. 5-7.

[19] *Ibid.,* Art. 8.

[20] *Ibid.,* Art. 12.

[21] *Ibid.,* Art. 16.

[22] *Ibid.,* Art. 20.

[23] *Ibid.,* Arts. 23-24. For the provisions of the ordinance of the Federal Council carrying into effect the provisions of the law, see *ibid.,* 1923, 341 ff. Note also *Rapport de gestion et comptes des chemins de fer,* 1929, 1-3. Adequate discussion of the organization before 1923 can be found in Georges Gariel, *La centralisation économique en Suisse* (2 vols., 1923), II.

[24] *R.O.,* 1910, 731 ff.; *ibid.,* 1910, 1010-1026.

[25] *Message,* 1930, 16.

to a certain extent the hierarchical structure. There are for the Federal Chancellerie and for the Federal Courts, for example, (1) the chiefs of the divisions, the vice-chancellors and the secretaries of departments, (2) the other superior civil servants and so on down to (13) the bailiffs and doorkeepers and (14) the personnel of the laboratories. The same general classification holds for the last three groups.[26]

Over the personnel included within these various classes the superior officials exercise their powers in two ways. The one method is by the power of giving orders and instructions to the civil servants *(commandement)*; the second is by the power of inspecting continuously the functioning of the public service and of restraining all faults which are committed *(surveillance).*[27] If one were to differentiate between these acts or the exercise of these powers in so far as they affected the officials themselves, their application would be seen to affect among other matters the nomination, the promotion, the discipline and the retirement of the officials. Regarding nomination the Federal Law contains the following provisions:

"Art. 4. The Federal Council fixes the special conditions required for appointment to the different positions. It may delegate this power to the departments which are subordinate to it. The Federal Court and the Federal Insurance Court fix these conditions for the civil servants whom they appoint.

"Art. 5. The Federal Council appoints civil servants subject to the reservations contained in paragraphs 2 and 3. It may delegate this power to the departments which are subordinate to it.

"The Federal Court and the Federal Insurance Court appoint their officials.

"The power to appoint federal railway officials belongs to the authorities indicated in federal legislation governing railway organization."

"Art. 62. The Federal Council lays down rules governing the service relations of persons hired by the Confederation who do not have the status of civil servants.'"[28]

[26] On October 5, 1929, a detailed decree was finally issued placing the various officials in their proper salary classes. *Übersicht der Ämterklassification nach Besoldungsklassen* (1929); *Arreté du conseil fédéral concernant la classification des fonctions* (1929), 3 ff. However, there are still functions of the same nature and same name which are included in different salary classes. *Message,* 1930, 17, 21 ff.

[27] Léon Duguit, *Traité de droit constitutionnel* (5 vols., 1921), III, 60.

[28] White, *op. cit.,* 363-364, 377. The powers conferred are limited in certain respects. Only persons of Swiss nationality, except in cases of special dispensation by the Federal Council, are eligible. *Ibid.,* Art. 2, 363. Appointment is to be preceded by a public competition for the vacant position, but the Federal Council may itself allow subordinate departments to except certain officers. *Ibid.,* Art. 3, 363.

An ordinance of the Swiss Federal Council in October, 1930, empowered the departments and the general directorates of the customs, the posts, and the telegraphs and telephones to fix the conditions of admission to each of their functions. In the making of appointments the Federal Council selects the civil servants of the departments included in salary classes one to eleven, those of the customs, postal and telegraph services and those of the Polytechnic School included in classes one to four. The general directorates of the customs, postal and telegraph services appoint their civil servants, for salary classes fourteen to twenty-six. The Council of the Polytechnic School appoints those for classes five to twenty-six. All other appointments not otherwise provided for fall into the hands of the departments.[29] In the railroad service the director of the *arrondissement*, subject to a variety of controls leading to the General Directorate, "nominates, promotes, dismisses and pensions the *fonctionnaires* and employees of the *arrondissements* upon the recommendation of the chiefs of the divisions."[30] These provisions clearly indicate that, subject to a few limitations, the Federal Council, the Federal Courts, and the General Directorate of the railroads possess almost complete discretion in the selection of personnel. The same observation holds true of promotions, for in the words of Art. 12 of the Federal Law, "the Federal Council defines the rules of promotion, though it may delegate the power to departments which are subordinate to it."[31]

Even in the matter of civil and penal responsibility the superior officials *(gouvernants)* play a conspicuous rôle. While, of course, the federal official is liable for the ordinary criminal offences just as any other Swiss citizen, he is amenable to the jurisdiction of the regular cantonal courts for penal offences committed in office only on the basis of an assignment by the Federal Council unless the case has been brought originally under a special grant of powers from the Federal Council.[32] It is to be noted that the Federal Council may deny the

[29] *Ordonnance sur les conditions d'engagement des fonctionnaires de l'administration générale de la Confédération*, 1929, 2-3: *Feuille fédérale*, Oct. 1930, 1.

[30] *R.O.*, 1923, 227; *Ordonnance sur les conditions d'engagement des fonctionnaires des chemins de fer fédéraux* (1929), 2.

[31] See White, *op. cit.*, 365; *Ordonnance . . . de l'administration générale, op. cit.*, 5-6.

[32] Fleiner, *op. cit.*, 269-270. The penal responsibility is provided for by Art. 107 of the Constitution and Arts. 53-57 of the Federal Penal Code of Feb. 4, 1853, as subsequently amended. This law provides for punishments in cases of bribery,

grant of authority provided it feels that no official misfeasance has been committed by the official.[33] In civil actions, in which the official may be held for full restitution of the damage caused by his dereliction, the processes brought against the officials chosen by the Federal Council must first be brought before that body. If the Federal Council denies its consent to the proposed action then the plaintiff is debarred from the federal courts, though he may under certain conditions bring action against the official in the ordinary cantonal courts.[34] The Federal Court, however, has exclusive jurisdiction over financial claims arising out of the service relationship.[35] The powers of the Federal Council were retained in full in the Federal Law over all administrative disputes not capable of a pecuniary evaluation affecting all appointees except the subordinates of the Federal Courts.[36] The latter, of course, retain full jurisdiction over the claims of their subordinate officials.

In disciplinary matters the supreme authority of the Federal Council and the Federal Courts over their subordinates was recognized by the Law of 1927.[37] The disciplinary punishments are:

1. The reprimand.
2. The fine up to 100 francs.
3. The withdrawal of transportation facilities.
4. The temporary suspension, with reduction or deprivation of salary.
5. The disciplinary transfer or demotion with an equal or lower salary, in case of necessity with reduction or deprivation of lodging bonus.
6. The reduction of salary within the limits of the sums fixed by the position.

---

unlawful acceptance of gifts, etc. See S. Bury, *Manuel de droit public* (1869), 322 ff. Otherwise the crimes which may be committed depend upon the laws of the canton in which the offender happens to reside. *Message*, 1924, *op. cit.*, 129.

[33] Ordinary "crimes and misdemeanors" over which the cantonal courts have jurisdiction may be transferred by the Federal Council to the Federal Court. White, *op. cit.*, Art. 36, 370.

[34] Fleiner, *op. cit.*, 272.

[35] Included in these matters which may thus come before the Federal Court are:
1. Claims of compensation for an invention, White, *op. cit.*, Art. 16, 366.
2. Claims for salaries and expenses. *Ibid.*, Arts. 37-54, 370-375.
3. Claims arising from the abolition of an office. *Ibid.*, Art. 55, 375-376.
4. Claims arising from an altering of the service relationship. *Idem.*

[36] *Ibid.*, Art. 58, 376. These matters include disputes concerning the rules of work, the right of association, etc. *Message*, 1924, 193. In conformity with Art. 14 of the Federal Law decisions of the General Directorate of the railroads relating to public expenditures may always be taken to the Federal Council on appeal.

[37] White, *op. cit.*, Art. 33, 369.

7. The reduction or elimination of ordinary salary increases.
8. The transfer to a provisional position.
9. The removal.[38]

According to an ordinance of 1930 the actual disciplinary power in the department would be exercised by the Federal Council and the chief of the department for all disciplinary punishments and the chief of the division for the reprimand, fines and temporary reduction in salary. Over postal, telegraph and customs officials the Federal Council and the chief of the department have jurisdiction in all disciplinary matters, while the general directorates of these services have the power of inflicting all disciplinary punishments except the transfer and dismissal of civil servants of classes one to four.[39] However, by the Federal Law of June 11, 1928, on Administrative and Disciplinary Jurisdiction, there was granted to the newly created Chamber of Claims of Civil Servants *(chambre des contentieux des fonctionnaires)* of the Federal Court final jurisdiction over cases involving the application of the two most severe disciplinary punishments, the removal and transfer.[40] Otherwise, the regular federal judiciary has no power of interferance in disciplinary cases not involving subordinates of the Federal Court.

With regard to retirement provisions, about 85% of the officials employed in the general administrative agencies and approximately 95% of those engaged in the railway services are insured in one of the

[38] *Ibid.*, Art. 31, 368-369. See for a complete summary of the disciplinary punishments *Rapport, S.S.B.P.*, 1928-1929, 97-98. In the telegraph and telephone services during 1929, some 193 disciplinary punishments were meted out, of which 155 consisted of fines up to 5 francs. *Annuaire, Administration des télégraphes et des téléphones suisses*, 1929, 9. There are certain limitations placed upon the action of the disciplinary authorities such as the requirement of an investigation before judgment is rendered and the right of the civil servant to receive aid from a representative. White, *op. cit.*, Art. 32, 369.

[39] *Ordonnance . . . de l'administration générale de la Confédération* (1929), *op. cit.*, Art. 26, 13. Since the *R.O.* for 1930 is not available and in view of the fact that the ordinance has been recently promulgated, I am assuming that it was issued in the form proposed in the *Projet du départment des finances du 14 septembre 1929*. These matters were dealt with in prior legislation affecting the railroads and are not considered in the similar *Ordonnance . . . des chemins de fer* (1929), *op. cit.* See *R.O.*, 1923, 227 ff.

[40] *R.O.*, 1928, 845. It must be borne in mind that the infliction of disciplinary punishments does not affect the penal and civil liability of the civil servants for the same acts. White, *op. cit.*, Art. 30, 368; *Message*, 1924, 21.

two Federal Insurance Funds.[41] Though, as indicated, appeals arising out of the disputes involving the insurance laws go to the Federal Court for adjudication, the control of the government *(gouvernants)* is limited only by certain legal provisions otherwise. The organs of the Insurance Fund for the General Administration are the Administrative Council and the office of the Department of Finance charged with the administration of the Fund.[42] Over both of these the Federal Council has final control *(direction supérieure)*, and the duties and powers of the Administrative Council are fixed by that body. The Fund for Pensions and Aid for the Railways is "administered by the General Directorate with the collaboration of the personnel," while the "administration is organized by a decree of the Council of Administration of the Federal Railways, and, in addition, by the special regulations of the General Directorate."[43] The control here as in the selection, promotion, and disciplining of the civil servants thus rests ultimately with few legal restrictions in the hands of the superior officials.

Such is the hierarchical arrangement in the Swiss public services at the present day. It remains to be seen whether the present relationships between the superior and the subordinate officials are undergoing a change, and, if so, to consider the forces and movements which may be making for a new synthesis.

[41] The general provisions of the Statutes regulating these Funds are discussed in some detail in Chapter IV.

[42] *R.O.*, 1919, 733; *ibid.*, 1920, 755.

[43] *Statuts de la caisse de pensions et de secours du personnel des chemins de fer* (1921), 29 ff. The reference to the Council of Administration indicates that this statute was enacted before the reorganization of the railroads in 1923.

CHAPTER IV

THE PERSONNEL OF THE SWISS CIVIL SERVICE[1]

We come now to the third characteristic of a bureaucracy, the determinate qualifications of the members of the organization required for the fulfillment of their several functions. As was pointed out above, the acquisition of such qualifications depends upon the prospect of a fixed salary, secure tenure, and regular promotion in anticipation of which the candidate undertakes the necessary training. It will be possible to show that here, too, the Swiss democracy has gone far towards developing an organized bureaucracy out of the inherent necessities of the situation. In analyzing the pertinent facts, we have taken up first entrance and promotion, second salary and pension, and third progressive rationalization of the technical aspects of the bureau.

In considering the recruitment of candidates for the public services in Switzerland the officials may be divided into four classes for purposes of convenience. The workers and artisans have, as a rule, attended the primary schools, and artisans are presumed to have served an apprenticeship of two and one-half years to four years in conformity with the general laws as well as the standards set by the Swiss Association of Arts and Meters. The auxiliary administrative service includes the functions performed largely by persons, mostly women, who are employed in the secretariats, in the divisions of control and in the postal services. The candidates for these positions have generally attended primary and secondary schools and a commercial school[2] for a short time. They are assumed to have made a study of languages, stenography, and other specialized subjects which will be of use in the performance of their duties. The administrative services of middle and superior degree are filled normally by those who have studied in schools corresponding to the American high schools (Mittelschulen). The superior officials usually are the possessors of a university training and frequently a legal one. The technical and scientific services are filled, as a rule, by individuals who have studied either in a university or in a technical school. However, there is not, as there cannot be, any

[1] The discussion in this chapter is based largely upon material contained in various typewritten reports and other special and unprinted information which the Swiss Federal Personnel Office was kind enough to furnish.

[2] These schools are maintained by the cantons and communes and receive subventions from the federal government.

general set of rules governing the selection of officials who perform these specialized and technical duties.

In general every person admitted to the services of the Swiss Confederation must fulfill two requirements. He must be able to pass a rigorous physical examination, and he must be a Swiss citizen of good character.[3] Outside of these general stipulations the various services apply different rules. In the central administration the candidates for the auxiliary administrative posts announced for competition[4] are given an examination in typewriting and shorthand. Frequently these offices are filled by promotion. The offices are filled for a trial period of three to six months and are not uncommonly held by individuals who have served an apprenticeship in the cantonal and municipal services.

In the customs administration the recruitment of women is carried on according to the principles governing selection in the central administrative agencies. Otherwise the personnel is divided into two groups, the civil officials and the frontier guards. The frontier guards must be at least twenty-eight years of age, must have performed military service and must have received a good education. An oral and written examination is given in which those who show familiarity with more than one language are given the preference. A four months' period of in-

[3] White, *op. cit.*, Art. 2, 363.
[4] The vacancies are announced in certain publications, the most important ones in the *Feuille fédérale*. The following illustration will indicate the methods used for "announcing posts for competition":

Address	Place Vacant	Salary (fr.)	Delay of Entry	Qualifications
Department of Interior President of Council of Federal Polytechnic School at Zurich	Curator of the Botanical Collections of Federal Polytechnic Schools	8,000 to 11,600	Dec. 14, 1929	Complete university course; scientific practice in the fields of botany and geography of plants; aptitude for advanced teaching.
Director of Federal Construction (This place will probably be filled by promotion) *Feuille fédérale*, 1929, Vol. III, 585, 586.	Administrative Assistant	8,000 to 11,600	Dec. 16, 1929	Profound knowledge of administration; three national languages

struction and a seven months' period of probationary service for the successful ones are climaxed by an additional training for four weeks and the final trials. From these frontier guards the civil officials of lowest rank are almost always recruited. The candidates for the middle and superior positions must have as a minimum a secondary school education and a familiarity with two languages. Those with university training are naturally better equipped, however, to pass the rigid examination covering languages, mathematics, economics, history and constitutional law. The civil officials likewise pass through a probationary period of twelve months before being finally admitted into the services.

In the postal administration individuals between the ages of sixteen and twenty-two, showing evidence of a good secondary school education and a knowledge of two languages, are eligible for candidacy to the offices of the middle and superior classes. The preliminary examination, given by a teacher, a representative of the General Director and a representative of the *arrondissement* directors, covers languages, mathematics, geography, history and civics. The examination, a rather difficult one, is designed to test the candidate's powers of exposition as well as his general information. A psychological test to ascertain the general aptitude of the applicant for the postal services follows. For a number of years the telegraph services have not recruited candidates to fill vacancies in the higher positions. However, they have had need of procuring technically trained men for the specialized work, and these it has secured to some extent from private industry. The railroad administration applies, as do the other services, the general rules applicable to the selection of women in the regular administrative branches. Artisan apprentices are chosen provisionally for the workshops from persons between the ages of fourteen and eighteen years. A preliminary examination necessitating a primary school training must be passed before the candidate is subjected to a psychological test of his memory, vision, attention, vivacity and dexterity. He likewise must serve a long period of apprenticeship. Officials of the stations are designated from apprentices who enter the services between the ages of seventeen and twenty-four years after having successfully passed an educational and psychological test. The examinations which are given to apprentices for the positions of conductors, engineers and brakemen stress languages and mathematics. The mechanics and mechanic helpers are chosen largely from the artisans and workers of the workshops. In some cases a university education and, in others, a technical training is required of applicants for positions in the technical and in the middle and superior administrative services.[5]

A cursory glance over these general methods utilized for the selection of personnel brings into clear relief certain striking features of the Swiss system. Concerning the nature of instruction required as a prerequisite for admission into the services it may be said that Switzerland does not emphasize the specialized instruction relied upon in the United States nor does she place the reliance upon the general background emphasized in England. Switzerland occupies a sort of midway ground. The insistence upon apprenticeships and periods of trial is worthy of mention only because of the great emphasis placed upon them. That an especial significance should be attached to linguistic attainments would normally be expected in a state which recognizes three official languages. The requirement of the use of psychological examinations on a rather broad scale constitutes an unusual feature. But, lest too much comparison be attempted where little comparison can be made, it must be repeated that the important services of the Swiss Confederation are more limited in scope and more technical in nature than those of most other states and that the existing conditions are unique in many ways.

In passing from the sphere of laws, regulations and decrees into the realm of so-called practical politics, one is immediately confronted with the oft-repeated statement that partisan preferment and personal favoritism have been almost non-existent in the making of appointments in Switzerland. The observation has been made so frequently that by virtue of mere repetition alone it has come to possess the stamp of orthodoxy.[6] Various reasons have been ascribed for this phenomenon. The weaknesses of party groups in the chambers with the consequent lack of partisan urge upon the appointing officials have been cited as a factor. The fact that the Federal Council must approve of appointments as a collective group has been pointed to as preventing abuses by individuals.[7] Nepotism is banned in the cantons by laws and in the confederation by a sentiment which are an historical survival of

[5] See *Rapport, S.E.V.*, 1929, 91-99. For a discussion of proposals for changing, see *Procès-verbal de la 4e séance de la commission générale du personnel des chemins de fer fédéraux*, July 3, 1929, 11 ff.

[6] See L. Dupriez, *Les ministres dans les principaux pays d'Europe et d'Amérique* (2 vols., 1893), II, 238-239; R. C. Brooks, *Government and Politics of Switzerland*, 121.

[7] Dupriez, *op. cit.*, II, 238.

the years when such action and such sentiment were necessary to prevent the formation of family oligarchies.[8] The chief explanation usually given is that the positions in the public services have not carried with them the remuneration and the honor which corresponding positions in other states have. They have consequently not been sought after as eagerly.[9] Some of these explanations would bear testing in the light of present-day facts and are, we believe, subject to some modifications. The charge of lack of remuneration, to the extent to which it is true today, might as well have been made in the United States where the offices are generally sought, although they are not, comparatively speaking, well paid. Those who attribute the absence of partisan influences to the fact that appointments are subject to the approval of the entire Federal Council (as a group), even if sound in theory, do not realize that in actuality the Federal Council makes few appointments. Furthermore, the recent growth of the Socialist and, to some extent, the Communist party is possibly making for a realignment of forces in the two chambers which may be felt in various ways.[10]

If we pass on to a consideration of the truth for which the various explanations are given, there may be found evidences of partisan influence. Bryce noted the charge that "the Federal Council is alleged to have been influenced in the exercise of its patronage by party considerations, appointing or promoting persons who are recommended by Members of the Assembly as having served the dominant party. . . ."[11] For example M. Bratschi, President of the Federative Union, contends that the representation accorded by the General Directorate of the Railways to the Federation of Christian-Socialist Transport Personnel "was due more to political pressure on the part of the Catholic-Conservative Party than to the importance of the Christian-Socialists as a group."[12] Complaints to the effect that too many of the offices of the central bureaus are given to German-speaking citi-

[8] J. M. Vincent, *Government in Switzerland* (1920), 88. For the historical explanation see V. Martin, *Histoire de la Suisse* (1926), 147 ff.

[9] Dupriez, *op. cit.*, II, 238; James Bryce, *Modern Democracies* (2 vols., 1921), I, 361.

[10] See Martin, *op. cit.*, 280. The probable future representation of the Socialist Party in the Federal Council is considered of particular importance by certain of the associations of personnel. See Chap. V.

[11] *Op. cit.*, 368.

[12] Robert Bratschi, "Le droit de discussion dans les enterprises fédérales," *R.S.*, April, 1930, 107-108.

zens are not unknown.[13] One of the chief arguments given in 1900, and subsequently repeated, in support of the initiative petition providing for the popular election of members of the Federal Council was "that it would eliminate the influence of parties."[14] Well-informed Swiss students of political processes are inclined to stress these facts and to justify the belief that these influences have played a more important rôle in the past than has usually been admitted and that these influences have been increasing within recent years.[15]

If it is true that the remuneration of officials has been in the past and is today lower than in most states, it is nevertheless true that changes within the past two decades have served to accord a great many financial privileges in the aggregate. At the present day the civil servants are divided for salary purposes into twenty-six classes. The following scale will illustrate the nature of the classification:[16]

	Maximum (fr.)	Minimum (fr.)
Class 1	17,000	13,400
Class 2	15,500	11,900
Class 3	14,000	10,400
......	......	......
Class 24	4,500	2,900
Class 25	4,200	2,800
Class 26	3,900	2,700

For securing the services of persons especially qualified or for retaining them in the service of the Confederation, payments which exceed by twenty per cent the maximum for each class may be made. On the other hand in districts where the cost of living is above or below the average, the minimum and maximum payments for each class may be reduced or increased as the case may be.[17] The directors general of the railways and the director general of the Department of Posts and Telegraphs do not fall within the regular classification and receive 25,000 francs. Other officials such as the district railway directors

[13] Brooks, op. cit., 121; Rapport, S.S.F.P., 1928, 3. The justification of such complaints is, however, contested. It is pointed out in this connection that, although only 1.74 out of every 1000 Swiss citizens belong to the Federal Civil Service, 2.07 out of every 1000 citizens in the French canton of Neuenberg are members of that service.

[14] T. Curti, Le referendum (1905), 348.

[15] Note the suggestion for the elimination of the limited "political interference" in Switzerland, R. C. Brooks, Civic Training in Switzerland, 141.

[16] Loi fédérale sur le statut des fonctionnaires, Art. 37, 12. These provisions are not included in White's translation.

[17] White, op. cit., Art. 37, 370.

and division chiefs of the general administration are likewise specially provided for. The initial salary corresponds as a rule to the minimum of the class to which the official is appointed, and upon the attainment of the normal maximum of the class an official is entitled to a regular increase at the beginning of each year. This increase is usually equivalent to one-fifteenth of the difference between the maximum and minimum salaries of the class. Those civil servants entitled to a promotion have, however, a right to a special increase.[18]

For each child under eighteen years of age a bonus amounting to 120 francs per child is granted, and for one month after the death of an official the salary of his office is granted to his survivors.[19] Furthermore, where the dependents are in need due to the permanent disability or death of the civil servant, the salary may be granted for a maximum of one year whenever and to the extent to which the capital value of a payment of a federal insurance fund remains beneath the amount of the annual salary. In addition there are various grants for travel and night service, bonuses for meritorious service of a specified number of years and other rights which accrue to the civil servant from a modification or cancellation of the service relationship.[20] It must be noted that the general provisions of the Federal Law apply to about two-thirds of all civil servants.[21]

Instead of having a regular pension system for officials Switzerland has worked out through the years a rather complicated compulsory insurance scheme. In general all of the agents of the Confederation except those who have left the service for the third time and those who

[18] *Ibid.*, Arts. 40-41, 371-372.
[19] *Ibid.*, Art. 47, 373.
[20] *Ibid.*, Arts. 44, 54-55, pp. 372, 375-376.
[21] Some interesting comparisons may be made from the following figures of the total expenditures of the Confederation for its personnel in different years:

Year	Administration	Posts	Telegraphs and Telephones	Railroads	Total
	(In thousands of francs)				
1852	734	1,156	———	———	1,890
1875	4,063	6,220	1,338	———	11,621
1913	11,416	21,124	5,504	———	38,044
1900	24,153	43,708	12,392	103,879	184,132
1921	70,536	102,189	39,457	240,887	453,069
1925	62,919	88,868	32,473	212,285	396,545

Kupper, *op. cit.*, 22.

are provided for from communal and other sources are included. The amount of the insurance is equivalent to the salary or salaries including special sums allowed for the increasing cost of living but excluding special sums allowed for houses and dependents. The insurance begins at the time of entry into the service and ends with the retirement except in cases of death or disability. From two sources are derived the funds from which the payments are made. Seven per cent of the annual salary of the insured, five monthly payments of any increase in the insured's salary, the expenses of the up-keep of the insurance offices and certain additional sums are contributed by the Government. Five per cent of his salary and four monthly payments of any increase in his annual salary are paid by the civil servant. These payments of the civil servant cease when the insured male reaches the age of seventy years or when he has been in the service for fifty years. Thirty-five years of service release a female employee from further obligations. The amount which the pensioned official is to receive depends both upon the salary of the official and upon the number of years of service. The scale for married officials is illustrative:

Amount receivable	Years of service
20%	1
25%	2
30%	3
—	—
48%	17
—	—
64%	27
70%	30

The proportion of the personnel expenditures to the total expenditures in the administrative services excluding the railroads will serve to indicate their growing significance to the Confederation:

Year	Total Expenditures	Personnel Expenditures	Percentage
	(In thousands of francs)		
1852	12,456	1,890	15.2
1875	43,236	11,621	26.9
1900	102,758	38,044	37.0
1913	190,923	80,253	42.0
1920	443,093	206,409	46.6
1925	537,089	184,260	34.3

Ibid., 23.

Orphans receive ten per cent of the last annual salary of the deceased until they reach the age of eighteen, but the sum is never to exceed thirty per cent for all the orphans dependent. Widows are the recipients of sums ranging from twenty-five to fifty per cent of their deceased husband's pension. Special consideration is given to disabled officials and to a class known as *déposants*.[22]

In addition to the regular compulsory insurance, the Confederation either allows or requires four types of insurance in case of accidents. Obligatory insurance is required of approximately five-sixths of the personnel of the Confederation for accidents occurring both in and outside of the service. Insurance is provided by the Confederation for about 1,200 officials in the military services. Certain officials of the telegraph and telephone and customs services who are not compulsorily insured and who are subjected to special dangers and officials of the central administration are provided for in a separate manner.[23]

[22] *Avantages spéciaux accordés par la Confédération à son personnel* (1925), 1-5; *Rapport du conseil fédéral sur sa gestion*, 1929, 14 ff. An incomplete and somewhat inaccurate summary may be found in *Monthly Labor Review*, Feb., 1928, xxvi, 66 ff. Reference has been made in a preceding chapter to the federal laws governing the system. The following statistics will indicate the present condition of the two Insurance Funds by showing the number of persons insured and pensioned:

I. The Pension and Aid Fund for the Railroads

	1929
1. Actives insured	
a. Completely insured	33,075
b. Partially insured	655
2. Pensioned invalids	8,732
3. Pensioned wives	5,335
4. Pensioned orphans	1,684
5. Others pensioned	400

Rapport de gestion et comptes des chemins de fer fédéraux, 1929, 13. For comparative purposes see *Die in der Schweiz bestehenden Einrichtungen für die Alters-, Invaliden- und Hinterlassenen-Versicherung*, 1925, 27.

II. The Insurance Fund for the General Administration

	1929
1. Actives insured	26,130
2. Pensioned invalids	4,183
3. Pensioned wives	1,911
4. Pensioned orphans	1,309
5. Others pensioned	100

Rapport du conseil fédéral sur sa gestion, 1929, 51.

[23] *Avantages spéciaux, op. cit.*, 5 ff.; Annex B.

The growing financial burden upon the Confederation which is partly explained by the salary and insurance systems in Switzerland has been largely instrumental in causing the Swiss to begin a serious study of administrative problems and personnel questions. In addition, the routine methods which inevitably creep into the work of the department and the worship of the *status quo* have combined to urge the necessity of breaking with the established habits of life and of work and of replacing these with a new division of labor as well as a new professional attitude. If the changes which have been instituted in Switzerland appear to be of little importance to the administrative reformer, the explanation is possibly due to the relatively efficient manner in which the Swiss bureaucracy has functioned in the past and the consequent relatively recent realization that changes were desirable. If the innovations seem to be of a superficial nature, the retort can be made that most administrative reforms fail to appreciate, not to speak of remedying, the really fundamental problems presented by modern bureaucracies. At any rate the recent efforts to secure economy and efficiency in the public services may be briefly reviewed.

In 1921 a special bureau was provisionally created in the Department of Finance charged with the general task of simplifying the services and methods of work and the more specific, and not inconsistent, duty of reducing the number of civil servants. Approaching its work through the second of its tasks, the bureau proposed various simplifications in the services and the fusions of several bureaus. ''In the face of the numerical size of the civil service, of the great diversity of personnel questions which were presented and of the importance and difficulties of the arrangement of the conditions of service by the Confederation as employer with its personnel as employees,'' the Federal Council decided upon the need of a permanent and legally recognized organ for treating these problems. While its activities were to be largely directed toward the suggestions for, and the aid in framing legislation affecting the personnel as a whole, this agency was to be empowered to make any proposals for desirable changes in the conduct of the separate branches of the service. With economy as its watchword, this bureau was to be charged with furthering the simplifications of methods of work, securing greater cooperation between bureaus and departments, increasing the output of work and reducing the number of officials to the minimum consistent with actual need.[24] The result

[24] *Message*, 1924, *op. cit.*, 202 ff.

was seen in the creation by the Federal Law of 1927 of a Federal Personnel Office in the Finance Department.[25] Its powers were outlined as follows:

1. "It prepares decrees, ordinances and regulations which the Federal Council promulgates in the execution of the present law.

2. "It prepares the decisions looking toward more scientific employment of the personnel appointed by the Confederation, or gives its opinion upon projects of this kind.

3. "It studies questions of principle concerning the personnel and insurance of personnel or gives its opinion on the subject.

4. "It gives its opinion on propositions concerning personnel questions of an individual nature; appointment and promotion, fixing of salaries and wages, housing bonuses, allowances, special payments and prizes, payment of wages or salary to survivors, secondary occupations, payment of damages, disciplinary measures.

5. "It gives its opinion upon petitions and suits concerning the service relationship of persons hired by the Confederation.

6. "It co-operates in the creation of personnel commissions.

7. "It prepares personnel statistics."[26]

Guided by the experience of the transport services, the Personnel Office has demanded on several occasions the creation of a commission of experts which would be charged with the examination of conditions of work in the administration. Before naming this commission, however, the Federal Council decreed that the departments, through their bureau chiefs, should make an examination and point out the present needs and defects, the possibilities of simplification and of expediting the work and feasible methods of reducing the personnel. Strange to say, if such results be strange, "the reports received declared unanimously that the divisions and the bureaus were organized on a simple and rational basis and that the existing system was proof in itself; the needs and faults would already have been corrected if they (the department heads) had perceived them." With the comment that "the

---

[25] The reasons for attaching this office to the Department of Finance are fully discussed in *ibid.*, 203. A minority of the Committee which considered the project in the National Council favored a different status for the Personnel Office. Certain ones as Bratschi, the spokesman for the minority, would have made it a superior authority of recourse in personnel matters under the Federal Council and independent of the Department of Finance. *V.E.R.*, 1925-1927, 194. Suggestions even point to its being placed under the Federal Assembly and not under the Federal Council. *Ibid.*, 194-195. See also *A.B.St.*, Sommer-Session, 1925, 171.

[26] White, *op. cit.*, Art. 65, 378.

future will see no change,'' the Personnel Office justifies the necessity of action on its own part and carries on with the work.

The general accomplishments of the Confederation during the few years in which it has been seriously considering the personnel problem and administrative reform do not look large in the aggregate. However, the Federal Personnel Office points with some justifiable pride to desirable innovations in organization and method. The changes in the customs administration have consisted in replacing superior officials by officials who fall within lower salary classes. Economy, it is insisted, has been secured without the sacrifice of any efficiency. While the hours of work were shortened and the number of vacations were increased after 1920, changes in methods have not operated to prevent a decrease of 3,000 units in the personnel of the administration of posts and telegraphs. Officials have been charged with the performance of more difficult tasks than formerly, and the unnecessary services rendered to the public have been eliminated in some cases. The introduction of automatic equipment in the telegraph services accounts largely for the reduction by thirty per cent in the size of the telegraph personnel. The union of the postal and telegraph offices under the same control in 1918 had already resulted in a better collaboration and a greater coöperation between the various bureaus affected by the change. Particularly in the distribution of letters and telegrams has the *liaison* worked to advantage. The railroad services, with an increase of fifty per cent in their mileage since 1920, have the greatest number of innovations to explain the decrease in the personnel by 5,000 units during the same period. The electrification of the railroads and the improvement of technical equipment have played a leading rôle. Acting after a commission of official and lay experts had made a careful investigation, the General Directors eliminated a number of offices which were not considered particularly necessary and extended the competences and duties of officials of the middle and inferior ranks. The supervising agencies were reorganized, co-operation between specified bureaus was made compulsory and larger and more centralized places of concentration for locomotives were substituted for the more numerous and smaller ones formerly in use. The workshops likewise saw many changes.

If the Confederation has given some special attention to the matter of administrative and mechanical changes, it has not neglected the equally important subject of the professional development of its personnel. While there are no coördinated steps being taken by the services as a whole, the separate branches have introduced their own requirements. In the central administration officials are encouraged and in some instances are required to attend professional schools. Work of an increasingly difficult nature is given them for the purpose of improving their capacities. Perhaps the customs service attaches the greatest importance to the professional development of its personnel. Frontier guards not only must serve a period of carefully supervised probationary service before final appointment, but they must also train at stated intervals later. The task of initiating civil officials into the practical work which their offices require is entrusted to well-qualified officials who have access to all materials which will be of value to the person receiving instruction. Transfers are utilized to acquaint the officials with the different branches of the service, and the taking of examinations for promotion is encouraged. Since linguistic proficiency is of especial value in these services, instruction in languages for auxiliary officials in the postal and telegraph administration is provided by the Confederation in commercial schools. Opportunities for training in the technical aspects of the work and frequent transfers for various classes of individuals characterize these same services. Similar observations could be made regarding the railroad administration. For example an official of Class II, after having served his two years of apprenticeship, holds the position of a candidate (*aspirant*) for one more year before being given a station. Professional instruction is given during these years of candidacy. In short it appears that Switzerland has by no means neglected the personnel problem in her attention to the administrative processes. Switzerland has realized, as some other states have failed to do, that the successful functioning of the public services depends on more than the creation of a theoretically perfect administrative structure or hierarchy.

CHAPTER V

IMPACTS UPON THE HIERARCHY IN SWITZERLAND: THE TREND TOWARD FUNCTIONAL AUTONOMY

The rapid increase in the size of governmental as of all business enterprises was bound to give increasing opportunities to the governmental employees to use collective pressure for the purpose of strengthening their bargaining position with the government, their employer. Not only can the employees of the government organize a lobby as other citizens do for other purposes, but they can strike as employees do in other enterprises. We do not say that they have a right to take such action, but they can certainly stop working and see what happens. But the possibility of using such strike as a weapon to force concessions which arise out of the technical emergencies of modern industrial civilization may be interpreted as an attack upon the hierarchy, one of the essentials of an organized bureaucracy. And it has been so interpreted by the eminent Léon Duguit and many more conservative lawyers, who violently disagree with the conclusions Duguit draws from his analysis.[1] If it is so interpreted, collective action by the civil servant assumes the portentous appearance of threatening the foundation of law and order and proposing the overturn of the government altogether. Upon further investigation it appears, however, that these governmental employees themselves think in terms of a concept of the civil servant which is greatly at variance with the more orthodox view, or perhaps it would be better to say they distinguish more or less clearly between the individual civil servant whose duty to subordinate himself is recognized and groups of government employees who have a right to bargain with the government just as private employees may concerning all matters pertaining to the conditions of their work. Such bargaining has a tendency, however, to extend to what the employees do, as the work council movement in private industry shows. If it does, it touches the foundations of democracy, as it diminishes popular control of governmental activities.

The dominant conception of the modern state is still that which

[1] Duguit, *op. cit.* III, and elsewhere. For a really broad, critical discussion of value beyond the legal verbiage see Elliott, *op. cit.*, Chaps. IV, XV.

considers it as a person; the state is, according to Esmein, "the juridical personification of the nation, the subject and support of public authority."[2] Law thus depends upon the existence of a superior authority over individual wills or upon the existence of sovereignty, and government, in the general sense, "designates the exercise by the sovereign of public authority; it is sovereignty at work."[3] The characteristic types of governments in existence today are, of course, the representative democracies, and in these, as well as in all states, there are certain human needs which must be met. For whatever reason undertaken, whether because they could not be properly performed by private industry or initiative or because of the necessity of monopoly, the fact remains that valuable and necessary services are performed for the individual by public agencies. Certain of these functions are so necessary to the public existence itself that there would be grave dangers to the life of the community if there were interruption. Hence, from the standpoint of the community, the problem of the most efficient and satisfactory method of carrying on these activities becomes a dominant one.[4] The satisfaction of these needs is in a large part an administrative function. If officials, then, carry on vital functions in the modern community reason dictates that the actions of the civil servant be controlled and regulated. This control is in the democratic states exercised by the highest officials *(gouvernants)* who are responsible to the community for the proper functioning of the public services. The subordinate agent is recognized as only a means to an end; the *fonctionnaire, en lui-même, n'est rien.*[5] The civil servant is recognized just as a creature of the law, as an agent of the government and nothing else.

But a growing spirit of dissatisfaction and a feeling of discontent, intensified by the impenetration of democratic ideas into the legislative branch of the government, have caused the government employee to consider himself in a new light. He has begun to recognize himself as a human being. And this tendency on the part of a governmental employee to look upon himself not as a legally created *homunculus,* but as a human being with human needs and human aspirations is most natural, even though perhaps disquieting to a community which

[2] *Elements de droit constitutionnel* (4th ed., 1906), 1.
[3] *Ibid.,* 13.
[4] For a good discussion see Gaston Jèze, *Cours de droit public* (1914), 241 ff.
[5] Hugot-Derville, *op. cit.,* 25.

has grown fat upon the robot-like performance of their duty by these servants of the public good.

The collective consciousness of these employees of the government, based upon their own interests, has crystallized around certain more or less distinctly voiced complaints. The most serious of these complaints quite naturally involves the salaries, pensions and special financial allowances of the officials. The human desire of the employee to improve his financial status cannot be reconciled with the desire of governments to limit their expenditures in so far as possible. With the partially inevitable growth in numbers there follows an increasing drain upon the public treasury which results in a smaller salary scale. Changes in cost of living do not receive recognition in salary laws, and individual hardships follow.

Another characteristic complaint has been that of favoritism, an evil which has assumed various forms. There is parliamentary favoritism which results when the acts of responsible officials are subject to parliamentary influence.[6] Ministerial favoritism, although it exists under all types of government, has taken under democratic government a particular form; that is, favoritism on behalf of the cabinet. "Cabinet influence becomes a convenient means of entering office among the better grades or, if one is already in the hierarchy, of passing over the heads of less favored colleagues."[7] The absolute dependence of the individual civil servant upon his superiors has contributed, where it exists, to one of the most serious causes of dissatisfaction. The possibility of arbitrariness on the part of the superior is increased where individual complaints are likely to be "lost" in the long passage down the hierarchical ladder.[8]

Quite naturally the civil servant has sought to alter these conditions and to secure an improvement in his material status. To do so he has had to turn to legislative bodies. The perennial demands of the official lead parliament to consider him as an "eternal supplicant;" deputies rise and refuse to be dictated to by these individuals, and a parliamentary antagonism gradually develops.[9] Moreover candi-

---

[6] Gaston Jèze, "Contribution à la theorie générale de la fonction publique," *Revue du droit public*, XLV, 1918, 500 ff.; Joseph-Barthélemy, *Le problème de la compétence* (1918), 237-238.

[7] *Ibid.*, 239.

[8] Cahen, *op. cit.*, 87 ff.

[9] *Ibid.*, 112.

dates, in their campaigning for office, make pledges to reduce the salaries of public officials and to make superficial reforms in the administration. Badly informed public opinion then comes to think of the civil servant as an intriguer and a professional parasite. Yet, no matter how justified and urgent all these complaints are, little has been done to remedy the situation. In fact, the air of suspicion which surrounded the bureaucracy as a heritage of the days of its monarchical glory[10] combined with the profound public conviction of bureaucratic inefficiency has prevented any enlightened public opinion in the matter altogether. Therefore, government employees have attempted more and more to help themselves. The ''civil servants, forming a hierarchy which the years have perfected, finally declare that they have their own technicians, their own factory experts; and obeying the same sociological necessities as the workers in private industry and commerce, they have come to discuss first the conditions of work and from this point the practical and moral control which is imposed upon them by law in the name of the state.''[11] It became clear, as a result, ''that in a choice between loyalty to his fellow workers and loyalty to a state which aimed at preventing these workers from attaining certain ends which they deemed good, there was no inherent certainty that the average trade unionist would feel a deeper claim on the part of the state.''[12] They began to see little by little the economic rôle which they played; they recognized the fact that, if their work ceased, a part of the economic life of the state would be arrested. The sequel is to be seen in the formation of associations, the presentation of collective demands and finally the resort to direct action. These attacks, to the extent that they would substitute varying degrees of autonomous control by the subordinate official for the present system and to the extent that they propose the use of direct action in the enforcement of their demands, represent assaults against the unified system of hierarchical control exercised in the name of the state.

It may well be that the second of these alternative conceptions of the civil servant or official will strike an unsympathetic note in the minds of all those who have tended to idealize the conditions of Swiss political life, but we feel that it is important to consider the actual facts in the light of the tendencies which the second conception embodies. Without

[10] See above, pp. 3, 13.
[11] Maxime Leroy, *Syndicats et services publics* (1909), x.
[12] Laski, *op. cit.*, 325.

committing ourselves to an exact evaluation of the force of these trends
we may find that they are significant concomitant aspects of the recent
development of the civil service in Switzerland, as elsewhere. Let us
then turn to the forms which the impacts upon the hierarchical principle have taken. And since it is only through their associations that
the various demands of the civil servants have been presented with
effectiveness, a consideration of the activities of these groups will indicate the nature of their proposals and the extent of their accomplishments.

It is entirely justifiable to say that the same explanations which
hold true in general for the development of a distinct movement toward
association and toward the acceptance of a new concept of their status
among the public personnel are applicable in Switzerland. There have
been in the eyes of the official specific abuses. The influence of partisan
considerations has already been dealt with;[13] the claim of arbitrariness on the part of the superior authorities has been voiced again and
again. In the eyes of the associations the disciplinary punishments up
to 1928 were "purely the actions of the superior authorities of the
administration, a fact which has caused a great deal of animosity between the personnel and the authorities."[14] The fear of arbitrariness
in the enforcement of the provisions of Article 13[15] as proposed in
the project of the Statute of 1927 resulted in many serious discussions
of the matter on the part of friends of the personnel in the legislative
bodies.[16] The insistence that the remuneration has been inadequate has
existed from the beginning[17] and reached its height during the discussion of the Federal Law on Civil Servants.[18] Most recently the same
question has arisen in the numerous discussions and complaints over
the classification of functions.[19] Various other demands for additional
rights, indicating a discontent on the part of the officials, have been
made at different times. The attitude toward the Administration will
be considered later, but it may be stated that there is a general feeling

[13] See Chap. IV.
[14] R.S., XVII, 1925, 63.
[15] See pp. 65 ff.
[16] Note, for example, A.B.St., Frühjahr, 1925, 98.
[17] This matter is adequately dealt with in Kupper, op. cit., 37-61.
[18] Message, 1924, 133 ff. Without considering the fundamental causes for the development of the salary problem in Switzerland, it can be pointed out that "civil
servant determinism" has played its rôle. Ibid., 1924, 44; ibid., 1930, 1 ff.
[19] Rapport, A.S.F.T.T., 1926-1928, 20-21; Journal de Genève, April 4, 1930, 4.

of opposition to it. The Swiss Federation of Postal Civil Servants insisted upon ''the necessity of opposing the resolute and fully determined will of the personnel to the united front of the Administration.''[20] In the parliamentary bodies objections to bestowing special privileges upon the federal personnel have been made on frequent occasions,[21] and in several instances the people have evidenced their hostility to the ''bureaucracy'' by rejecting proposals to provide pensions for federal officials and to increase salaries.[22] As a consequence, all of the conditions which would normally lead to the development of associations and to a certain feeling of unity among the subordinate personnel seem to have prevailed for some years in Switzerland.

The right of association has been granted in Switzerland since the beginning of the present federal structure. By constitutional provision citizens had the right of forming associations providing there was nothing illegitimate or dangerous to the state in these collective activities. The cantons were ''to take the measures necessary for the suppression of abuses.''[23] This provision was considered to be applicable to the public official as well as to the ordinary citizen, but it did not in fact prevent the formation of various associations which recognized the right to strike.[24] A serious attempt to restrict the right, which had thus existed prior to that time in fact if not in law, was included in Art. 13 of the project of the Federal Council of the Federal Law on Civil Servants. The proposed Article contained the following provisions:

''Sec. 1. The right of association is guaranteed to the civil servant within the limits of public order.

''Sec. 2. The civil servant is forbidden to take part in an association which pursues ends or utilizes means which are dangerous to the state.

''Sec. 3. The associations which recognize, favor or utilize the strike are unlawful.''[25]

---

[20] *Rapport*, 1928, 15.

[21] See *A.B.St.*, Frühjahr, 1925, 98.

[22] Simon Deploige, *The Referendum in Switzerland*, (C. P. Trevelyan, trans., 1898), 153; Curti, *op. cit.*, 335, 337; W. E. Rappard, ''The Initiative, Referendum and Recall in Switzerland,'' *Annals*, 1912, 137.

[23] *Constitution*, Art. 56.

[24] All of the associations which were members of the Federation of Trade Unions up to 1927 recognized this right. Some provided for it by specific provisions in their statutes. *Statuts, S.S.F.P.*, (1922), Art. 46; *Statuts, S.E.V.* (1921), Art. 1.

[25] *Message*, 1924, 239.

The committee which considered these provisions in the Council of
States in the spring session of 1925 reported favorably upon the provisions of the project.[26] Obviously the Federal Council was attempting
both to restrict the former sphere of associational liberty and to accord to itself a great deal of discretionary power by the inclusion of
the phrase "within the limits of public order." Strong opposition to
this course of action was evidenced by the submission of three minority
reports[27] and by the final decision for a reconsideration. As the result
of this opposition the majority of the committee in the following session of the Council of States had modified its recommendations so as
to include only sec. 1 as the Federal Council had recommended it,
to eliminate sec. 3 and to reword sec. 2 in the following manner:

"Sec. 2. A civil servant is forbidden to take part in an association which
recognizes or utilizes the strike of the civil servant, pursues ends or utilizes means
which are illegitimate or dangerous to the state."[28]

In this form the article was finally passed. When the article was considered by the National Council the majority of the commission, which
reported, recommended the adoption of sec. 1 as proposed by the first
minority of the committee in the Council of States, the adoption of
sec. 2 as passed by the Council of States and the elimination of sec. 3
of the original project.[29] In the following form, consequently Art. 13
passed the National Council[30] and with some minor changes was embodied in the Statute as enacted into law:

"Sec. 1. The right of association is guaranteed within the limits fixed by the
Federal Constitution.
"Sec. 2. Civil servants are forbidden, however, to join an association which per-
mits or employs the strike in the civil service, or which pursues ends or utilizes

[26] *A.B.St.*, Frühjahr, 1925, 98.
[27] The first minority favored striking out secs. 2 and 3 and altering the
phraseology of sec. 1 to read as follows:
"Sec. 1. The right of association is guaranteed to the civil servant within the
limits fixed by the Federal Constitution." *Ibid.*, Frühjahr, 1925, 98-99.
[28] *Ibid.*, Sommer-Session, 1925, 241. The first minority in the spring session still
adhered to its original proposals.
[29] *V.E.R.*, 1925-1927, 45. The minority report on sec. 1 favored the proposal of
the Federal Council while the minority report on sec. 2 proposed the elimination
of secs. 2 and 3 of the original project and of sec. 2 as passed by the Council of
States. *Idem.*
[30] *Ibid.*, 73.

means which are illegitimate or dangerous to the state. The application of this rule is vested exclusively in the Federal Council.'"[31]

The discussions in the National Council preceding its passage were marked by the somewhat acrimonious debates of M. Perrin, Vice President of the Federative Union, and M. Musy, the president of the Confederation. M. Perrin demanded the removal of the proposed restrictions upon the right of association of the personnel and suggested that the Federal Council was more interested in restricting the right of association than in the suppression of the strike.[32] According to M. Mercier, ''all of the federal personnel, all of the members of our organization, whether they are or are not members of the Federation of Trade Unions and whether they are or are not opposed to the strike of the civil servant . . . are unanimous in declaring unacceptable Art. 13 and in considering that it is an intolerable restriction upon the rights of the personnel.''[33] Such an attitude was a result of the belief that ''all civil servants are citizens and should be put on the same plane of equality with other individuals in so far as their rights of association are concerned.'' In reply M. Musy emphasized the distinctions between ''the status of an employee in private industry and the status of a civil servant'' to justify his insistence that the original recommendations of the Federal Council be supported.[34] There were clearly two points of view expressed, and a comparison of Art. 13 in the law with Art. 13 of the original project would, even in the absence of clear evidences, be proof that a compromise had been reached.

With the right of association granted since 1848, it was to be expected that the movement toward association should begin early. It was, however, only after organizations for industrial ends had gained some headway among the ordinary workers that loose unions of a local character among the postal officials came into being. As time went on, other associations were formed with broader aims. The Swiss Union of Railway and Steamboat Employees was organized in 1887 and was followed in 1891 by the Swiss Union of Postal, Telegraph and Customs Officials. With broader ends in view than their predecessors, these associations began to interest themselves in such matters

[31] White, *op. cit.*, 365.
[32] *V.E.R.*, 1925-1927, 65.
[33] *Ibid.*, 68.
[34] *Ibid.*, 58-59, 71.

as hours of work. The year 1893 witnessed the inception of the Swiss Postal Union, and the year 1897 the beginnings of the Union of Swiss Customs Officials.[35] The movement, once begun, soon spread to other classes of federal officials, and with its growth went a concomitant feeling that some unified endeavor would be necessary to secure the ends desired. In the spring of 1898, as a consequence, the General Federation of Civil Servants, Employees and Workers of the Confederation was formed. This Federation drew its membership only from the postal, telegraph and customs services and included only about one-fourth of the officials of the federal services. This organization proved of short duration, for it was dissolved in 1904.[36] In the meantime the General Assembly of the newly founded Federative Union of Civil Servants, Employees and Workers met in 1903 at Basel with twelve associations of personnel represented. Though it was bitterly opposed at first by many of the smaller associations which feared that their interests would be overlooked and by others which feared that political neutrality would not be maintained,[37] this Federation has shown a steady growth. It is now known as the Federative Union of Federal Personnel and of the Public Transport Services (U.F.P.F.)

To the progress of this movement the fact that 56,033 members or 84.3% of the total Federal personnel were organized in 1925 bears striking witness. Of this number 52,353 persons or 78.8% of the total personnel were in unions or federations affiliated with the Federative Union.[38] By 1929 the membership of the Federative Union had increased to 58,506 or to approximately 90% of the total. The following federations are affiliated with the Federative Union:

	Membership in 1929
1. Swiss Federation of Railway Officials........................	36,129
2. Swiss Federation of Employees of Postal, Telephone and Telegraph Services	8,248
3. Swiss Federation of Personnel of Public Services (only part of federal personnel groups)	670
4. Federation of Metallurgical Workers........................	468
5. Swiss Federation of Postal Civil Servants...................	3,924

[35] Kupper, op. cit., 28-31.
[36] Ibid., 33.
[37] Ibid., 35.
[38] Ibid., 36; La répartition du personnel fédéral dans les organisations professionelles (1925).

6. Swiss Federation of Civil Servants of Telephone and Telegraph Services 2,130
7. Swiss Federation of Civil Servants of Customs Service........ 677
8. Swiss Federation of Postal Clerks........................... 2,704
9. Federation of Civil Servants of Central Administrative Services 1,206
10. Swiss Federation of Employees of Customs Services.......... 2,050
11. Swiss Federation of Supervisors of the Railways............. 300

58,506[39]

There are a few associations which are not affiliated with the Federative Union. Particular mention might be made of the Federation of Christian-Socialist Transport Workers.[40] A few federal officials are members of the Swiss Federation of the Personnel of the Public Services, an organization which includes primarily cantonal and municipal officials.[41] The remainder of the personnel is not organized. Internationally the Federative Union is affiliated with the International Federation of Civil Servants which was organized in 1925[42] and which has recently

[39] *Rapport, U.F.P.F.*, 1928-1929, 5. The Swiss Federation of Railway Officials, the largest of these bodies, has affiliated with it the following eleven associations:
1. Workers' Union of Swiss Transport Enterprises
2. Swiss Union of Locomotive Personnel
3. Association of Platform and Station Personnel
4. Swiss Union of Switchmen
5. Swiss Union of Train Personnel
6. Swiss Union of Personnel of Inspection
7. Swiss Union of Personnel of the Railway Administration
8. Swiss Union of Personnel of Private Railways
9. Swiss Union of Maintenance Men
10. Swiss Union of Workers of Railway Shops
11. Swiss Federation of Pensioned Railway Employees
Rapport, S.E.V., 1929, 214-308.

[40] This Federation had a membership in 1925 of 1200 individuals and is affiliated with the National Federation of Christian Unions. *Gewerkschaft des christlichen Verkehrspersonals der Schweiz*, 1929, 16. Other associations which were not affiliated were the Union of Olten (superior civil servants of the Railways) with a membership of 730, the Union of the Personnel of the Military Department with a membership of 800 and the Union of the Employees of the Military Workshops with a membership of 350. *La répartition, op. cit.*

[41] The total membership of this Federation was 11,993 in 1926 of which 905 were civil servants, employees and workers of the Confederation. As indicated above, a part of these are affiliated with the Federative Union. *Industrial and Labor Information*, XXIII, 1927, 362; *Monthly Labor Review*, XV, 1922, 204.

[42] *L'Atelier*, II, 1925, 432-433. Switzerland was not represented at the first meeting of this body. *Industrial and Labor Information*, XIV, 1925, 178.

shown a tendency to coquette with the International Federation of
Trade Unions.[43] The Swiss Federation of the Personnel of the Public
Services is affiliated with the International Federation of the Personnel of Public Services, a body which in 1929 voted to amalgamate
with the International Federation of Civil Servants.[44] There are other
affiliations such as that of the Swiss Federation of Railway Officials
with the International Transport Workers Federation.[45]

The purpose of each of the associations in Switzerland is in general
"the improvement of the economic and social status of its members
and the furthering of the development of their general and professional instruction." This pronouncement of ends is reproduced almost
verbatim in the by-laws of all the associations.[46] With certain exceptions all of the associations disclaim any political and religious align-
ments.[47] The Christian-Socialists, while excluding every discussion
of a "political or confessional nature," recognized that the "Federation stands from the point of view of principles upon the Christian
philosophy of life."[48] Disclaiming any political or religious align-
ments the Federative Union has for its purpose the "safeguarding of
the professional, economic and moral interests of the whole of the
personnel." It is to attain these ends by the "organization and execution of common actions for the whole of the personnel, by supporting
actions undertaken by one of the constituent organizations and by
participating in economic movements affecting salaried persons and
consumers."[49] Its organs are an assembly of delegates, a central committee, a smaller directing committee and a committee on administration.[50] This general type of organization is found in all of the sub-

[43] The Congress expressed itself in 1927 as being in favor of closer relations
with the International Federation of Trade Unions. *Ibid.*, xiv, 1927, 179. It was
invited during the same year to send a representative to the Congress of the International Federation of Trade Unions. *International Trade Union Movement*,
vii, 1927, 116. See also *ibid.*, viii, 1928, 13.

[44] *Industrial and Labor Information*, xxxi, 1929, 310.

[45] *Fourth Year Book, International Federation of Trade Unions*, 1926, 486.

[46] Note *Statuts, S.S.F.P.*, (1922), Art. 2; *Statuts A.S.F.T.T.*, (1921), Art. 2;
Statuten des schweizerischen Posthalterverbandes (1912), Art. 2.

[47] See, for example, *Statuts, S.E.V.*, (1921), Art. 1.

[48] *Statuts, Association Chrétienne-nationale du personnel des postes, télégraphes
et téléphones* (1923), Art. 2; *Statuten des Verbandes christlichen Bundesbeamten*
(1929), Art. 2.

[49] *Statuts, U.F.P.F.*, (1922), Art. 3.

[50] *Ibid.*, Arts. 9-30.

ordinate associations. The secretariats of these bodies deserve special mention, however, in view of the fact that the Federative Union does not have a corresponding agency.[51] Practically all of the constituent organizations of the Federative Union make provision for publications of various types.

There can be no doubt but that among these members of the various associations there is a certain fundamental feeling of solidarity. They were united in favoring the establishment of an administrative court and in support of the passage of the Federal Law on Civil Servants. But care must be taken lest the impression be left that the officials in the Swiss bureaucracy present a united front in all matters. Particularly, complaints may be heard from different groups regarding the attitude of the Federative Union toward the classification of functions. The Swiss Federation of Employees of the Customs Service, while recognizing the efforts of the Federative Union in raising the personnel to its present status, had to declare "that it has not defended our just demands in a manner which we should desire."[52] The Swiss Federation of Postal Civil Servants admitted the existence of some excitment within its ranks occasioned by "certain attempts of sister associations to obtain the status of civil servants for their members."[53] In view of this objection the statement of the Federal Council to the effect that "the associations of personnel in the end refused to demand, with certain qualifications, the status of civil servants for the rural agents"[54] in the postal services is explainable. A somewhat amusing but significant complaint came from the Swiss Federation of Employees of Postal, Telegraph and Telephone Services. This body objected to "the lack of friendliness and even of courtesy on the part of certain civil servants toward the workers."[55] Between the Christian-Socialists and the associations affiliated with the Federative Union there appears to be a feeling that borders almost on bitterness. The Swiss Federation of Railway Officials claims that "all of their (Christian-Socialist) activities have been concentrated in propagandist efforts to secure new members and to disparage our Federation." In the elections of members to commissions in 1929, the Christian Socialists

[51] Note, for example, *Statuts, S.S.F.P.,* Art. 37.
[52] *Rapport,* 1928, 6.
[53] *Rapport,* 1928, 43.
[54] *Message,* 1930, 5.
[55] *Rapport,* 1928, 82.

were reported to have turned "all of their heavy artillery, including the efforts of the clergy, pressure on families and the influence of the Catholic Conservative Party organization" upon their opponents and to have celebrated their success in winning three seats with a "boyish glee."[56] Even charges of duplicity have been made.[57] On the other hand, the Christian-Socialists feel that "the delegates of the personnel in the Joint Arbitration Commission consider themselves less as representatives of the entire personnel than as the exclusive representatives of the Federative Union" and that, consequently, their organization should have its own representatives.[58] It is suggested the differences between these groups are the natural and inevitable result of a certain divergence of interests. It is in the failure to recognize these differences, which are confined not alone to Switzerland and which we consider not as incidental but as fundamental, and in the assumption that there is a typical civil servant, that Duguit and his school go astray. Consequently, when we for brevity's sake speak of the "attitude of the personnel," it will be done with the understanding that the limiting qualifications just set forth are implied.

Whatever differences of opinion there may be, there can be little doubt of the influence which the associations of personnel have had upon the legislative and administrative agencies. With some success pressure was originally brought to bear to secure alterations in the salary scales.[59] The influence of the associations in the original project for the Statute of 1927 is evident, and even the Federal Council recognized that the final provisions represented in a large measure the results of agreements between the representatives of the state and of the officials.[60] In the discussion of the project in the legislative bodies, changes were made as a result of the opposition of representatives of the personnel. Art. 13 and the provisions for the maximum and minimum salaries of the twenty-six classes in their final form are

[56] *Rapport*, 1929, 32-34; *Rapport*, U.F.P.F., 1928-1929, 21-24.
[57] *R.S.*, xviii, 1926, 87-88.
[58] *Jahres-Bericht, Gewerkschaft der christlichen Verkehrspersonals* (1929), 29.
[59] Holcombe, *op. cit.*, 255 ff.
[60] Three separate memoranda were submitted in 1921 by the Federative Union, the Federation of Civil Servants of Central Administrative Services and the Federation of Christian Socialists. The tentative project which was drawn up was submitted to the associations for their criticisms before a final draft was made. *Message*, 1924, 1-3, 511; *V.E.R.*, 1925-1927, 1-5.

good illustrations of that opposition.[61] While the exact extent of their influence upon legislation cannot be evaluated, it is clear that the representatives of the personnel are numerous and active in the Swiss lower chamber. Upon the administration the influence is no less evident. The Federal Council drew up a tentative outline of an ordinance for the establishment of disciplinary commissions which, in essence, corresponded to "that which our colleague, Bratschi, indicated would be our last concession."[62] As a result of conferences with the Federal Council "representatives of the personnel were able to secure a number of concessions, particularly as regards the inclusion of groups within class 26 of the salary scale."[63] On Sept. 9, 1929, the Directing Committee of the Federative Union discussed with the Federal Council modifications in the classification and the desirability of prompt ratification of the recommendations of the Joint Arbitration Commission. This "end was achieved since the Federal Council approved the proposals of the Commission on Oct. 4, 1929."[64] In addition to bringing pressure to bear upon the Federal Council certain of the associations of personnel have looked with longing eyes "to the time when they will be represented in the highest executive authority."[65] Consequently, when a vacancy occurred in 1929, the largest of the Federations, the Swiss Federation of Railway Officials, felt that "the true party of the working people (Socialist Party) . . . with one-fourth of the seats in the lower chamber was entitled to this seat." Its reasons for this desire may be best stated in its own words:

A number of facts prove to us that our penetration into parliament is most effective. It is a great disadvantage for a party . . . not to have the power of exercising a decisive influence on the administrative machinery. That influence is only possible if it can be exercised in the executive authority. . . . *It is clear that a progressive spirit penetrating the administration and that authority can have a great influence on the relationship with the personnel.*[66]

[61] *La Tribune du fonctionnaire*, Nov. 16, 1929, 4; Kupper, *op. cit.*, 6. Compare the provisions of the original project in *Message*, 1924, 248 with the provisions of Art. 37 of the Statute. *Loi fédérale sur le statut des fonctionnaires*, 12. These provisions of this article are not included in White's translation.

[62] *Rapport*, U.F.P.F. 1928-1929, 25. Bratschi is President of the Federation of Railway Officials and of the Federative Union.

[63] *Ibid.*, 12-15.

[64] *Rapport*, S.E.V., 1929.

[65] *Ibid.*, 7.

[66] *Ibid.*, 149. Italics mine.

It is these reasons, rather than the failure of the Socialist Party to secure representation in the Federal Council, that are significant, and it is these reasons which will encourage certain of the associations of personnel to further efforts. But if only a few of these associations have recognized the feasibility of securing representation in the Federal Council, all have witnessed the possibility of participating in "the direction of the administration" through various commissions in which the personnel is represented. Nowhere can the diverging viewpoints of the administration and the associations be more clearly seen than in the debates over these matters from 1925 to 1927. The attitude of the associations is best indicated by the following statement emanating from the Federative Union:

In this particular case what the great majority of the salaried personnel united in their associations desire is a complete democratization of the federal enterprises. But, such a democratization can only be attained by granting to the commissions of personnel or to other organs not merely the right of giving advice but the right of participation with executive power *(avec force executive)*.[67]

To this point of view came the retort of the Federal Council that "it is necessary for the law to clearly specify that these personnel commissions can have only a consultative rôle and no right of action obligatory upon the administration." "Every system," which followed any other rule, "would simply be incompatible with the responsibilities of the administrative organs."[68] In even stronger language the Federal Council recognized that there were proper limits to the activities of these associations and that these limits were reached when demands came from the associations to represent their constituent members in the various disciplinary cases which were subject to the jurisdiction of the Federal Council. To the request of the officials, the Federal Council replied:

We have persistently held to the point of view that the rule now in force constitutes a guarantee of the maintenance of order which ought to exist in the relationship between the superior and inferior in a service such as the railroads which is based upon hierarchical principles. . . . It is necessary to create a spirit of confidence in the superior and to convince the subordinate agent that his superior is his true representative. . . . But, that confidence will be broken and will tend to disappear, if the bond which unites the personnel to the Confederation should be weakened, if the civil servant is imbued with the idea that the best ways of de-

[67] *Message*, 1924, 218.
[68] *Ibid.*, 1924, 217.

fending his interests are to appeal not to his superior but to the associations of personnel and their organs.[69]

The movement toward the institution of delegations of personnel in the federal services received first mention in 1906.[70] Some progress was made during the succeeding years, and the momentum thus gained showed its effects in the various concessions made by the Federal Council in the project of 1924. Since a consideration of the specific commissions is neither possible nor essential,[71] a brief description of the four types of commissions in which the personnel is represented in the railway services will be illustrative. In the first place there are the commissions of the Pension and Aid Fund and of the Sick Relief Fund. These commissions are not only authorized to give their opinions in matters, but they are likewise charged with the enforcement of the statutes providing for the various funds except where jurisdiction is specifically given to other authorities. There are also the Personnel Commissions, bodies which have the function of advising the administration on matters of a technical and administrative nature. These agencies include the General Commission for the entire personnel, five special commissions for the most important services and commissions for each of the workshops. It should be noted that the General Commission is presided over by the President of the General Directorate and that the questions which may be discussed are limited in their scope.[72] More important are the disciplinary commissions. Though mentioned in the Statute of 1927[73] they were dealt with in more detail in the Law on Federal Administrative and Disciplinary Jurisdiction of 1928.[74] These bodies have, however, only the jurisdiction which is bestowed upon them by the Federal Council and consist of three members of which the Federal Council selects two. The per-

[69] *Ibid.*, 1924, 196.

[70] *Ibid.*, 1924, 204 ff.

[71] The matter of personnel commissions is discussed in some detail in Paul Anliker, *Die Personalausschüsse* (1924), 49 ff. An excellent brief account is Robert Bratschi, "Le droit de discussion dans les entreprises fédérales," *R.S.*, April, 1930, 101 ff.

[72] These bodies were first recognized by statute in 1927, although they had been in existence before that date. See White, *op. cit.*, Art. 67, 379. The nature of the discussions may be judged from *Procès-verbal de la 4e séance de la commission générale . . . tenue le 3 juillet, 1929.*

[73] White, *op. cit.*, Art. 33, 369.

[74] *R.O.*, 1928, Art. 43, 847.

sonnel is represented finally in certain joint arbitration commissions *(commission paritaire)* which consider questions of a social nature and matters affecting the remuneration and conditions of employment of the civil servant. The members of the commission of the Law on the Hours of Work, which was created in 1920, are appointed by the Federal Council and have only advisory powers. Perhaps the most important commission in which the personnel is represented is the Joint Arbitration Commission created by the Statute of 1927. This body consists of twenty members and a president, ten of the members being selected by the personnel of the Confederation through a system of proportional representation. Its functions, which it has exercised in a vigorous fashion, are outlined as follows:

"Art. 66. At the invitation of the Finance Department the Joint Arbitration Commission gives its opinion (a) on projects for executory regulations proposed by the Federal Council in the application of the present law; (b) on propositions having the effect of modifying or completing the present law; (c) on questions of principle concerning the personnel and salaries in general."[75]

Designed to foster a spirit of coöperation and mutual trust between the administration and the subordinate officials, these commissions have rather in some cases furnished opportunities for the irreconcilable viewpoints of the two groups represented to clash openly. In the debate in the Joint Arbitration Commission over the classification of personnel in 1929, the ten representatives of the personnel voted against a fixed classification while the ten representatives of the administration voted for it. The "President (Kasser) voted in favor of the proposition, and this decision was final."[76] In the second session of the General Commission of the Railway Services in 1929, Robert Bratschi, the President of the Federative Union, saw fit to comment upon the attitude of the administration toward the personnel during the past few years.[77] M. Schraft, the President of the Commission, alleged in reply that the speech of Bratschi was in the nature of a polemic and could not be tolerated in the General Commission. The reaction to

[75] White, *op. cit.*, 379. The methods of procedure in this body may be found in the various *Protokolle der paritätischen Kommission des eidgenössischen Finanzdepartements*. See particularly the discussion on classification beginning January 10, 1929. *Ibid.*, II, 48 ff.

[76] *Jahres-Bericht, Gewerkschaft des christlichen Verkehrspersonals*, 1929, 28.

[77] No record of this speech was available.

this affair by the Swiss Federation of Railway Officials is summarized in the following statement:

This regrettable incident is of great importance from the point of view of the relations between the General Direction and the commissions of personnel. We thought the past year would witness some improvement in these relations. The facts show that we were too optimistic. The judgment rendered, 'the commissions of personnel are a good thing, but they ought not to have too much power,' seems to dominate the situation. They (the administration) support the commissions of personnel as long as they concern themselves with trivial matters. But, if they consider a problem of some importance, they place a damper upon it in order that the members must realize that they are minor personages *(petits employés)* who do not understand the bigger problems.[78]

And well said it was, for there was involved here a bigger problem than probably either the Federal Council or the Swiss Federation of Railway Officials realized. For, despite the seeming unimportance of these "intermediary bodies between the superior and the subordinate," their existence gives evidence of a fundamental movement, and that movement claims no deep affection for the continuation of the *status quo* in the present system of administrative organization.

Still, it has not been so much the phantom of the associations of officials which have been agitating for various changes but the spectre of the possibilities inherent in and the demands emanating from trade-unionism which have threatened most fundamentally the basis upon which the hierarchical system of administrative organization rests. Trade-unionism does not necessarily imply any more than the mere federation of various types of associations of employees. But it is well known that the weapon of trade union organizations is the strike, and it has been said that "the strike is the fact which subordinates the functioning of the public services, that is, the satisfaction of public needs, to the particular interest of the agents."[79] The suspension of work has been, as Lefas recognized, not only "incompatible with the notion of public service, but also with the permanence of employment which it above all involves and with the hierarchical discipline which is such an essential feature of bureaucracy."[80] Considered from one

---

[78] *Rapport*, 1929, 124-125. For a similar evaluation of these commissions see the speech by M. Perrin, Vice President of the Federative Union, *V.E.R.*, 1925-1927, 66.

[79] Jèze, *op. cit.*, 93.

[80] *Op. cit.*, 206-207.

aspect the strike thus becomes a revolt against the hierarchical control by the state in that it substitutes the power of the trade union and its leaders for that of the hierarchical superiors.

The history of the Swiss official, in so far as his activities in the trade union can be distinguished from his activities in the association, is instructive.[81] Though Switzerland was not a country offering a particularly fertile field for the early development of the trade union movement among the public officials,[82] this movement has gone on in a halting fashion after a somewhat late start. The first organization of any importance was the Trade Union of Munitions' Workers in Berne in 1892, followed by similar unions in 1893 in Thun and other cities. In the same year unions of telephone workers had their inception, and these organizations joined in 1894 to form the Federated Central Union of Telephone Workers. The year 1897 saw the Union of Confederated Workers in Thun come into existence.[83] While the movement continued to spread, the fact that the Secretary of the Swiss Federation of Trade Unions was unable to secure statistics from the local unions in 1906 indicates that no great progress had been made by that time.[84] Later years witnessed a more rapid development, and by the end of 1923 some 40,450 public officials or 60.6% of the total were affiliated with unions which were members of the Federation of Trade Unions.[85] By 1925 the number of affiliated federal officials had climbed to 45,047[86] and in 1929 to 45,515. The federations included in 1929 were the Swiss Federation of Railway Officials, the Swiss Federation of Employees of Postal, Telephone and Telegraph Services, the Swiss Federation of the Personnel of the Public Services and the Federation of Metallurgical Workers.[87] From the beginning these groups recognized the "struggle of the classes" in their by-laws in more or less

[81] "Though there is a general agreement in the demands of the civil servant, there is a difference in the ways in which they can be attained. The first are grouped in associations, the others in trade unions. The first appeal to legal methods. The second reject these and wish to speak of 'contracts of work,' of means of common right which furnish these a sanction, including the right to strike if there is need." *Ibid.*, IV.

[82] Holcombe, *op. cit.*, 254.

[83] Kupper, *op. cit.*, 31-32.

[84] Holcombe, *op. cit.*, 253.

[85] *La répartition, op. cit.*

[86] *R.S.*, XVI, 1926, 170-172.

[87] *Rapport, U.F.P.F.*, 1928-1929, 5.

the same form in which the Federation of Trade Unions recognized it until recently; that is,

The trade unions of Switzerland, recognizing the proletarian class struggle, form the Swiss Federation of Trade Unions.[88]

It is in other words a body which clearly has recognized the right of the strike.

Switzerland was not to escape her problems of the strike in the public services. From a strictly legal standpoint the Swiss official may have stood in a special relationship to the Confederation. The Constitution may have provided that the civil servant could not enter any union the purposes of which might be classed as illegitimate or dangerous to the state, and unions of civil servants which recognized the right of strike may have been considered as illegitimate or dangerous.[89] But facts do not always square with legal fiction. In November, 1918, a series of events was to occur which brought this truth home. Though the facts are not entirely clear, it is obvious that the authorities of the canton of Zürich requested the aid of federal troops to deal with a threatened outbreak against the cantonal government. Upon the refusal of the Federal Council to rescind its action in acquiescing in the request, the so-called Committee of Olten, the Central Committee of the Federation of Trade Unions and the Directorate of the Swiss Socialist Party called a general strike on November 10, 1918.[90] Immediately an "Appeal to the Civil Servants, Employees and Workers of the Confederation" was issued by the Federal Council. Recognizing the fact that "certain of the federations of officials of the Confederation ap-

[88] *Statuten, Schweizerischer Gewerkschaftsbund*, 1925, Art. 1. Of course this Federation is affiliated with the International Federation of Trade Unions, a fact which is of little significance because of the recognition of the "autonomy of the trade union organization" and because of the general impotency of the International Federation. *Fourth Year Book, International Federation of Trade Unions*, 1926, 641. The rules of the International Federation may be found in *International Trade Union Movement*, VIII, 1928, 17.

[89] Fleiner, *op. cit.*, 360. There was no legislation specifically covering the right of strike in the public services up to 1927. *Railway Strikes and Lockouts* (1927), 199.

[90] *Le Temps*, Nov. 14, 1918, 4. Short and not entirely satisfactory accounts may be found in Arthur Studhalter, *Der Beamtenstreik nach schweizerischem Recht* (1925), 14; C. H. Picavet, *La Suisse* (1920), 250 ff. The viewpoint of a former president of the Swiss National Council is to be found in Felix Bonjour, *Real Democracy in Operation* (C. L. Leese, trans., 1920), 210 ff.

pear to wish to associate in the movement,'' the Federal Council went on to say:

> We can only admit, in this dangerous and serious time confronting us, that some civil servants and workers of the Confederation are abandoning their posts. In entering the service of the state you entered into a contract with the state involving some duties which you cannot legally lay aside. You are bound to the state by a bond which forbids that you take this action. . . . We recall to you your duty and we hold you responsible for all the consequences which its violation would entail.[91]

This appeal to legalism and fear did not prevent a majority of the railway officials and some 1,346 postal officials from heeding the call of the strike leaders. As a consequence of this action the Federal Council, whatever the legal justification for its own action, issued on November 11 an ordinance which placed the civil servants, employees and workers of the military service, federal and cantonal, as well as those of the transportation services under the military laws. In addition the participation of the personnel of the state in a strike was declared to constitute a crime.[92] As a result of this determined policy the strike was of short duration and ended on November 14.[93]

But regardless of its duration or its limited application Switzerland had witnessed a strike in which officials of the Confederation had participated, and succeeding events were to show that it had not been forgot. After a series of moves with a similar aim[94] the famous Article

[91] *R.O.*, 1918, 1198.

[92] *Ibid.*, 1918, 1199.

[93] *Le Temps*, Nov. 15, 1918, 2.

[94] There was a postulate presented to the Federal Council in 1919 calling for the interdiction of strikes. *Rapport du conseil fédéral*, 1922, 32. In 1921 the ''Haberlin Law'' was passed by the National Assembly. Article 47 of the proposed law provided:

''All who incite, threaten or publicly profess belief in the overthrow of our political order by violence, or threaten the public safety of the state or the cantons, be it by words, writings or pictures either within the country or abroad, or undertake any activity which necessarily tends toward the violent overthrow of the system will be subject to imprisonment.

Should these incitations, threats or propaganda be circulated among civil servants, employees or workers of the Confederation or cantons, . . . of the transport or essential services, the term of imprisonment will be not less than six months.'' *The Labour Monthly*, II, 1922, 273. This measure was never placed on the statute books, as it was defeated in a popular referendum. *Feuille fédérale*, II, 1927, Supp. 8.

22 was included in the project of the Federal Law on Civil Servants. This article contained the following sections:

"Sec. 1. Civil servants are forbidden to strike or to urge other civil servants to do so.

"Sec. 2. Associations or coöperative societies are forbidden to deprive a civil servant of his membership or to damage him in his economic interests for non-participation in a strike.

"Sec. 3. Agreements made by associations or coöperative societies as well as statutory or other arrangements contrary to these prohibitions are void.''[95]

In the discussion leading up to the final adoption of these provisions in the project, the associations recognized its ''absolutely reactionary character.''[96] The Federal Council in its report admitted that, in the course of the joint meetings with the associations of personnel, the prohibition of the strike was the object of lengthy discussion, and ''that it was impossible to cause their representatives to approve the proposed article.''[97] Such an opposition was of no avail in the face of the belief of the Federal Council that the ''prohibition of strikes springs naturally from the nature of the service-relationhip.''[98] In clear and concise words the Federal Council retraced the ground which had been covered so frequently from the tribunes of foreign states. In the words of this Swiss executive body:

It is by virtue of the necessity of living in security that a state organizes its public services. It is for assuring an uninterrupted functioning that their administration is placed in the hands of the civil servant. It is consequently quite natural that the law should forbid any obstacle to this continued functioning. . . . The motives are all the more compelling in a democratic state where the nation itself determines the conditions of employment. . . . In our country the strike of the civil servants assumes the aspect of a strike against the entire people.

The administration which is created for the public interest should never be an army which the civil servants can turn against the group.[99]

In the debates in the legislative bodies the advocates of the adoption of this article, while using a mass of verbiage, added little to the statement of the Federal Council.[100] The friends of the personnel severely

[95] *Message*, 1924, 242-243.
[96] *R.S.*, XIV, 1922, 82-83.
[97] *Message*, 1924, 98.
[98] *Idem.*
[99] *Ibid.*, 5.
[100] See, for example, the speech of Baumann in the Council of States in *A.B.St.*, Frühjahr, 1925, 113 ff. and the speeches by Schupbach and M. Musy in the National Council in *V.E.R.*, 1925-1927, 79 ff., 96 ff.

condemned the proposed provision in the Statute because of the desirability of the strike "in an extreme case when all other possibilities have failed" just as it rests in the hands of others who are engaged in productive enterprises.[101] Bratschi insisted that these provisions would not be an emanation from the people but rather from the Federal Council and the Federal Assembly.[102] Nevertheless, the Article passed in its original form with thirty-two dissenting votes in the National Council[103] and only one dissenting vote in the Council of States[104] to become Article 23 of the Federal Law on Civil Servants.

But in the face of these legal provisions, there still stands the unchanged attitude of the personnel. M. Perrin, the Vice President of the Federative Union, after pointing out that the situation which existed in 1918 remains unchanged today, made the following pragmatic retort:

> Every one knows that in strikes the reprisals depend upon the forces opposing them both in private industries and in those of the state. The strike itself . . . cannot be prevented by a law any more than it can be organized by statutory provision.[105]

And so we find the two clear views presented regarding the use of direct action by the civil servant. There is the attitude of the superior official, the head of the hierarchical organization, who thinks in terms of the assault upon the orderly functioning of the government. There is the attitude of the subordinate official who conceives of the strike as a necessary means of attaining certain objects and of remedying certain abuses which affect him as an individual. But whether conceived of as an assault upon the state or as a necessary means of safeguarding the vested interests of the individual servant the strike remains, as it must always remain, an attack upon the hierarchy. It

[101] *A.B.St.*, Frühjahr, 1925, 114 ff.

[102] *V.E.R.*, 1925-1927, 83.

[103] *Ibid.*, 102.

[104] *A.B.St.*, Sommer-Session, 1925, 118.

[105] *R.S.*, xix, 1927, 231. However, the inclusion of Art. 23 in the Statute caused the Federation of Trade Unions to amend Art. 1 of its by-laws (quoted above) as follows:

"The Swiss Federation of Trade Unions undertakes the task of protecting the interests common to all federations and their members, while having as its aim the promotion of the national economic well being." *Industrial and Labor Information*, xxiv, 1927, 118.

may well be that the strong traditional loyalty which has characterized the evolution of Swiss political institutions will neutralize these destructive tendencies. It may consequently be that the glamour which many publicists are wont to throw around the political life of Switzerland will continue to be justified. But it must be insisted that the same syndicalist movements which have threatened the existence of organized bureaucracy in other modern states have appeared in the Swiss public service.

CONCLUSION

The detailed analysis of the Swiss Civil Service has shown that a fairly highly organized bureaucracy has developed in the Swiss Government. The elaborate judicially safeguarded distribution of functions or offices is public and determinate, since the basic distribution is provided for by legislation and the more specialized distribution is undertaken by ordinances. The structure as a whole is a distinct hierarchy with strict subordination and discipline, also enforced and limited by legislation and ordinances, and interpreted by a court. Finally, the requirements for qualification for the various functions are elaborate and organized with reference to the rational needs of the functions themselves. The attendant developments of a fixed salary, secure tenure and regular promotion are also found. In short, the various aspects of a fully organized bureaucracy are seen in distinct outline even through this rather cursory examination.

The period which saw the organization of this bureaucracy is, however, characterized by the fact that politically Switzerland has had popular government; in fact, in many ways a more extreme type of popular government than has ever been attempted elsewhere on the continent of Europe. This would suggest that popular government under certain conditions is well qualified to organize and maintain a bureaucracy. What are these conditions? There are those who would immediately inform us that Swiss "national character" explained it all, that the Swiss were sober, intelligent, honest, and so on and so forth; in short, all those things which human beings ought to be but seldom are. I consider this argument extremely weak and so will leave it to those who are convinced by faith to make of it what they can. Another important condition, it would seem, is the small size of the country. But even though Switzerland is small, Switzerland is not small enough to be compared with a Greek πόλις or a New England town, communities which were so small that an effective supervision of the officials by the community could be considered an effective means of control. As a third *differentia specifica* might be urged the Swiss historical and political tradition, the so-called love of liberty and similar things. But the historical tradition of Switzerland before the advent of the New Federation in 1848 was a typical administration by notables, the social and mercantile aristocracy, and the development of the civil service after 1848 took place in clear and conscious hostility to this historical tradition. A Swiss historian has pointed out that it was practically impossible for a member of the old families to get into the public service for a long while after 1848.

It does not seem as if *differentiae specificae* will do as a satisfactory explanation for this development of a Swiss bureaucracy. We must look for structural peculiarities in order to explain the situation fully. In the first place should be mentioned, it seems to me, the comparatively independent executive which is in a position to become professionalized through long service and thus amalgamated with the lower strata of the hierarchy. The collegiate organization of this body strengthens its *neutral* position between people and representative assembly on the one hand, and the service bureaucracy on the other.

But fundamentally, the essential point is that the development of a bureaucracy is nothing peculiar to the government. The great industrial enterprises of our time also require large staffs for their successful operation. Whenever these bureaucratic "cells" impinge upon purposes of the community as a whole, there arises a tendency to subject these services to central control. This tendency takes the form of an expansion of the existing governmental services either for purposes of complete operation (telephone, telegraph, railroads as in Switzerland) or at least for purposes of supervision and control. The general tendency toward bureaucratization merely finds expression in these centralizing efforts, inasmuch as bureaucracy as such tends toward monocratic control. This does not mean, however, that democratic sentiment is not as such opposed to the power of the bureaucracy. In fact, it manifests itself by organizing considerable impediments to successful bureaucratic administration. The short tenure of office in Switzerland may be cited as an instance of that sort. But on the whole the technical necessities of the modern industrial system have been of such urgency in Switzerland as elsewhere that they called forth adequate machinery in spite of ideological objections.

It is altogether common to misstate the nature of responsibility and to interpret the relation between the people and their representatives on the one hand, and the administrative bureaucracy on the other hand, too much in terms of antitheses. Our industrial system has produced complex needs for the maintenance of public safety and order. These needs the community wants to be satisfied. But it only perceives dimly the difficulty which stands between it and the fulfillment of this wish. Is it surprising that the public finds the services of the government too expensive when it never wearies of complaining about the high cost of everything else? But, while the latter has no particular effect, the former tends to operate as a constant interference with the essential requirements of the bureaucracy. This tendency to interfere is intensified by the irritation felt over the "red tape" methods and the aggressive expansiveness of the bureaucracy. But as long as a "privatization" of the functions can be prevented, the fierce enthusiasm of the functionary for his function, of the official for the power of his office, is desirable for the accomplishment of the ultimate purpose for which they exist. In this sense it may be said that a bureaucracy lusty for power is greatly to be preferred to a bureaucracy satisfied to grow fat on the livings which it has secured for itself. It also must be said that definite machinery is needed to counter-act the tendency of the public to pauperize the public servant. This leads us to our last point.

For it remains to say a word concerning the significance of the syndicalist impacts upon the hierarchy, without entering into the legal controversies which have raged over this point. In the first place, it deserves notice that in actual fact the strike has not been used to any extent in Switzerland. As the civil service or bureaucracy increases in relative size compared with the population, it is not likely that they will become more frequent. The strike will always be reserved for very serious controversies.

But inasmuch as the governmentalization of industries depends upon and necessarily involves the continuous increase of the governmental bureaucracy, of necessity any difference between the "public" and the "bureaucracy" must tend to disappear. In the socialist state all industrial activity is governmentalized and consequently the people and the bureaucracy have become one. It is a curious misrepresentation of the facts if Lenin describes this change as "the disappearance of the State." The state disappears only in the sense that nobody is there to see it any more.

At this point it is apparent why it is absurd to "forbid" the strike of civil servants. It is as absurd as to declare a revolution unconstitutional, or to outlaw war. On the contrary, none of these events can be "legalized"; they show that every legal order rests upon a fact of nature, a social reality beyond all law, namely, the groups of human beings to which it applies. And therefore, just as *the* state or *the* government as such does not become problematical by the impending possibility of a revolution (nor by its actual consummation) but only the particular form of government which such a revolution proposes to destroy, so a strike in the civil service does not threaten the destruction of *the* bureaucracy as such, but only the particular legal form of the then existing bureaucracy against which the strike is directed. If this were fully realized, the hysterical frenzy which characterizes many discussions about this problem should give way to a sane realization of the needs of the human beings employed in our vast governmental bureaucracies. Upon their successful functioning depends the well-being of modern industrialized communities.

Here our study would end, if we were to live up to the scientific detachment which we have advocated, and which rests satisfied with formulating tentative hypotheses concerning the facts as we find them. But as the natural scientist often succumbs to the temptation of letting his imagination dwell upon the engineering possibilities of a scientific hypothesis, so we political scientists love to turn statesmen and to ask ourselves what we would do, if we could, provided our hypothesis were right. If we yield to this temptation—and with Oscar Wilde I frankly confess that I love nothing so much as to yield to a temptation—then we might ask now:

What is the solution of the difficulties which the strike presents? Is there an institutional safeguard in accord with the trend inherent in the evolution of the modern bureaucracy, if the legal prohibition is of no avail? I believe there is. In the wider governmental realm the threat of revolution has been mitigated fairly adequately by granting the public a limited amount of participation in the basic decisions. Within the narrower governmental realm of the civil services or bureaucracies a similar thing has been demanded and promises to be useful. It is the gradual admission of the civil servants as a group as co-determinants of the fundamental decisions affecting their part of the service, i.e., the railroads. Such participation of the civil servants themselves in the making of the basic decisions does not deserve the hostile reception which it has hitherto had. Just as the works councils[1] have their limited field of distinct utility, so the *Bureau Council* (Civil Service Committee)[2] would be valuable, not so much because of the technical improvement in the service as because of the feeling of par-

---

[1] See C. W. Guillebaud, *The Works Council* (1928).

[2] See some material on the operation of such committees in England and Germany in *The Civil Service in the Modern State.*

ticipation in responsibility which such a council would give to the public servants themselves. Many people who have reflected upon this matter have tended to make the same mistake that has so frequently been made with regard to the participation of the members of the larger group, the body of citizens, in the wider realm; that is, to evaluate such participation in terms of the technical contribution made by it instead of looking at it from the angle of the functioning of the whole. To repeat here a fundamental if somewhat platitudinous truth, a group of human beings is not willing, except in certain cases of extreme emergency, to be treated like dumb animals. Whether or not their material "interests" are taken care of a little better or less well does not matter to them in comparison with whether they feel that they have had a chance to participate in deciding what those material interests are. The civil servants in large public services too wish to become self-respecting fellows in a common enterprise and not cogs in a machine directed by a superimposed government. Barring the times of emergency there is no reason to believe that the hierarchy will not gain in the long run. Max Weber's idea that the trend of bureaucracy is toward monocratic control is probably correct only in the sense in which it has been true for the governments as a whole; the unitary control may be exercised only within the limits set by the entire group. When looking at the evolution of modern bureaucracies from this angle, one dimly perceives a federative commonwealth of mutual servants. Each great service would have its own internal controls, but these would be held together by an individual or a group or both, controlled in turn by the entire people. In short, we find that bureaucracy and democracy are not antithetical, but that they belong to each other as structural aspects of a fully organized living community. The group as a whole can act by majority decisions. Such decisions dispose of the fundamental issues. There is no apparent reason why this system of associational group action is going to undermine the authority of the superior officials when dealing with their individual subordinate colleagues. If it does anything, it will strengthen the hierarchical principle, because the increased corporate consciousness will be a bulwark against the disturbing interference of allegiance to political parties. Buttressed by the backing of an administrative court in matters of discipline and in conflicts of competence and supported by corporate action in matters of administrative discretion of more general significance, the superior will be able to demand a degree of subordination which it is difficult to maintain where accusations of partisan bias are a constant threat to the authority of the superior.

Finally, such partial self-government within each service might provide an effective check against the inclination of the public at large to hinder the healthy development of the civil service in a democracy. For, even though the final decision would not be taken away from the public, the united opinion of all those who operate the particular service might become a powerful force in moulding the opinion of the public at large. For this opinion is nowadays, after all, compounded of the opinions of the more limited groups which together constitute the community.

BIBLIOGRAPHY

I

Amtliches stenographisches Bulletin der Bundesversammlung, 1925-1927.

Annuaire statistique de la Suisse, 1893-1929.

Advantages spéciaux accordés par la confédération à son personnel (1925).

Beamtenjahrbuch, 1930.

Bericht der Grossratkommission . . . des Kantons Basel-Stadt (1926).

Bulletin de statistique suisse, 1929.

Bundesgesetz über das Dienstverhältnis der Bundesbeamten, Verhandlungen der eidgen. Räte, 1925-1927.

Constitution of Switzerland.

Entscheidungen des schweizerischen Bundesgerichtes. Teil-Staats- und Verwaltungsrecht, 1929.

Feuille fédérale, 1924-1929.

Fourth Year Book, International Federation of Trade Unions, 1926.

La répartition du personnel fédéral (1925).

Message du Conseil fédéral à l'Assemblée fédérale à l'appui d'un projet de loi sur le statut des fonctionnaires fédéraux, 1924.

Message du Conseil fédéral à l'Assemblée fédérale concernant l'état des fonctions dont les titulaires ont qualité des fonctionnaires (1930).

Political Handbook of the World, 1929.

Procès-verbal de la 4e séance de la commission générale du personnel des chemins de fer fédéraux tenue le 3 juillet, 1929.

Projets du département des finances, 1929-1930.

Protokolle der paritätischen Kommission des eidgenössischen Finanzdepartementes, 1929-1930.

Protokoll der 6. Sitzung des Fachausschusses IV des Personals der schweizerischen Bundesbahnen, Oktober, 1929.

Railway Strikes and Lockouts (Washington, 1917).

Rapport du conseil fédéral sur sa gestion, 1922-1929.

Rapports de gestion des chemins de fer fédéraux, administration des postes suisses etc., 1927-1929.

Rapports de gestion et comptes, S.E.V., S.B.P., U.F.P.F., etc., 1927-1929.

Ratschlag und Gesetzesentwurf betreffend die Dienstverhältnisse und die Besoldungen der Beamten, Angestellten und Arbeiter des Kantons Basel-Stadt (1925).

Recueil officiel des lois, 1910-1929.

Statuts, S.E.V., S.B.P., U.F.P.F., etc.

Swiss Civil Code (Ivy Williams trans., Glasgow, 1925).

Texte des lois et ordonnances (Berne, 1926).

Übersicht der Ämterklassifikation nach Besoldungsklassen (1929).

II

Ammann, J., *Theodor Curti* (Rapperswil, 1930).

Anliker, Paul, *Die Personalausschüsse* (Berne, 1924).

Archiv für Sozialwissenschaft und Sozialpolitik.

Baer, F., *Die schweizerischen Kriegsverordnungen* (5 vols., Zürich, 1916-1919).

Barthélemy, Joseph, *Le problème de la compétence* (Paris, 1918).

Bonjour, Felix, *Real Democracy in Operation* (London, 1920).

Brooks, R. C., *Civic Training in Switzerland* (Chicago, 1930).

——, *Government and Politics of Switzerland* (New York, 1921).

Bryce, James, *Modern Democracies* (2 vols., New York, 1921).

Bury, S., *Manuel de droit public* (Lausanne, 1869).

Cahen, Georges, *Les fonctionnaires* (Paris, 1911).

Catlin, G. E. G., *The Science and Method of Politics* (New York, 1927).

——, *A Study of the Principles of Politics* (New York, 1930).

Clark, J. M., *Studies in the Economics of Overhead Costs* (Chicago, 1926).

Clery, Rabinet de, *Pouvoir législatif* (Paris, 1921).

Constant, Benjamin, *Réflexions sur les constitutions et les garanties* (Paris, 1814).

Comer, J. P., *Legislative Functions of National Administrative Authorities* (New York, 1927).

Curti, T., *Le referendum* (Jules Ronjot trans., Paris, 1905).

Demartial, G., *Le statut des fonctionnaires* (Paris, 1909).

Delbrück, Hans, *Geschichte der Kriegskunst* (6 vols., 1900-1929).

Deploige, Simon, *The Referendum in Switzerland* (C. P. Trevelyan trans., London, 1898).

Dickinson, John, *Administrative Justice and the Supremacy of Law* (Cambridge, 1927).

Duguit, Léon, *Traité de droit constitutionnel* (5 vols., Paris, 1921).

Dupriez, L., *Les ministres dans les principaux pays d'Europe et d'Amérique* (2 vols., Paris, 1893).

Elliott, W. Y., *The Pragmatic Revolt in Politics* (New York, 1928).

Encyclopedia of the Social Sciences (1930), Vol. III.

Esmein, A., *Eléments de droit constitutionnel* (4th ed., Paris, 1906).

Fleiner, Fritz, *Schweizerisches Bundesstaatsrecht* (Tübingen, 1923).

Frankfurter, Felix, *The Public and Its Government* (Oxford, 1930).

Gariel, Georges, *La centralisation économique en Suisse* (2 vols., Genève, 1913).

Gibert, Max, *La discipline des fonctions publiques* (Paris, 1912).

Gosnell, Harold F., *Boss Platt and His New York Machine* (Chicago, 1924).

Grasserie, Raoul de la, *Les principes sociologiques du droit public* (Paris, 1911).

Grotius, Hugo, *De Jure Belli ac Pacis* (1750).

Guillebaud, C. W., *The Works Council* (Cambridge, 1928).

Guy-Grand, Georges, *La démocratie et l'après-guerre* (Paris, 1922).

Haller, J., *Papsttum und Kirchenreform* (Berlin, 1903).

Hauriou, M., *Précis de droit administratif et de droit public* (10th ed., Paris, 1921).

Hauck, Albert, *Kirchengeschichte Deutschlands* (5 vols., Leipzig, 1887-1929).

Hoerni, Robert, *De l'état de nécessité en droit public fédéral suisse* (1917).

Holcombe, A. N., *Public Ownership of Telephones on the Continent of Europe* (Cambridge, 1911).

Hugot-Derville, René, *Le principe hiérarchique* (Paris, 1913).

Jèze, Gaston, *Cours de droit public* (Paris, 1914).

——, *Les principes généraux du droit administratif* (Paris, 1904).

Kupper, Ernst, *Die Besoldungspolitik des Bundes seit 1848* (Zürich, 1929).

Laski, Harold J., *The Problem of Administrative Areas* (Northampton, 1918).

——, *Studies in the Problems of Sovereignty* (London, 1917).

——, *A Grammar of Politics* (New Haven, 1915).

——, *Authority in the Modern State* (New Haven, 1927).

Lefas, A., *L'État et les fonctionnaires* (Paris, 1913).

Le Play, M. F., *La réforme sociale* (3 vols., Paris, 1864), III.

Leroy, M., *Syndicats et services publics* (Paris, 1909).

——, *Les transformations de la puissance publique* (Paris, 1907).

Lippmann, Walter, *Public Opinion* (New York, 1929).

Lowell, A. L., *Government and Parties in Continental Europe* (2 vols., Cambridge, 1896).

MacIver, R. M., *The Modern State* (London, 1926).

Martin, V., *Histoire de la Suisse* (Paris, 1926).

Merkl, Adolph, *Allgemeine Verwaltungslehre* (Vienna, 1927).

Merriam, Charles E., *New Aspects of Politics* (Chicago, 1925).

Michels, Robert, *Political Parties* (Trans. by Eden and Cedar Paul, New York, 1915).

——, *Corso di Sociologia Politica* (Milano, 1927).

——, *Sozialismus und Fascismus in Italien.*

Muir, Ramsay, *Peers and Bureaucrats* (London, 1910).

——, *How Britain is Governed* (New York, 1929).

Picavet, C. H., *La Suisse* (Paris, 1920).

Robson, W. A., *Justice and Administrative Law* (London, 1928).

Rice, Stuart A., *Quantitative Methods in Politics* (New York, 1928).

Schmitt, Carl, *Die Diktatur* (München, 1928).

——, *Verfassungslehre* (Leipzig, 1928).

Smend, Rudolph, *Verfassung und Verfassungsrecht* (Leipzig, 1928).

Sombart, Werner, *Der Moderne Kapitalismus* (Leipzig, 1902).

Studhalter, Arthur, *Der Beamtenstreik nach schweizerischen Recht* (Bern, 1925).

Verfassungsausschuss der Länderkonferenz Beratungsunterlagen (1928).

Vincent, J. M., *Government in Switzerland* (New York, 1900).

Weber, Alfred, *Ideen zur Staats- und Kultursoziologie* (Karlsruhe, 1927).

Weber, Max, *Wirtschaft und Gesellschaft* (Leipzig, 1924).

White, L. D. ed., *The Civil Service in the Modern State* (Chicago, 1930).

——, *Principles of Public Administration* (New York, 1926).

Whitehead, A. N., *Cosmologies Ancient and Modern* (Lectures at Harvard University, 1930-1931).

——, *Science and the Modern World* (New York, 1925).

Willoughby, W. W., *Principles of Public Administration* (Baltimore, 1927).

III

American Political Science Review, 1929.
Annals of the American Academy of Political and Social Science, 1912.
Bibliothèque universelle, 1913.
Foreign Affairs, 1930.
Industrial and Labor Information, 1921-1929.
International Trade Union Movement, 1927-1928.
Journal des débats, 1918.
Journal de Genève, 1930.
L'Atelier, 1925-1927.
La Tribune du fonctionnaire, 1929-1930.
La Vie socialiste, 1929.
Le Temps, 1918.
Monthly Labor Review (U. S. Department of Labor), 1915-1928.
New York Times, 1918.
Political Science Quarterly, 1930.
Press Reports of International Federation of Trade Unions, 1928.
Revue syndicale suisse, 1922-1930.
Revue du droit public, 1914, 1918, 1928.
Revue politique et parlementaire, 1907, 1918, 1922.

INDEX

BAIT

KENNETH ABEL

Delacorte Press

Published by
Delacorte Press
Bantam Doubleday Dell Publishing Group, Inc.
1540 Broadway
New York, New York 10036

Library of Congress Cataloging in Publication Data
Abel, Kenneth.
    Bait / Kenneth Abel.
        p.   cm.
    ISBN 0-385-31190-7
    I. Title.
    PS3551.B336B5   1994
    813'.54—dc20   93-11471   CIP

Manufactured in the United States of America
Published simultaneously in Canada

March 1994

10 9 8 7 6 5 4 3 2 1

RRH

For my wife and daughter

1

"Let him die. Save us all trouble."

Laughter. He tried to lift his head. A hand settled on his forehead, shoved him back.

"He's up."

"Got a vein?"

Cold metal on his forearm. His sleeve was torn back. A hand rolled his hand into a fist, squeezed. A sting as the needle went in. The strap tightened around his wrist with a jerk.

No pain. There should be pain. If you feel it, you make it.

That's what they told you, the guys with the bullet scars on
their bellies, grinning at you when they lift their shirts. Too
fast to think, they said. Before and after, nothing in between.
One minute, you're standing there, and the next . . . A
flash in a dark hallway, so bright you can almost see the
bullet streak toward you. Your hand, slick with sweat, trying
to get the gun down, but there's nothing to shoot at in the
dark. At the end of the hall, the sound of a window breaking. And then, behind you, Jerry thrashing on the stairs.
You're trying to hold him down, but he's jerking away,
moaning, there's blood everywhere, and suddenly he's not
moving anymore, he's smiling, the asshole, shaking his
head, blood coming out of his nose, saying, *it's the ones you
don't feel that* . . .

In the hospital, Jack Walsh was still a cop. Private room.
Card from the union on the table, a drawing of a guy in
traction, tongue hanging out, a pretty nurse peeking under
the sheet, saying "Well, *that's* not broken." The other side,
they called it. You took the bullet, woke up to flowers, three
weeks of hospital food, soap operas through a thick haze of
morphine. You're a hero, just for being alive. You get a
medal for breathing, the joke goes, two if you can fill the
bedpan.

It was the lawyer that ruined it.

He showed up early in the afternoon, poking his head
through the door.

"Well, you're up." He pushed the door open, squeezed
into the room. A heavy man, wheezing, his shirt tight across
his stomach. He squinted behind his glasses. "The doctors
said you'd sleep a few more hours. But I figured, what the

2

hell? I'm here, I'll have a look. Save myself a trip, you know?"

He settled into a chair, grasping his briefcase between his knees. He leaned forward, thrust out a damp hand.

"Don Markoff. Feel up to a talk, Jack?"

"You understand, Jack, the department has to do this."

The lawyer balanced the briefcase on the edge of the bed, digging through a thick wad of papers.

"It's a disclaimer. It just says you weren't on duty when the accident occurred, that you were operating the vehicle without the authorization of the department, not in your capacity as an officer. It's a liability thing. You understand, Jack?"

He drew a paper from the briefcase, placed it delicately on the bed.

Jack's leg hurt. Suddenly, like someone had yanked a blanket off him. Burning, they tell you. Like a hot poker shoved right through you, so you want to pour water on it. He tried to focus on the lawyer's words. *Accident,* he said. *A disclaimer. . . . My capacity as an officer.* He shook his head. That wasn't it. What this felt like was—he wanted to say gravel popping under a truck's wheels. Like someone took a hammer to the front of his leg, went right up from the ankle to the hip, cracking the bone.

"You with me, Jack?" The lawyer frowned, tapped at the paper with one finger. "I've got to have your attention on this. You're covered, but the department needs this before it can process your claim."

"Tell me again."

The lawyer gave a sigh. He was gonna have trouble with

this one. Handsome guy, strong face, all that dark hair, like a Kennedy maybe, one of the kids. Eyes that look right into you, even through the drugs. Cop's eyes. But you could see the liquor in his face. Swollen. He picked up the paper, held it out.

"You sign this, you're just saying you weren't on duty. You don't have to admit anything about how it happened, that's for the Review Board. You're just saying that the department shouldn't be responsible. You got it?"

"You think I could get a nurse in here?"

"In a minute, Jack. This is important. You're gonna live with this for a long time. In my experience, it doesn't hurt to cooperate. The duty log says you signed out Friday night at 10:42. The call came in at 3:38, Saturday morning." He grinned. "You had yourself a time, didn't you? They got some nice blood work on you, found a bottle in the car. There's a witness, old guy in a cab, says you didn't even slow down. Went right through the light. How's that look, Jack? The girl, she was telling 'em on the scene how you had a few at the hotel. . . ."

Ah, shit. *Chris.*

The lawyer caught his expression, smiled.

"You're a married guy, aren't you, Jack? That girl's gonna be a problem for all of us. Hardly a scratch on her, but you watch, she's got a lawyer by now, gonna retire on the department if you don't sign this. And the kid . . . Well, you want the truth, that's gonna be your worry, not mine. His people don't go to court. Not by choice, anyway."

"What kid?"

The lawyer paused, rubbed at his chin.

"They didn't tell you?"

"Tell me what?"

"The kid, Jack. In the other car."

His leg was on fire now. He tried to shift his weight, but his hips wouldn't move. He pulled the sheet back. The cast extended up his left leg, encasing his hips. The lawyer was watching him.

"The kid died, Jack. He had one of those little Mazdas, the convertible, you know? Brand new, red one. Got it for his birthday, I heard. I saw it this morning, Jack. Looked like when you step on a beer can. They had to cut it in half to get him out." He gestured toward the door. "Nobody's been in here to talk to you?"

"Just you."

"Jesus, you don't even know who you killed." He sat back, tugging at his collar.

"You fucked up, Jack."

Kate Haggerty crossed the street, carrying the sack carefully. Four coffees, three black with sugar, one light. Three years of law school, a year of clerking, two with the U.S. Attorney's office, and she was getting coffee. She walked up the block past the auto body shop, the hair salon, the fish market, to where the van was parked in a lot across from the funeral parlor. She wasn't complaining. This was her operation, Riccioli had made that clear. It was a stroke of luck. The emergency room doctor knew her from college. He recognized the kid, figured she might want to know. She'd called the judge, could run the subpoena out to his house in half an hour. The judge agreed to sign it, but he wanted Riccioli's name on it.

"That's fine, young lady." The judge's tone was patient, as with a child. "Now you just call up your boss and have him sign the paper. You understand?"

Yeah, she understood. *Young lady.* The way they looked at her when she stood before the bench, the half-smile, thinking, *such a pretty girl.* Eyes on her runner's body, watching her move. Wondering why she pulled that pretty red hair straight back. She clenched her teeth, dialed Riccioli's house.

"They're gonna take him to DiNapoli," she told him. "That's where the family goes."

"Do it," Riccioli growled, his voice still thick with sleep, then hung up.

Three hours later, the van was in place, the microphones transmitting the sounds of footsteps, a coffeepot gurgling, a man belching. It was a long shot, she'd admit. Still, it was her show to run. If the guys hunched over their headsets in the back of the van wanted coffee, she'd get it.

She tapped at the door. It opened a crack, and she climbed in.

The ambulance bearing the mortal remains of Vincent D'Angelo turned into the narrow drive just before noon. Haggerty watched the driver swing the door open, slide the stretcher out, dropping the wheels. An attendant appeared at the door, and they wheeled the stretcher up the shallow ramp.

"Used to be a good-looking kid. He did commercials, you know? On the TV." The attendant's voice was thin over the headset, distant. "I seen one just the other night. Toothpaste."

Haggerty saw one of the men make a note in a log.

"Mosca," the man said. "The mortician's assistant. He's been in there all morning, since they got the call."

"His head went through the windshield, got stuck there."

6

The other voice was deeper, a faint accent. Spanish, Haggerty figured. The driver.

"Ain't that some shit."

"You wanna sign this, Tony?"

"Give it here. You want coffee? Cups under the counter." A rustle of paper. "His father tells us he wants an open casket. You believe that?"

"You gonna tell him no?"

"Do I look stupid?"

A faint clink, then another. Haggerty imagined the attendant bending over the body, picking bits of glass from the flesh with a tweezer, dropping them onto a tray.

"Jesus, look't him. How'd you like to be the asshole did this to Johnny's boy?"

Russo swung the Lincoln into the driveway, under the blue awning.

"Keep going. Around back."

Listen to him, Russo thought. Like he's telling you where to pick up his laundry.

He parked it next to the ambulance, walked up the ramp to ring the bell. When the door buzzed, he pushed it open, waved to the car.

"Here we go." Harmon raised his camera. "Johnny-boy."

A stocky man in a pale suit, gray hair swept back, got out of the car, hurried up the ramp. The camera whirred, tracking him.

"Just Russo." Harmon murmured. "He's traveling light."

At the rear of the van, one of the quiet men flicked a switch. The reels of tape began to turn slowly.

Russo stepped back, holding the door.

"Gray van," he said. "In the lot across the street."

Johnny D'Angelo paused in the shadow of the door, lowered his sunglasses. He smoothed his hair back, straightened his tie. His eyes looked tired.

"Assholes," he said. "They've got no shame."

"You see 'em spot us?" Harmon lowered the camera as the door swung shut.

"Pretty quick."

"They've had practice. You're not gonna get much here."

"We get what we get." Haggerty watched the ambulance driver emerge, back out, swinging wide around the Lincoln. "How's he look?"

"Like shit." Harmon slipped the lens cap onto the camera, made a note in his log. "Sometimes I hate this job."

Riccioli didn't look up from the papers scattered on the desk before him. It was a thick file, the tab marked in Riccioli's broad scrawl, "Johnny D." Haggerty watched him flip through the pages quickly. She knew the contents. A brief police sheet, mostly from the early sixties. Three years at Lewisburg on an auto theft and transport charge. Probation officer's statement, "Attitude—poor." Informants' reports from two decades, the name marked in red. In recent years, entire pages ran red. Photographs, starting with a mug shot of a young tough, hair slicked back. Later, a man talking on a street corner, entering a restaurant, surrounded by reporters on the steps of a courthouse. Finally, three shots of dead men—one slumped in a car, blood streaming from his head; another sprawled in the street, his eyes staring; the last, an elderly man in an expensive silk suit, slouched at a café table, the back of his head blown off. Flipping to the end, she had been startled to find copies of the boy's death certifi-

cate, an autopsy report, and—barely two hours after the van had dropped her at the steps of the Federal Building—a transcript labeled "DiNapoli Funeral Parlor, 7/8/92."

"So you got nothing." Riccioli rubbed his eyes. For a moment, he looked like he needed sleep. When he looked up, it was gone.

"Funeral arrangements. He didn't stay long. They left him alone with the kid, maybe five minutes. I couldn't even hear him breathing."

"You figure he spotted you."

"Took him thirty seconds, maybe."

Stay cool, she told herself. *You're frustrated, but he doesn't have to see it.* Riccioli liked to sweat the younger lawyers, peering at them from under his eyelids, asking the obvious until they stumbled, finding a flaw where none was visible. She sat back, watching him scan the transcript. *It was a shot. They've been running tapes out of the pizza joints for three years now. You come up empty in one day, he's gonna start yelling?* Johnny, they had discovered, was a very clever boy.

"What about the cop?"

"A drinker. Put in more than six good years, promotions, transfer to narcotics. He lost a partner about eight months ago, watched him bleed to death in the North End. After that . . ."

"You talk to him yet?"

"Not yet."

"The girl?"

"Treated and released. I heard she came back to work at the courthouse this morning. They had to send her home."

"All right." Riccioli sat back, fixing her with his eyes. He was a thin man, his face tanned from a recent vacation. Ten, maybe twelve years older than me, Haggerty thought. Mid-

forties. Worked his way through law school, played the politics shrewdly. Not bad for a grocer's son. A corner office, windows on three sides, huge mahogany desk, expensive leather couch. On the wall near the door, a picture of the president, smiling broadly, clasping his hand. In recent months, she'd heard talk of a run at the statehouse. The file on his desk looked worn, well-thumbed.

"I want you to pursue this," he said. Haggerty fought the urge to smile. "There's probably nothing here, but it's worth a look. Let's get the van back over there. The man's grieving. He's angry. I want to know what he's saying, even if it's just ordering flowers."

"And the cop?"

Riccioli swung his chair toward the window, silent. He twisted a pen between his fingers.

"Get his story, then let the department handle it." He paused, drew a pad toward him. Absently, he drew a box, put an X inside it. "We play this one up front. The media asks us, we're calling it accidental death, but we're looking at vehicular homicide. Nothing special about this, you got it?"

"They're not gonna buy that."

"No, they're not. But that's our line. We're respecting the family's privacy, you know? It's a tragedy, but these things happen."

He closed the pen, slipped it into his pocket. The pad disappeared into a drawer. He stood, reached for his coat. Haggerty rose, clutching at the papers on her lap.

"When they press you, give 'em the cop." He smiled. "Maybe our friend Johnny would like to know who killed his son."

2

Ice. These little towns, they let the snow freeze on the side-walks, then the wind blows it smooth as glass. Jack Walsh eyed the long walk into town, his leg aching. Twenty minutes for the bus.

Athol. Like a kid with a lisp. A name to conjure with during nine months in MCI. What better home for a failed cop, an ex-con, a drunk facing the cold morning sober? The place looked the same as he remembered it, just poorer. A mill town, waking to its own hard morning-after. *You can't escape your past.*

One bus in the morning, running up the hill from the flats where the mill workers live, past the high school, then a long, slow loop past the mills along the river. Only the mills all moved to Georgia ten years back. Everyone broke, living on credit. No jobs anywhere in the county—none in the whole state of Massachusetts lately. Movie house closed, radio station off the air. Three cops in the whole town, sitting in the doughnut shop every morning, watching traffic. When he was a kid, he rode that bus to school, carved his name on the back of the last seat. Couldn't wait to get out. Now, he's standing on the edge of the road, wind cutting his face like bits of glass blowing through the pines, praying for that bus to come, knowing that if he gets on, pushes his way to the back, his name would be there. Some life.

A mistake, the lawyer had called it. Tough luck when it happens to you, but better than being the other guy, right? Still, if you're a cop, something like this happens, you start looking for work.

The first reporters showed up at the hospital the same night. He could hear them arguing with the cop in the hall. Lying there in the dark, he felt like one of those chickens hanging in the window of a Chinese restaurant. He could imagine the picture. Stretched out on the bed, his leg dangling from its strap, face turned toward the camera, surprised. *The Cop Who Killed Johnny's Boy.* That's how you sell newspapers. He listened to them shouting in the hall, the nurses joining in now, trying to push them toward the elevators, the cop pressed against the door, telling them where to put their cameras. The department did that much, at least, kept the sharks off him for a few days.

So they got Anne, instead. Caught her coming into the lobby that night, cops trying to hustle her through the

crowd of reporters, the lights making her look even paler. *The Wife.* Thank God she didn't bring the kids.

By the time she got to the room, she'd stopped crying. Closed the door behind her quietly. Just stood there, looking at him. Let him feel her silence. Finally, she laid her bag on the edge of the bed, glanced around the room.

"How do you feel?"

"Like shit."

And she nodded. What else could he say?

"I took the children to my mother."

"Do they know?"

"Not yet."

He shifted his weight. His leg ached. Beyond the window, he could see rain in the glare of a streetlight.

Whenever he thought of that night, that's what he remembered. The rain falling. A cone of pale mist. The sound of Anne quietly sobbing.

The bus appeared in the distance, headlights flickering as it bumped up the hill. The snow had begun to fall again. He shifted the cane to his left hand and dug in his pocket for change. The first step was tricky. Wedge the cane into the ground, get a grip on the inner edge of the door, heave. Worse when it's snowing, when the slush from a dozen pairs of shoes makes the floor slick, the ground so soft the cane twists out of your hand. Two women, clerks down at the Food King, watched him lurch down the aisle, their eyes blank.

"A small town likes a story," his brother Larry had said during the drive out. Eyes on the road, a careful driver. "I can give you a job, a place to stay. But you can't hide from it here. We get the papers, too."

Local boy, a dozen years gone. He had a friend in the bottle. One girl too many.

The bus rattled up the hill. He stared out the window, thinking of the girl. He hadn't noticed her at first, leaning against the counter while he filled out the requisition form, her fingers riffling the pages of a thick paperback. He'd felt her looking at him, her eyes amused behind those little round glasses, like the hippies used to wear. Blond hair pulled back into a thick braid. When he handed her the form, she smiled. He watched her walk back into the file stacks to pull the folder, her legs taut beneath the faded jeans. He picked up the book. It was in German.

"You can read this?" he asked when she returned to the counter.

"If I work at it."

"What's it about?"

"Death." She smiled. "I think."

He dropped the book on the counter.

"Sounds like fun."

"It's for a class."

"You a student?"

"Night school."

"What do you study?"

She shrugged.

"Human nature." She peeled the pink carbon off the back of the form, scribbled her initials in one corner, and dropped it into a tray on the counter. She tucked the pencil behind her ear, tossed a stray lock of hair back with a flick of her wrist.

"Learn anything today?"

"You ask a lot of questions."

"I'm a cop."

14

"Glad you're not a proctologist."

It took a minute, but when he laughed, she rewarded him with a smile that made his knees weak.

"Points for accuracy." She pushed the file across the counter. "But you gotta work on your time."

Two days later, he made time to take the file back, lingered by the counter to watch her carry it back into the stacks. Not beautiful exactly. Put her next to Anne, she'd look plain. But her small body glistened with youth. She looked untouched by time, hurt, the slow uncoiling of hope. She flirted easily, with a confidence that swept aside fear. Watching her bend to slip the file onto a shelf, he felt his heart tighten with desire.

Later, when he trailed one finger up the inside of her bare thigh, he discovered a tiny scar, a pale half-moon etched in the soft skin at the top of her leg.

"What happened here?"

"I grew up in Florida. We used to ride our bikes to the beach in our bathing suits. We had a shortcut through a fence. A nail cut me. I had to get a shot."

He bent, touched his tongue to the tiny ridge of flesh. She squirmed, raised her hips to meet him. . . .

He pushed the image from his mind. In recent months, he sometimes woke in the pale half-light before dawn, his body hot with the memory of her. Gripping his hips with her slim legs, her cries as they rocked against the mound of pillows on the creaking hotel bed. He drove the memory from his head with images of his children's faces, Anne sobbing in the hospital room, the boy's forehead, streaked with blood, when they pulled him from the crumpled car.

It was this image that had haunted him in the hospital. When the papers got hold of his Academy picture, matching

it with a shot from the kid's high school graduation, he stopped shaving, letting the beard hide the flicker of pain in his jaw at each shuffling step. *Get used to it,* the doctors told him. *You'll have it for the rest of your life.*

In bed for two weeks, then the wheelchair until his ribs healed enough for crutches. With therapy, they had him walking within a month. Quick, the doctors called it. But he had worked at it, sweating through hours of exercises, passing the nights flexing the muscles in his thigh and calf, again and again, while the television flickered. By that time, he had known the indictment was coming. He was told nothing, but lying there in the dark, the sweat beading on his forehead, he could picture the scene. The courtroom, crowded with reporters. The prosecutor, playing to the cameras. And the court, sensing the public interest, coming down hard. He would do time. Bad enough for a cop if he's healthy. On crutches, with enemies, he wouldn't stand a chance.

Two weeks after the accident, he resigned from the department. At his trial, the boy's family sat in the front row. He recognized D'Angelo from the newspapers, watched him twist in his seat, smoothing his tie, to whisper to a blunt-faced man in the row behind. The man stared at him, nodding. Walsh sat in silence as a parade of officers from his Division testified about his years of service, the injuries he had suffered, his grief at his partner's death. The judge, hunched over his papers, avoided his gaze. Told to stand, he found his knee had stiffened, had to lean on the table to keep from falling. In the brief silence that followed, the boy's mother burst into tears. A young woman quieted her. From the corner of his eye, he saw D'Angelo tug at his collar, his face flushed. His eyes met Jack's, and he smiled

sadly. Leaning forward, he raised one hand, blew gently across his palm. *Like a speck of dust.*

His lawyer, hired by the department, considered the sentence a victory. Eighteen months in a state medical facility. He would serve no more than ten. His injuries would keep him out of the general population, where a cop could meet with an accident. He would spend his days in physical therapy, his evenings in counseling sessions for substance abusers. The department would notify the warden of his case. Two cops from the South Shore had done time there on a misappropriations charge, spent three years shooting pool with the guards, sleeping in a storeroom next to the guard station.

"They had a VCR." The lawyer grinned. "An account down at the video store. Used to order out pizza."

Pizza. Jack smiled. *I can call D'Angelo's.*

But the lawyer had been right. He had done his time without a hitch. Nine months, eighteen days. Sleeping in the infirmary, an intern's room off the chronic ward, fitted with a heavy lock that allowed the warden to claim him as a secured prisoner and let Jack sleep without jumping at every sound. He worked out, shifted papers in the infirmary office each afternoon. In the evenings, he went to AA— thirty prisoners crowded into a classroom, somberly reciting their failures. *My name is Jack, and I'm . . .*

Beyond the steamed windows of the bus, the winter fields looked faded as an old photograph. He felt the old women's eyes on him. Maybe they remembered him. As a kid, he'd worked in his father's store every summer. Hauling boxes out of the trucks, dragging them down the aisles to stock nails, light bulbs, garden shears, combination locks. At night, hitching the few miles into Gardner with his friends

to try the bars. Flirting with the girls behind the counter at the Chicken Fry, the local guys glaring at them from the parking lot. A couple of fights, a lot of tough talk. It had seemed like something was happening at the time.

Now look at him. Riding the same bus into town. Spending the day perched behind a counter, cane propped against the stool, watching a local kid drag boxes along the aisles, slide a razor across the edge, peel the top back. Larry, sitting in the tiny office at the rear of the store, frowns at his columns of figures. Some nights, as the kid pushes a broom along the aisles, the cash registers spitting their totals onto long strips of paper that curl along the floor, he half expects to see his father on his toes beyond the window, stretching to drag the security grate down. Like nothing has changed, the other life a dream that fades in his coffee.

Except that now, as the bus clatters over the tracks, past the old graveyard, he can almost see his father's stone among the pines. In his pocket, a letter from his wife's lawyer, which he will carry on his lunch hour across the square, past the courthouse, up a painful flight of stairs, to show the lawyer who handles his brother's collections.

The lawyer, a heavy man in a wrinkled suit, squints at the pages, shakes his head, pushes the letter back across the desk.

"They're gonna sue you," the lawyer says. "Third-party complaint. Then they file for a judgment to get out of it, making you the sole defendant. This way, the kid's family can't get the house."

Jack nods, knowing this. The lawyer sits back in his chair, watching him fold the papers and slip them back into his pocket.

"It's just procedure," he says. "What're they gonna get from you, your cane? You got nothing, so they get nothing. What's to worry about? You're safe."

Safe. A thin snow swirls around him as he crosses the square. He makes the walk often. Each week, an envelope arrives from an expensive law firm in Boston. Witness depositions. An action by the insurance carrier. Letters from one lawyer to another, with his name typed in at the bottom. *And send it to the cop.* D'Angelo, sitting in his lawyer's office, smoothing the fabric of his tailored suit.

He's yanking my chain. Reminding me that he hasn't forgotten me.

The snow stings his eyes. At each step, a weight bounces off his hip—a slim .25 Beretta with an extra clip, stitched into the broad hem of his down jacket, held in place by a double loop of elastic, a strip of Velcro at the fold where, with a slight tug, the pocket drops free. Below the counter at the store, he had bolted a pair of wing clips to a ledge one evening, easing the tension with a screwdriver until they gripped the barrel of a .410 pump with a pistol stock. Another, with the barrel sawed off to an inch, hangs from a pair of clips beneath the bed frame in his cabin. Many nights, as the wind howls through the trees beyond the window, he wakes with his body tensed and sweating, his hand reaching. A police-issue flak jacket dangles from a hook on the bedroom door. He eyes it as he dresses each morning, feeling naked as he slips his shirt on.

He limps on through the whipping snow, his eyes scanning the cars parked along the square, watching the traffic for a sudden slowing, a passenger alone in the rear seat, a window open despite the cold.

Safe.

3

From his office window, Johnny D'Angelo looks down upon the back lot of South Boston Auto Repair, James P. Gallo, Prop., a business in which he has no documented interest. At one end of the lot, a row of crumpled cars stands behind a wall of melting snow. During the last year, each car has been sold at least four times, the names on the transfers drawn from residents of nursing homes in the western part of the state. Only days after each sale, accident reports are submitted to the insurance companies, with damage listed a few hundred dollars below the car's value. It is a very profit-

able business, which, by virtue of its three employees' vast appetites, deposits a large percentage of its income at the end of each week into the cash registers of its neighbor, D'Angelo's Pizza.

Johnny D'Angelo shakes his head.

Stupid, he thinks. *They should push that snow out of the way. Some insurance guy has a slow afternoon, comes down here to look at the car. Maybe he remembers there hasn't been any snow in the last three weeks, starts thinking about how that car could get wrecked when it hasn't moved.*

He swivels his chair to face his desk. Across from him, Jackie Mullen from the South End leans forward, tapping one finger on the desk as he talks. Johnny shifts in his chair, not looking at him. *Fat Jackie. Like a meatball in that cheap suit.*

"This guy, he's into me for thirty-two hundred this month alone. Over fifteen thousand for the year. I got two guys in the hospital. He tried to run 'em down with a fuckin' Buick."

Fat Jackie settles back in his chair, one hand raised like he's trying to stop a bus.

"You and me, we've had our problems over the years. But we always worked it out. But this guy, he's way outta line. I'm supporting him and his whole family here. Don't get me wrong, it's not the money, Johnny. I got money. You hear what I say? Fuck the money. It's the lack of respect. I'm supposed to let him walk away from this, just 'cause he's gonna marry your daughter? I ask you."

He spends too much time staring out the window lately, his stomach twisted with pain. *Jimmy's a good guy. He doesn't think, is all. Lets things slide, I gotta send someone down there to get him to move that snow. Can't figure it out for himself.*

And yet, as he reaches for the phone, raising one finger to

silence Fat Jackie, he knows it isn't the snow that bothers him. Nor the letter dangling from the sign for the last three weeks. (*Sout Boston Auto Repair, just like you say it,* Jimmy'd said, trying to get him to laugh.)

Even Russo can figure it, standing with Jimmy while a kid drags a shovel out of the garage.

"You gotta think," he tells Jimmy. "He sits up there staring at that oil spot on the pavement over by the fence. Only he doesn't want to look at it, so he looks at the sign, or the snow, or whatever." He shakes his head. "It's gonna take him a while, Jimmy. He's gonna be on you about something until then."

And as he says it, they can see him in the window, one hand smoothing his tie with a practiced gesture, silver hair combed straight back, his face expressionless. Russo lets a hand fall on Jimmy's shoulder, gives it a shake.

"You want my advice, Jimmy?" Russo sweeps his arm across the parking lot. "You get some black paint, get a truck in here during the night to move the cars for a couple hours and do the whole lot. He doesn't see the oil every day, maybe it won't bother him so much."

"I don't know, Tommy. Used to be, he had a gripe 'bout me, he told me. I didn't have to hear it from you."

"What d'ya want, Jimmy? It's like when we gotta go up to the North End, up by where Vinnie got killed. He makes me drive all the way down Hanover through all the traffic, so we don't have to pass the street. He doesn't want to see it, you know? We get where we're going, he's in a bad mood. Tells me the shocks need work. Or he's in a restaurant, I can see him through the window yelling at the waiter. Poor guy didn't do nothing, but he's angry. Like with you."

"You think he's angry at me?"

Russo shrugs, tugs his collar up against the wind. *Not my problem,* he thinks. *Some guy over at the police yard wants the car off his lot, has it towed it over to Jimmy's, dumps it in the back. And Jimmy, he gets shook at the police truck pulling up in back, so he lets 'em. Leaves it sitting out there, what, six weeks? He's looking at it every day, seeing Vinnie's face like he was on the table, bits of glass in a little dish next to his head.*

When he glances back at the window, it is empty.

As Johnny settles into his chair, Fat Jackie leans forward once more. He doesn't like waiting, staring at D'Angelo's back while he watches some fucking kid shovel snow. He can feel the anger on his face, his skin hot. But he holds his temper, knowing if he walks out he'll get no satisfaction. He plays along with it, waiting his chance. Now, as Johnny's eyes meet his own, he leans into him, keeps his voice quiet, takes his best shot.

"He's not your kid, Johnny. I known him since he was stealing cigarettes out of the machine down at the Trailways. He's a punk, and he's done violence to my people."

He raises one finger, same as Johnny did, holds it there for a moment to make the point.

"Where I come from," he says, his voice almost a whisper, "we don't let that slide."

Johnny looks at him, his eyes tired.

"I'll take care of it," he says.

According to papers filed with a grand jury convened by the United States Attorney for the District of Massachusetts, D'Angelo's Pizza, Inc., employs thirty-two people at six retail outlets, another twelve at a central warehouse, and an administrative staff of seven, including its president and

sole stockholder, John Anthony D'Angelo. The company employs an additional seven people at two subsidiaries, D'Angelo Restaurant Supply and DRS Farms, Inc.

After an evening slogging through the financial records, Haggerty had to admit she was impressed. The restaurants offered a documented cash source, with register receipts to support the entire operation. The trick was that some of the sales were legitimate—a fact, Haggerty saw from the file, that had sunk Riccioli's last indictment. The restaurants sold pizza (*By the Slice! By the Pie!*) from an outlet two blocks from the federal courthouse. Haggerty smiled, shook her head. Try telling a juror the place is a front when he's just eaten lunch there.

Yet, a former employee had testified—reluctantly, Haggerty noted—to false receipts, a night manager who kept the cash registers chattering until dawn, recording sales that never took place. *A good system*, Haggerty thought. *No way to prove the money's dirty.* On the other end, the company bought all its supplies—flour, tomato sauce, cheese, kitchen equipment—from the two subsidiaries, leaving a hazy trail of invoices and checks that hid the fact that no money was spent. *From one pocket to the other*, Haggerty thought. *Lots of cash comes in, but nothing going out.* Pure profit.

The way Riccioli figured it, the money—from drugs, truck hijacking, insurance fraud, kickbacks—was laundered through local banks as receipts from the pizza joints. For decades, criminal prosecutions had failed as witnesses, under the stares of mob lawyers, grew forgetful. In recent years, the prosecutors had turned to accountants where the police had failed. The guys on the federal organized crime task force had a joke: *The mob has a retirement plan, death and taxes.* By selling a few pizzas, D'Angelo could avoid the tax

weasels. Haggerty had heard that during the last audit the IRS boys had come away shaking their heads, claiming that the restaurants showed a documented profit. On the books, the income from the six pizza joints scattered across the city was larger than the combined sales of the two largest burger chains, statewide. A lot of pizzas.

Haggerty pushed the records aside, stretched. She needed a run, a shower, more sleep. Too many hours in the office, chasing leads that had been checked dozens of times. For over a year, the D'Angelo file had remained in her files, unopened. A week of surveillance during the funeral of D'Angelo's son had produced nothing, and Riccioli had abruptly pulled her from the case. As a last gesture, to satisfy her own mania for order, she had scribbled a note to a file clerk she was cultivating at the Department of Corrections, requesting—along with the name of her hair stylist—notice of the disposition of the charges against the police officer, sentence imposed, and estimated date of release. The clerk's note returned a few days later, and she dropped it into the file and forgot it.

When, almost a year later, she found on her desk a Notice of Release for "Walsh, John D., Vehicular Homicide," it took her a moment to make the connection. She set her briefcase on the floor, slipped off her shoes, and slumped into her chair. It was late, and she was tired. The streetlights shimmered through a thin rain beyond the window. The tiny office was strewn with files, stacks of papers, exhibit boxes. The ancient leather chair was cracked, the stuffing spilling out in several places. She had draped it with a Navajo shawl, held in place by strips of masking tape. At idle moments, her fingers sought the fringes taped to the base of the chair, twirling them into elaborate knots. She picked up the

paper, tapped it with one finger. Footsteps receded down the dark hall. *The cop!*

She pushed back from the desk with one foot, tugging at a heavy file drawer. The folder was covered with a thin layer of dust. At the back of the file, she found three sheets, captioned in boldface, "Update to Main File," that Janice, her secretary, had slipped into the folder when she was out. The sheets were dated in the last four months.

Someone's been working the file, Haggerty thought. *Funny no one mentioned it.*

She shrugged. It wasn't her case. If Riccioli wanted to reassign it, that was his business. She had too much work as it was, too little time off, no life beyond the walls of this tiny office.

She stuffed the release form into the file, and shoved it into the drawer. She hooked the edge of the metal drawer with her toes to shove it closed, then paused. If the file was active, she should keep up with it. Riccioli knew she had done the background; if he assigned it to her, there would be no time to catch up. She sighed, lifted the file back onto her lap.

The tax reports took hours. When she found her mind drifting, she got up, switched off the office light. In the darkness, she fumbled for the desk lamp, feeling her senses grow alert. She bent the lamp down, so the only light in the room was the glare that reflected off the pages. An old law school trick: eliminate the distractions.

Confused by the details of corporate structure, she sketched a series of boxes on a legal pad, marking one "Pizzas," the next, "Supplier," which she linked by a dotted line to "Farms." Below that, she drew a series of arrows, charting the flow of money from the restaurants to the subsidiary

companies, and, by a complicated series of transfers, back into the main company. *A very clever boy, our Johnny.*

When she felt that she had glimpsed the faint trail of money from the cash registers in the restaurants to the private accounts at the bank, she stuffed the reports back into the file. Again, as she slid the thick folder into the drawer, she hesitated. The updates. She pushed the chair back to her desk, noted the dates from the forms on her legal pad. She bit her lip for a moment, then retrieved the release form on the cop.

All right, maybe it means nothing. Maybe you're obsessive. Disappointed it never came to anything. That's what Riccioli will think. Still, it can't hurt to get it in the file.

She gathered her papers, glancing at her watch. Nine-fifty. The file room closed at ten o'clock. She would have to sign the file out and get it back first thing in the morning. Another late night.

When she got home, she spread the file on her couch, flicked on the television to chase the silence from the tiny apartment. The furniture—a battered couch, an oak coffee table painted an unspeakable brown, and her father's old leather recliner—had emerged from her parents' attic when she left for college, following her to law school. She kicked off her shoes, scratched the soles of her feet on the edge of the table. One day . . .

Taking up the file, she added the release notice to the jumble of papers at the back of the file and initialed the change on the file log, alerting the file clerk to send out update notices. Next, she flipped through her own reports on the surveillance two years before, looking for comments in Riccioli's cramped hand. A red marker had noted

D'Angelo's spotting the surveillance van, an exclamation mark in the margin. *So do it better, asshole.*

She flipped to the back of the file. There were only two new entries. She consulted the dates on her legal pad, confirmed that a third update notice had gone out only three weeks before. She sorted through the clipped pages more slowly, found nothing more recent than January.

"Well, shit." She would have to ask the file clerk, a silent woman who loathed disorder in her files. Haggerty could imagine her scowling, glaring at her with suspicion. She shrugged. "Not my fault."

She set the file aside, stretched out on the couch with the new entries—a recent IRS report concluding that there was insufficient evidence for prosecution on tax fraud charges, and, stapled to a blank sheet of paper, an embossed wedding invitation, folded once, addressed to Thomas Riccioli, United States Attorney. Inside, in a flowing script:

Mr. and Mrs. John A. D'Angelo
request the pleasure of your company
at the wedding of their daughter
Maria D'Angelo
and
Francis Anthony Defeo
Sunday, February 10, 1991
at 2:00 p.m.
St. Vincent's Church, Boston

"That's balls!" she laughed. "Good for you, Johnny."

Attached to the sheet was a news clipping, "Assault Charges Dropped," and a photograph of a young man pushing through a crowd of reporters. Beside the photograph, Riccioli had scrawled, "Frankie Defeo meets the

press." She glanced at the clipping, a fight in a bar in Revere spilled out into the parking lot. Frankie had taken an axe handle from his car and broken three ribs on some kid from Saugus. The kid filed charges, then refused to testify when the case came to trial. *Little league stuff,* Haggerty thought. *Must be ambitious, though, marrying Johnny's girl.* She remembered a photograph of the daughter from the cop's sentencing, clutching her mother's arm, shouting at the press. Pretty girl, small, with angry eyes, a cascade of black hair across her shoulders.

Haggerty tried to imagine the girl's life—the little girl visiting her father in prison, the police cars in the driveway after school, urgent phone calls in the middle of the night, her mother dragging her from bed to hide with a neighbor. And in high school, the boys watching her from a distance, leaning against the fence at the convent school as she walked past, their eyes following her to the car, where Tommy Russo chewed his cigar.

Haggerty smiled. She knew these boys, had met them at the fence when the afternoon bell rang. The nuns watched from the windows, taking notes on which girls tugged their skirts up at the afternoon bell, accepted drags on a boy's cigarettes, or, shielded by a crowd of boys, slipped into a car for the ride home. But Kate Haggerty, a lawyer's daughter, had gotten grades and gotten out. If she smiled at the memory of the boys at the fence, it was because distance is kind to such boys, smoothing their rough edges, giving their crude jokes, their dangling cigarettes, their battered cars the innocence of a life that holds no claim anymore. *And if you can't get out,* Haggerty wondered. *If you're marked by the rumor of violence, the need for silence? If the boys at the fence watch you with wary eyes, what then?*

30

"You marry one," she murmured. "The first one who has the courage to ask you."

She turned back to the news clipping, the photograph of Defeo pushing his way through the crowd, his eyes empty. A small guy, but wiry. His face was pale, the dark hair combed back. He had a weak mouth, curled up at one edge in a sarcastic grin.

A boy who wants that life, who watches with envy as the car drives you away.

"This wedding thing, it's gonna kill me."

Russo could see him in the rearview, flicking the ash from his cigar through a crack in the window.

"Angela, she's got this list. The fucking florist, the photographer, the band. It's three feet long, Tommy."

He leaned forward, peering through the windshield. A block away, a car pulled into the parking lot of the International House of Pancakes, stopping in the pale light of the streetlamp. A Chevy, blue. He settled back in his seat.

"You think I'm kidding? She calls 'em all at least twice a week. The colors are wrong. The song list is too short, some fucking thing."

"Keeps her busy."

"Am I complaining?"

"Yeah, Johnny."

"All right. Give me a break here, Tommy. It's making me crazy, that's all I'm saying. Like we're launching a ship here, or something."

His cigar glowed in the darkness.

"She's busy, she's happy," Russo said. "Got no time to think, you know?"

"Maria came to me, I figured, you know, it's too soon. I

told her, 'Your mother, she's not ready for this. She's still thinking about Vinnie, right?' I mean, Tommy, I'd wake up in the middle of the night, and she's crying. Every night this happened. I get up in the morning, she's got the covers up over her head. I come back a couple hours later, she's still there. How's she gonna make a wedding?''

The cigar glowed. *Like it was his fault,* Russo thought. *Angie screaming at him. What's he gonna do about it? Doesn't he care? And him just sitting there, listening to it. Asks me one day, can we get a guy inside the prison? I told him, we got a dozen guys in there. They can't get at this guy. Sleeps with the guards, for Christ's sake. Just wait, I told him. He's gonna get out of there one day.*

Tell her, he says, shaking his head. *Tell her.*

''Maria, she wants to go right in there, give her the news. What am I gonna say, no? So next thing I know, Angie's outta bed, she's in the kitchen on the phone to Mr. Charles, making an appointment to get her hair done. Telling me she's gotta start looking for a dress, for Christ's sake.''

He flicked at his lip with one finger.

''I'll tell you, though, I gotta get outta there, she starts with that list.''

''Here he comes,'' Russo said.

A second car turned into the restaurant lot—a Lincoln, the leather roof shining under the lights.

''Look at him in that car.''

''He's got an account down at the Soft-Wipe. You can see him over there every morning.''

Johnny grunted. He pressed a button, and the window rolled down. He leaned forward.

The Lincoln parked in front of the entrance. As the headlights died, the Chevy pulled out, tires squealing. It swung

past the Lincoln, came to a sudden stop. A man leaped out of the passenger side, approached the car. Even from their distance, they could see the driver look up, surprised, raising one fat arm as the man yanked the door open, lifted the gun . . .

Jackie Mullen felt the door jerked from his grasp. He looked up, saw the gun reflected in the window, raised one hand. The gun swatted his hand aside, nestled in the hollow of his ear.

"Wait," he whispered.

Three faint pops, echoing along the wet street. Jackie slumped across the front seat. The gunman trotted back to the Chevy. It pulled out with a screech, bumped over a curb in a shower of sparks. Headlights flaring, it rounded the corner and pulled to a stop beside them.

Johnny nodded to the driver, looked past him at the gunman.

"All right, Frankie," he said. "Angie said to remind you 'bout the fitting tomorrow. Mr. Tux, on Washington."

The passenger nodded, a flash of teeth, and the Chevy roared off. Johnny settled back in his seat, the cigar glowing.

"Okay, Tommy. Let's go."

4

The note was on Haggerty's desk when she arrived at the office a few minutes after seven: *See me. Riccioli.* She dropped her briefcase beside the desk and the file in a chair by the door.

Riccioli, phone to his ear, waved her into a chair. He listened in silence, scribbling notes on a legal pad. A secretary came in with a sheaf of papers, which he tore open.

"They just arrived," he said into the phone.

He flipped through the papers, peeling off a police report, which he set aside.

"And the car?"

He scowled, scribbled a note on the pad, spun it around and pushed it across the desk to Haggerty.

You took the D'Angelo file. Why?

She took out a pen, but he held up one finger, pulled the pad back, flipped the page to make a note.

"All right," he said. "I want witness statements, not just from the restaurant patrons, but everyone. You got a grocery distributor down the block, a couple of machine shops that used to have a swing shift. Put some people out there tonight, see what they come up with. This one's on my red list."

He kept Haggerty waiting while he dictated a memo to his secretary, reminding her to have the police reports distributed to all attorneys who were active on the D'Angelo file. Haggerty, fumbling in her pocket for a pen, looked up in surprise as she heard her own name. Riccioli, his back to her, clicked off the recorder and spun the chair to face her. He considered her a moment in silence, then ejected the tape from the dictaphone and tossed it into a tray on the edge of his desk.

"What do you know?"

"I was just doing a routine update, staying current."

"You have an interest in this file?"

"The cop was released ten days ago. I just got the notice."

Riccioli was silent for a moment. He turned to stare out the window.

"Do you anticipate any activity from that angle?"

"Hard to say. Johnny spotted the surveillance at the time, so he knew we were interested. That might have scared him off. On the other hand, to let something like this go . . ."
She shrugged. "It's hard to forgive in his business."

36

"The A.G.'s staff thinks he's trying to go up-market," Riccioli said. "They think he wants to clean up his act, get out of the messy stuff. The theory is he's planning to turn the whole thing over to one of his people and run the restaurants straight."

"It doesn't make sense."

"No?" He turned to look at her. "Explain."

"There's no retirement option. Next guy would always be looking back over his shoulder, wondering where the loyalty lies. He gets itchy, thinks he's got to clean the slate."

"Richard the Second," Riccioli murmured.

"I'm sorry?"

He shook his head. "Go on."

"Johnny's made a lot of enemies over the years. They see he's out of the business, it means he's put down his guns. If they decide to take a shot at him, he can't hit back."

"Unless the new guy is family," Riccioli suggested. "Then he avoids both problems. You figure your kid won't come after you, and he can't let someone else take you out."

"But the son's dead."

Riccioli smiled, shook his head.

"Vinnie wasn't for the business. We kept an eye on him, but his father never let him near the action. That was fine with him, I think. He wanted to be an actor, did a few commercials. Liked to chase the girls. It's the old story, the father spends his life building it up and the son doesn't want it."

"You're figuring Frankie Defeo," Haggerty said.

"He's a tough kid."

"But small-time."

"So was Johnny when he started. And Frankie has guts. He took a risk going after the daughter. He could have ended up in a ditch on the South Shore."

"Or the heir apparent."

"We figure he showed up a few weeks after the son died. Saw an opportunity, I guess. Johnny made it as a hitter. He took the dirty jobs, showed he was tough. But that was twenty years ago. Now you got wiretaps to think about, tax indictments, all the stuff we've thrown at Johnny over the last ten years. Maybe he looks at this kid moving on his daughter, he sees an operator. A tough guy, but someone who can play the angles, too."

"I guess this explains the invitation," Haggerty said.

"Johnny likes his little jokes."

"But you don't buy it."

Riccioli studied her. His eyes were tired. He reached for his coffee cup, and she could see by the way he gripped it that it was cold. He'd been here a while.

"The A.G. boys are pretty convinced."

"It's just a theory."

"They've got a source."

"Ah." That explained the missing update—an informant, his reports restricted to the top levels. Haggerty felt disappointed. He'd been testing her, letting her make her case when he had information that proved her wrong.

Riccioli picked up the police report and tossed it across the desk.

"Somebody took out Jackie Mullen last night. Put three bullets into him outside a pancake house on the South Shore. According to surveillance, he met with D'Angelo in the morning."

"Did they get it on tape?"

"Every word. Mullen was threatening Frankie Defeo."

"And Johnny?"

"Very cool. Heard him out and said he'd take care of it. Play it for a jury, it'll sound like conciliation."

Haggerty's mind raced. D'Angelo knew he was under surveillance. Any important business, he left the office, made his calls from public phones. Why would he agree to meet Mullen there? Unless he wanted it on tape.

"So you figure he's immunizing himself," she said quickly. "He's talking for the tape, pretending he wants to avoid violence."

"Maybe."

"You think Defeo did the shooting?"

"It's his score. Johnny would want it settled before the wedding."

"But he'd be giving us Defeo."

"The district attorney is bringing an indictment this morning."

Haggerty stared at the police report, her brow furrowed.

"I don't get it. Why?"

Riccioli glanced at his watch. He gathered his papers, rose.

"That's the question of the day, isn't it."

Frankie Defeo had coffee at the T&D Diner in Day Square every morning. He arrived around ten, sat at the counter, near the window. He folded his newspaper to the sports section, then watched the traffic.

He knew, from recent experience, that habits were dangerous.

"What gets a guy killed," Johnny had said pointedly, watching him slip the gun into his pocket, "ain't that he's got enemies. Fuck it, I got enemies. We all got enemies. What gets a guy killed is he likes pancakes in the middle of

the night. Or he buys his newspaper at the corner store. He goes to see his girlfriend on Thursdays, parks his car around the block so his wife don't see it. You follow me?"

But Frankie Defeo was a fatalist. Crazy, they called it in the neighborhoods. The kind of kid who'd jump the third rail and ride the back of a subway train to beat the fare. A kid who stole because stealing was easy and working was dull. Walking into a liquor store when he was fifteen with a .22 in his jacket pocket, the owner laughing at him, whipping that huge .357 from under the counter, still laughing when Frankie jumped through the plate-glass window.

Frankie grinned. More guts than brains. Sitting there in the window of the T&D every morning, should have a target on his back.

"Somebody wants me," he had told his friends, "they'll know where to find me."

This morning, it was two guys in bad suits. He spotted them getting out of an unmarked in the Dunkin' Donuts lot down the block, looking over at the diner. *Cops*, he figured, *'cause the hitters don't dress that bad.* They waited at the opposite corner until a uniform pulled into the Texaco across the street. When they started toward him, he sighed, waved the waitress over. He slipped a business card out of his wallet.

"Gina," he said, "you wanna be an angel, call this number for me?"

Even as a girl, Angie Tomasino had seen it coming. When her girlfriends had sprawled on the floor of her living room, scribbling their married names for every boy in the neighborhood, it hadn't taken long for her destiny to appear. "Angela D'Angelo," they sang, delighted with the cruelty of fate. And though Johnny D'Angelo was six years older, a

tough boy who spent his nights unloading trucks in unlit alleys, they nudged her toward him at parties, called out to him in moaning falsetto as he drove past, tossing them a grin. She could feel his gaze on her as they shoved her forward, giggling. When, months later, he shouldered his way through the crowd at a party, holding her with his eyes, she bit her lip, threw her head back, and met his gaze.

"Angela D'Angelo," he said, smiling. "It's got a ring to it."

"That's the only way it'll happen," she said.

He cocked his head, the smile lingering.

"What?"

"A ring."

He laughed, pushed past her to the keg. Later that night, hearing shouts from the street, she had peered through a window to see him pinning a local boy to the ground, punching him. His shirt was spattered with blood. Watching it, she had felt strangely excited, as if she were somehow a part of it—the circle of shouting boys, the flash of headlights from passing cars, the dull thud of the punches. She could not pull herself away, watching until the distant wail of a siren scattered the boys. Rising, Johnny put the tip of his shoe against the boy's throat.

"It's over," he said. "Friends now?"

The boy swallowed hard, nodded. As Johnny stepped back, he glanced up at the house, catching her eye. He stood there for a moment, the siren growing louder, just looking at her. When she let the curtain fall, he turned and walked away.

It was almost a year before they spoke again. By then, he had begun to make a name for himself, had beaten an arrest for car theft, was waiting for trial on another. He saw her in

the bakery where she worked on Saturdays, walked clear past the window, then came back. He stood for a moment, looking in at her, making her remember him that night, the blood on his fists and shirt. He dropped his cigarette, pushed the door open, and came over to the counter where she was standing.

"Hiya, Angela D'Angelo."

"Johnny."

"You're selling cookies now?"

"Saturdays."

"Your parents, they think you're a good girl, huh?"

And he smiled at her, inviting her to smile with him.

"You want some cookies, Johnny?"

He looked down at the counter, ran his finger along the glass over the rows of cookies.

"These any good?"

"They're all good, Johnny. I gotta say that."

"Lemme have one of these."

She opened the case, took a piece of wax paper and lifted out an *Ossi di morti*, passed it over the counter.

"Thirty-five cents."

He dropped the coins in her palm, held the cookie out to her.

"Here."

"What?"

"I hate these." He ran his finger along the counter. "How about these? You like these?"

"They're okay."

"Gimme one." He laid some more coins on the counter, pointed. "And one of these."

She took the cookies out, but he'd already moved down

the counter, his finger trailing along the glass. She took out a box, unfolded it.

"That's okay, I don't need a box."

"You gonna eat these here?"

"Nah, I hate cookies."

She looked at him.

"Johnny, what're you doing?"

"What else you like?"

"I can't eat all these cookies."

"How about one of these chocolate things?"

"Stop it, Johnny."

"Not till you come out with me."

"You never asked me."

He came back along the counter, gave her that smile.

"So I'm asking you."

Just like that, she told her daughter. She had thought about it a lot in the last few weeks, at night mostly, after a day of talking to florists, looking at reception halls, choosing menus. When she and Johnny got married, it was a ceremony at St. Stephen's and the reception at the KofC hall on North Margin Street. A few streamers across the ceiling, some flowers, all her high school friends wearing their prom dresses. Who could afford more? So this time, she was gonna do it right, give her daughter the kind of wedding she used to dream about, the kind you see in those magazines. *Besides, we gotta do it right, 'cause of who your father is. It's a social event. People are gonna talk about it. We're setting the tone for the community.*

She smiled, coming up the front steps. If her friends had known, when they used to tease her. *Angela D'Angelo.* Now, they had to drive out to Newton, past the country club where the rich lawyers played golf, and peek through the

43

gates, up the curving drive, to see her house. She liked to imagine them, standing out there, trying to decide whether to ring the bell, biting their lips.

She set her packages down on the hall table, stepping over the pile of mail that had spilled through the slot. Standing there, she counted the envelopes. Thirty-two, today alone. That made two hundred and eighty-four since the invitations went out ten days ago. Johnny had laughed at her, ordering the response cards.

"What is this?" He waved the card at her. "Like they're not gonna come. These people, they're hoping they get invited."

"You gotta do this, Johnny. That's just the way it's done."

"All right." He tossed the card on the table. "But anyone says no, I want to know about it."

And he had been right. For six days, she had been slitting the envelopes open, piling the acceptances on the kitchen table. Nobody had sent regrets. Every night, Johnny asked, teasing her with it.

"So what's the story, anyone coming to this thing? We gonna be sitting there in an empty hall, listening to the band?"

She set the regular mail aside, took out her letter opener. She got pleasure from these slim cards, the formality of the manners: *Mr. and Mrs. Thomas Russo will attend*. People she saw every day, in the supermarket, at Johnny's office, became different in these cards. Like you could already see them in their gowns and tuxedos, toasting Maria with their champagne glasses. It made life seem more graceful, more real. *These are people*, the cards seemed to say, *like the pictures in the society pages*. This was tradition, family, the kind of thing that makes you feel like you have a place.

44

Her fingers worked quickly, taking up each envelope, slipping the letter opener under the flap. A flick of the wrist to slit it open, a quick glance at the card, then she tossed it onto the pile on the table. As her fingers closed on one envelope, she paused. Too thick. There was something folded inside. She glanced at the front, no return address. She shrugged, tore it open.

In her bedroom, Maria D'Angelo had the headphones on and U2 turned up loud. She bent over one bare foot, brushing the red polish onto the nail with careful strokes. In the slight pause between songs, she heard her mother scream.

She took the stairs two steps at a time. Her mother was in the kitchen, her face pressed against the refrigerator, sobbing.

"Momma? You okay?"

Her mother waved her off, turned her face away.

"What happened?"

She shook her head, her shoulders trembling. Maria glanced at the pile of cards on the table, the unopened envelopes in a neat stack. On the floor beside her feet lay the letter opener and a crumpled page. She bent, picked them up. It was a response card, a single page stapled to the back: *Thomas Riccioli will not attend.* She flipped the card up. A photocopy of a form, the title in thick block letters—Notice of Release.

5

The girl unlocked the bicycle from a post near the entrance of the parking garage, and tied her knapsack to a rack behind the seat with an elastic cord. She knelt, tucked her jeans into her socks, then unhooked the helmet from beneath the seat.

"Look't this. I love those things. She looks like she's wearing a fuckin' hard-boiled egg on her head."

"You wanna start the car?"

Russo sighed. The girl had one leg over the bike. She balanced like that for a moment, clipping a pair of dark lenses over those weird little glasses.

"We're gonna lose her, Johnny. It's rush hour. She'll cruise between the cars, we're still sitting there. You want her followed, you should get one of those bike guys, the messengers. Give him a hundred bucks, he'll stay on her ass. She sees him, she figures he's making a delivery, you know?"

"Did I say tail her?"

Russo started the car.

"Where to?"

"Get on the highway. Let's take a ride up to Medford."

Ah, shit, Russo thought. *Sight-seeing.*

From the street, the house wasn't much to look at—an aging two-family on a small lot. Six rooms down, five up. The yard was overgrown, and it needed a coat of paint. A plastic slide and a couple of kid's bikes were strewn across the narrow drive at the side of the house. Russo could see the wife in the kitchen window, her head bent, looking down at something in her hands. Dishes.

In the weeks after the accident, they'd spent hours parked on this street, sitting in the dark. Russo knew every house on the block, what time the people got home, which ones had kids, or dogs that had to get walked, the windows where televisions flickered late into the night. The cop had moved out when he got out of the hospital, moved into an apartment over in Brighton with two other cops who'd split with their wives. Johnny had kept a tail on him right through the trial, until Dukie, the tail, had started talking about splitting the lunch tab with the guys from the U.S. Attorney's office, asking them for copies of the pictures to give to his kid.

"So fuck him," he had said to Johnny at the time. "They're just waiting for you to get restless. A clean shot or

no shot, right? Let the court have him for now. We'll wait our turn."

And Johnny had sat in silence, the tip of his cigar glowing, his face turned to the pale light of the windows, the shadows of the children moving across the shades.

"I'm gonna walk up to the corner, get a pack," Russo said, twisting in his seat. "You want anything?"

Johnny shook his head.

"Ask about the cop," he said.

Russo shrugged, flicked off the dome light, and got out. He walked up the street to the corner spa. An old man sat behind the counter, watching a soccer game on a portable television.

"Camels," Russo said. "You got coffee?"

"Yes. Very good." The old man nodded, his accent thick. A postcard was taped to the side of the register, a city in sunlight beside the sea, *See Beirut Now!* Russo smiled, shook his head. Everyone's homesick for somewhere.

The old man poured the coffee into a cardboard cup, squeezed the lid on. He snapped a bag open, set the coffee inside and tossed in two packets of sugar and a creamer, a napkin, a plastic stirrer. Ask for coffee, get a picnic. He reached for the cigarettes, paused.

"Camels, yes?"

"That's right."

The old man dropped the cigarettes into the bag. His hand hovered over the register. He pursed his lips, searching for the numbers, pecked out the sale. Russo tossed a twenty on the counter.

"Maybe you can help me," he said. "I had a friend used to live up here. Loaned me money a while back. I wanted to

pay it back, but I lost his number, you know? Jack Walsh. He's a cop."

"Yes?" The old man frowned, his brow wrinkled. He considered Russo's face, frowned, shook his head. "I am sorry."

He counted the change onto the counter, turned back to the television.

As he walked back up the street, Russo could see that Johnny had the window down, the smoke from his cigar swirling in the flicker of passing headlights.

It's coming, he thought. *Gnawing at him, like he's got a gutful of hate, he's gonna die if he don't spill it.*

He paused on the sidewalk before the house, peeled the plastic from the top of the cigarette pack, shook one loose. He shook the match out, flicked it into the gutter. The wife was watching him from the window, her face still.

It's coming, lady, he thought. *And it's gonna be bad.*

Anne Walsh watched the man walk away into the shadows. A moment later, she heard a car door close.

Cop, she thought. *The way he looked up at her.*

She'd been expecting it since Jack was released. Before the trial, she had tried to get used to the idea of cops watching the house, keeping track of who visited, checking her packages, taking plate numbers off her neighbors' cars. She had grown up in the life, watched her father grow old in the uniform, married a cop she'd met at a barbecue held for her father's retirement. She'd become a teacher, working with abused children in a state facility, but she'd never lost the eye. She could spot an unmarked on the street, could tell an all-night diner from a greasepit, and always scanned the block before walking to her car. In her purse, she carried a

tiny pistol, her father's solemn gift on the day she moved into her first apartment.

When she met Jack, watching him squeeze onto a bench opposite her at the long picnic table, flashing his rugged smile, she had fixed him with a cool glance, hoping to discourage him. Cop's girl, cop's wife. She was determined not to share her mother's fate, lying awake through the late shift, wondering how she would raise the kids alone if . . .

But if he got the message, he gave no sign of it. He shrugged, struck up a conversation with her mother that lasted through the ice cream. During quiet moments, she could feel him looking at her, but when she glanced up at him, she found his attention fixed on her mother's words, a slight smile on his face. When the group at the table broke up, he rose with the women, swept up an armful of paper plates and followed her into the kitchen.

"I hear you don't date cops," he said, dumping the plates into a garbage bag. He held it open for her to scrape the blackened grill.

"Not cops I don't know."

"Jack Walsh," he'd said, smiling. He leaned over the sink to run water over his hands, pulled a paper towel from the roll. "Ask your father about me."

And then he was gone, the screen door slamming behind him. She could hear him calling out his good-byes in the yard below, caught a glimpse of him pushing through the gate.

What's to ask, she had thought. *Movie cop. Thinks he's Mel Gibson, crashing through doors with his gun out. If he passes a mirror, he might blow the collar.*

She grinned, shook her head. In the backyard, her mother

was bent over her father's chair, whispering in his ear. They glanced up at her as she pushed through the screen door, her mother smiling. Her father, she noticed, was less cheerful. Later, as the crowd thinned, he waved her over, pulled up a lawn chair beside his own.

"Your mother worries you might be lonely," he said. "She thinks you work too much."

"And what do you think?"

"I think you're smart to stay away from cops."

"Got anyone in mind?"

"Your mother does."

"He said I should ask you about him."

"Big mistake."

"Yeah?"

He drained his beer, leaned forward to pitch the empty can into a garbage bag.

"Jack Walsh is a good cop," he said.

"He seems to think so."

"He's got good instincts, works the street better than I could."

"But . . ."

"Women like him. He's a handsome guy. You go for coffee, the waitress flirts with him."

"So you're saying he stays busy."

"I'm saying he's not your type."

She laughed, pushing out of her chair.

"I could have told you that."

To her surprise, he let two days pass before calling. His voice was pleasant over the phone, quiet, but with a touch of laughter, so you pictured him smiling. *Smooth*, she thought. *He gets lots of practice.*

"So did you ask your father about me?"

"We talked."

"Your basic neutral answer."

"You anxious to know what he said?"

"I can guess. He told you I'm a ladies' man. As a cop, I've got more guts than sense. Maybe I've seen too many movies."

She smiled.

"That about it?"

"Pretty much. If you figured he'd say that, why did you tell me to ask him?"

"Are we talking strategy now?"

"I'm curious."

"That's a good sign."

"Call it *idle* curiosity."

"You want the whole plan? You're a smart woman, independent. You're not gonna date a guy your father likes. I figure I'll do better as the black sheep. Maybe you'll take a risk."

"So you're the boy my father warned me about."

"It sometimes works."

He'd picked her up at nine. Just coffee, she told him as she got into the car, and he smiled. To her surprise, she enjoyed herself. He told her stories—not about his work, but scenes from his childhood: a cop's son, who swore he'd never end up like his dad.

"Before he made his twenty, bought the hardware store, he worked property crimes out of Area D. He used to sit there at night in the dark, the TV flickering but no sound on. A beer in one hand, another on the floor next to his chair. Just sat there, watching cop shows, like he was trying to

figure out why it looked so different. I'd see him sitting there, and I'd think, 'Not me. No way.' "

He smiled.

At midnight, he drove her home, walked her to her door.

"You've blown your image," she told him, unlocking the door.

"How's that?"

"You're not so bad."

"New strategy. Gotta keep you off balance."

And with that, he smiled, kissed her on the cheek, and walked back to his car.

Two nights later, she invited him in.

She dried her hands on a dish towel. The kitchen floor was scattered with toys. In the corner, Becky was busy taking all the pots out of a cabinet. From the living room, she could hear the faint *blip, blip* of a video game.

"Danny," she called out. "Homework!"

"I am!"

She heard papers rustling.

"No television, no video. You've got school tomorrow."

"I'm almost done."

She gathered up the toys and dumped them in a wicker basket. She made up Becky's bottle, used it to tempt her away from the cabinet long enough to straighten up the pots.

That was it, she thought. The night, a few weeks before the accident, when she'd woken in the middle of the night to find him gone. She got out of bed, her legs suddenly weak with fear.

You didn't hear the phone, she'd reminded herself. *They'll call if . . .*

54

And then she heard a cough. She threw a robe over her shoulders, went downstairs. She found him in the living room, sitting with the lights out, the television flickering.

When he looked up at her, he was crying.

6

Just before dawn was worst. He would wake, suddenly, his heart pounding, the sheets bathed in sweat. Most days, he would lie there a few minutes, until his pulse slowed, then get up, make coffee, watch the sun come up. On weekends, he tried to make himself go back to sleep. Pulled the sheets up over his head and imagined that he was sailing—a clear sea, a warm night, the boat rocking gently. But his jaw ached with tension, the muscles in his legs cramped until he had to draw them up, digging into the flesh with his fingers. At last, exhausted from the effort, he would get up, turn the

shower up so hot it stung his skin, leaning his head against the wall, while the water pounded the tension out of him.

Awake, he couldn't remember the dream. Still, it didn't take a fancy shrink to figure it out. He woke feeling like something had swept over him. A feeling in the belly like you get when there's shooting. As if you had looked away at the wrong moment, and some crucial thing had slipped past you. Out of control, like a car sliding on a slick . . .

He yanked the shower handle, so the cold water hit him before he could jump back. Gasping, he reached for a towel. His cane hung from the edge of the counter.

The house was dark. On his second day in town, he had bought a set of curtains at a discount store. Thick and ugly, like the kind in roadside motels. Except he needed them, not to keep the daylight out, but to blind the windows at night. The last thing he wanted was to throw a shadow on the blinds when he moved through the house. Like a target.

On Saturday, he wasn't scheduled at the store until noon. He ate his breakfast in the flicker of the television. A coyote, in a flying scarf and goggles, a pair of wings strapped to his back, soared through a crimson sky. *Danny used to watch this,* he thought, *eating his cereal on the living room floor, climbing up into my lap.*

He pushed the thought away. A tiny cloud of smoke raced along a winding road. The coyote wiggled his eyebrows at the camera, adjusted his goggles, dove.

A car crunched over the gravel in the drive. Jack dropped his spoon, knocked the chair over backwards as he flung himself toward the hall, where his coat hung. He pressed into the corner; the gun dropped into his hand with a slight tug at the coat hem. When his breathing steadied, he edged across the door to the narrow window, peered through. A

woman was climbing out of a battered Volvo, pulling her scarf up against the wind. She carried no bag, and her hands were empty.

He dropped the gun into the pocket of his bathrobe, and, suddenly conscious of his uncombed hair, limped back along the hall to the bathroom. His cane was still dangling from the kitchen table. *Funny*, he grinned. *Like that coyote, a little cloud of dust behind me.*

The porch step creaked. At the door, he hesitated, one hand resting on the gun in his pocket. *No chances.* He glanced through the window. She was chafing her hands together, blowing into her cupped palms. No deep pockets, the coat buttoned up to the neck. *Offer to take it, get behind her, where you can watch her hands.* As she raised one hand to knock, he swung the door open.

She looked up, surprised.

"Mr. Walsh?"

He remained silent, watching her face shift as she caught her balance, the lips tightening, the eyes growing guarded.

"Mr. Walsh, I'm Kate Haggerty from the U.S. Attorney's office in Boston. I'd like a few minutes of your time."

The kitchen was clean, she noticed. He set the chair on its feet, wiped the floor where the spoon had fallen with a paper towel.

Heard me coming, she thought. *He's expecting visitors.*

She accepted his offer of coffee, watched him limp across the small kitchen. He was thinner than the pictures, his face tired. She looked for a drinker's flush around his eyes, but saw none. It was a handsome face, she decided, tragic. *A man who lives with pain. Making himself taste every ounce of*

regret. When he turned back to the table with the coffee, she looked away quickly.

He settled into the chair, wincing as he stretched his leg out. He stirred his coffee, waited.

"I'm sorry it's so early," she offered. "You're not as far from Boston as I thought."

"About half a lifetime."

She smiled.

"Have you been back?"

"Not much reason." He smiled. "Plenty of reason not to."

"That's what I'm here to discuss."

"What's to discuss? I'm not very popular these days."

"Have you been threatened?"

"No one has to threaten me. If they want me, they'll know how to find me."

"You're not exactly on display here."

"You found me."

"I got your address from your probation officer. I had her pull your file. She has the only copy."

He shrugged.

"So they'll get it some other way."

Haggerty frowned, looked away. Watching Walsh brood over his coffee, she found his pain too convincing. He expected trouble, that was obvious. He would sit here in his gloomy cabin, waiting for the unspoken threat to become real, even believing it a kind of justice. *He thinks he deserves it,* Haggerty realized.

"Tell me about your partner," she said.

He looked up, surprised.

"What?"

"Jerry Friar. According to your personnel file, you filed a DD 5 Complaint with Internal Affairs after his death. . . ."

"That was a long time ago."

"You made some serious charges."

"I was angry."

"Why?"

He glared at her. For the first time, she glimpsed the rage that lay beneath his grief. His eyes clouded over, and he shifted his gaze to the window.

"You read the file," he said.

For a moment, she hesitated. The file revealed only that a hearing had been scheduled, and then abruptly canceled ten days later. Perched on a narrow bench in the hall outside the parole officer's cramped office, she had pondered the two dates, until, flipping back through the pages, she had realized why the date stuck in her mind. *Three days,* she had thought, growing excited. *He filed the complaint three days after his partner was killed. What did he know that the Review Board didn't? What could get him mad enough to risk his career, then just drop it a few days later? What makes a good cop into a drunk?*

"I want to hear your side," she said.

"What's this got to do with D'Angelo?"

"You tell me."

He considered her, shook his head.

"You've got a question, you ask it."

"All right," she leaned forward, held up one finger. "Jerry Friar was killed in a drug buy in the North End. Nothing happens there without D'Angelo knowing about it."

"You're thinking like a prosecutor," he said. "It doesn't work that way on the street. Some kid sells a little smoke, makes some money, decides to move up to Burmese Yellow. He's working out of a triple-decker, got customers coming up the back steps. Now Johnny's gonna know about it even-

61

tually, because the distributor gets his stuff from the Chinese in New York, and they keep records. But this kid, he's got six months before they catch up with him. And when they do, Johnny just sends someone to let him know he's gotta start paying his taxes. He says yes, and he's back in business. That's about as organized as it gets. D'Angelo, he's just like the IRS, only you can reason with him."

"What about Friar?"

"Just like I told you. Some guy selling out of a triple-decker. We knock on his door, he starts shooting. Jerry's coming up the stairs and catches it in the chest. Just ran out of luck."

"This was during Operation Clean Sweep."

"There was an even pound of crap."

"What do you mean?"

"Big publicity. The mayor on television, the D.A. Even the U.S. Attorney." He looked at her. "In the end, what happens? The reporters get some film, the mayor gets reelected. Jerry takes a bullet, bleeds to death on the stairs. The guy . . . gets away." His fingers kneaded the muscle in his leg, digging into the flesh. "Nothing changes."

"So you were angry."

"I got over it."

"Two weeks later. First you filed a complaint."

"We all make mistakes. I make a lot."

"Tell me about the complaint."

He looked away. Beyond the window, the trees stirred in the wind. A memory swelled within him—a streetlight throwing shadows across an empty room. *No, not empty . . .* He shook his head, pushing it away.

"Let's go back," Haggerty suggested. "You said you knocked on the door, and the suspect began shooting. Of-

ficer Friar was coming up the stairs when he was hit. Is that correct procedure? Doesn't that leave him in the line of fire?"

"You should be a lawyer." He smiled.

"So, as I understand it, the Review Board could have drawn two conclusions. Either Officer Friar failed to take cover as you entered the apartment, or you moved too fast, leaving him exposed when you knocked on the door."

He remained silent.

"Maybe that's why you filed the complaint, to cover up your mistake." She paused, watching his face. "That could put a burden on a man, knowing that his screw-up got his partner killed."

He tipped his chair back, stretching for the coffeepot. He filled her cup, slipped it back onto the counter.

"But that's not what happened, is it?"

"No."

"Want to fill in the blanks?"

He sipped his coffee.

"You're doing fine."

"All right," she said. "Let's try again. At what point did you identify yourselves as police officers?"

He smiled thinly.

"We didn't."

"So you knocked on the door, and the suspect just started shooting."

"Funny, isn't it."

She sat back in her chair, considering.

"I have only your word for this."

"No, you don't. I never said it."

"But you were willing to testify before Internal Affairs. You filed a complaint."

"And then I withdrew it."

"Why?"

"I came to my senses." He looked at his watch, pushed his chair back. "I have to get ready for work."

She caught his arm.

"You're saying the guy knew you were coming."

He stood, took the cane from the edge of the table.

"I didn't say that," he said.

The Volvo bounced over the gravel drive, paused at the edge of the road, then turned east.

"She's gone."

Harmon lowered the camera, let the curtain swing back. He noted the time in a log, grinning.

"God, you remember the legs on her?"

Cardoza loosed his headphones, letting them dangle around his neck.

"Too cold," he said. He scribbled a series of numbers beside the time in the log. "She'd freeze it off."

"I'd risk it."

A flash of color caught Harmon's eye. He raised the camera, got two quick shots of Walsh locking the kitchen door, a few more as he limped down the driveway.

"He's heading out."

Cardoza leaned over to the edge of the stairs, called out.

"Brodie! Let's move."

A toilet flushed. Brodie clomped down the stairs in his boots, grabbed his coat at the door. "Bus stop?" Cardoza scanned the road with the telephoto.

"He's walking east."

"The lake again."

"Stay warm."

Brodie hurried out. Harmon picked up Walsh at a break in the trees, got a tight shot of his face. Worried.

"Looks like a tough night."

"Tough life, you ask me."

7

Detective Lieutenant Tony Keenan waited for the patrol car to disappear around the corner. After six years in Narcotics, running buy-and-bust operations in the Irish projects of South Boston, Keenan shared the dealer's hostility to beat cops. The last thing you wanted in the middle of a buy was a couple of uniforms, their mouths stuffed with glazed donuts, gaping at you from a passing cruiser. More than once, his crew had found themselves, guns drawn, facing down some late-shift heroes, the buy blown.

Part of the problem, Keenan knew, was that he had the

look. He was a small man, his eyes narrow and intense. On the street, he wore his dark hair pulled back into a short pony tail. He kept a pair of dark glasses tucked in the breast pocket of his jacket, which, he figured, fit the image. A toothpick jutted from the corner of his mouth. *Maximum trafficante*. His crew laughed at the slicked-back hair, the salon tan. They called him Luis, savoring the pun on his rank.

When the patrol car vanished behind the row of warehouses, Keenan reached up, unscrewed the bulb in the dome light, and got out of his car. He paused at the rear of the car, opened the trunk, and took out a small canvas bag. He checked the street in both directions, then walked up the street past a loading dock to a narrow ramp, where a yellow floodlight flickered and spit in the cold drizzle. At the top of the ramp, a narrow strip of duct tape was visible on the fire door. Keenan smiled, walked farther up the street to an empty lot. A chain-link fence ran along the street, topped by a loop of razor wire. He ran his hand along the fence until he found the cut in the wire, the thin strip of plastic woven through the loops. He pulled the plastic free and slipped through the hole, tugging the bag after him.

He made his way through the shadows along the warehouse wall to a basement window set into a recess in the wall. One pane of the window was missing, and when he squeezed his hand through to slip the latch, his fingers came away coated with a thin film of oil. The window opened silently. He dropped the bag through the window. Gripping the edges of the window frame, he lowered himself through, dangled for a moment, then dropped into the darkness.

He fished a penlight from his coat pocket, played it across the cavernous basement. Crates were stacked to the ceiling.

The narrow aisles were spanned by cobwebs. Something skittered through the darkness to his left. Keenan picked up the canvas bag. Pushing the webs aside with one hand, he picked his way toward the distant stairs.

The police cruiser slowed, its searchlight drifting across the loading dock, up the ramp, past the fire door.

"Hold it," Officer Eddie Shea said.

He swung the light back to the door.

"I told you I saw something. It's taped."

His partner, Officer Frank Breden, threw it into park.

"Good eye," he said, picked up the radio.

Keenan could smell him on the stairs. The stink of his cheap cigarettes lingered in the narrow stairwell, getting stronger as Keenan moved quietly up the stairs toward the third-floor landing. He was seated on a crate near the stairs, his back against a fire wall. A thin man, with blunt features, his dark hair swept back and oiled. *Mestizo,* Keenan thought. *Straight from the barrio.*

Beside him, a narrow window looked out over the bright floor of the warehouse below. He smoked, one hand toying with the cigarette pack on the crate next to him. A rifle lay across his lap.

Keenan slipped out of the unlit stairway, moving quietly. He was only a few yards away when the man glanced up, his eyes registering surprise. Keenan let the canvas bag drop against the stock of the rifle, smiling. The man sat very still, watching him.

"Evening." Keenan nodded toward the window. "He down there?"

The man nodded. His gaunt face was green in the light from the frosted window. Keenan eyed the rifle.

"That for me?"

The man gave a thin smile, shrugged.

Keenan picked up the pack of cigarettes, shook one loose.

"You mind?" he asked. "These things, they got a wicked stink. I could smell you two floors down."

The man was silent, watching him lay the pack on the crate, bring the cigarette slowly to his lips.

"Light?"

The man hesitated, then shrugged, raised up on one hip to slip his hand into his pocket.

Tight pants, Keenan thought. *A ladies' man.*

His left hand drifted under the hem of his coat. As the man raised a slim gold lighter, Keenan leaned closer. The knife blade caught the flame, flashing under the man's chin. He gave a startled grunt. The flame sputtered, died. One hand drifted up to touch his throat. He looked at it, surprised by the blood dripping from the fingers. He leaned back against the wall, slowly.

Keenan lifted the rifle from his lap, laid it on the floor. He took the cigarette from between his lips, flicked it against the man's blood-soaked shirt, a shower of sparks tumbling into his lap.

"They'll kill you, these things."

"You're late."

Sagria was seated at a table in the tiny office. A lamp swung on a cord above his head, gleaming on his bald head. Keenan looked around for the suitcase. Sagria watched him in silence.

70

"In due time, my friend." He gestured to the bag. "I see you have brought what we discussed."

He reached for the bag.

"May I?"

Keenan's hand closed on the handle, slid it off the table.

"Get the money."

Sagria smiled, shook his head. He stood slowly, smoothing his tie. He crossed to the door, reached up to a cooling vent, and pulled off the grill. A briefcase was wedged into the duct.

"Satisfied, Lieutenant?"

He returned to the table, leaving the briefcase.

"I want to see it."

Sagria waved a hand toward the bag, casually.

"Be my guest."

Keenan walked over to the duct, stepping into the tiny squares of light from the window.

Now, he thought. *As I reach up for the bag. A clean shot through the window.*

He slipped the briefcase from the duct and walked back to the table. Sagria frowned.

"You got a problem if I count this?"

The frown vanished. A smile, the hand extended, palm up.

"Please."

Sitting in his chair, not moving a muscle. He knows something's wrong. Now he's got to run with it.

Keenan laid the briefcase on the table, pressed the latches with his thumbs. It was locked. He sighed, shook his head.

"You gonna give me the key, or I gotta break it open?"

Sagria's eyes were on the window, the darkened warehouse beyond.

71

"You consider this a misfortune, Lieutenant. Dealing with me. Am I correct?"

"Like stepping in dogshit. It's part of the job."

"Ah, but you're wrong. Your job, Lieutenant, is to arrest me." He gestured toward the briefcase. "This, I think, is another matter."

He ran a hand over the top of his head, then smoothed the fringe of hair above his ears. His eyes remained on Keenan's face.

"May I show you something, Lieutenant?"

Sagria slipped his hand into his pocket, drew out a bullet, flattened on one side where it had whanged off something hard. He smiled at Keenan, leaned forward across the table, laid the bullet before him.

Keenan looked at it for a moment. He picked it up, held it up to eye level. A big bullet—nine-millimeter, he figured. The flattened edge meant bone, a head shot maybe. A guy lying on his side, so the bullet leaves the skull, hits the pavement and ricochets, ending up in a wall. Some cop digs it out, realizes he's found a treasure. Keenan turned it in the light, tracing the spiral pattern from the gun barrel. And then, suddenly, his mind flashed on a scene of carnage, a wall splattered with blood.

Keenan laid the bullet on the table. Two shots for each guy. That meant three bullets still missing. Three nines each with a thin spiral carved in the lead—a ballistics signature— as they had spun from the barrel of a Glock 7 registered to Lieutenant Tony Keenan, Narcotics Division, on a departmental UF 10, Force Record Card.

Keenan sighed. *Stupid mistake.* He kept two throwaways in his locker, and another—an old .45 automatic, the serial numbers filed—taped beneath the seat of his car. That night,

almost two years before, he'd parked near the docks, the kid who fingered the couriers grinning at him, watching him slip the .45 from under the seat and drop it into the pocket of his coat. They'd found the Colombians sleeping on a pair of cots in the back room of a bait shop. He got in their faces with the .45 and the badge, put them on the floor, face-down, spread. He put the gun behind one's ear, a fat guy, his breath whistling through his bad teeth.

¿Dónde está?

¿Qué dijo?

He'd pulled back on the slide, let it snap, chambering a round. The man stiffened, sweat breaking out on the back of his neck. The kid watched them from the door. He bounced the .38 against his thigh, smiling.

¿Cómo se llama?

Machito.

¿Dónde está, Machito?

The man took a moment, thinking about it. Keenan got his other hand in the guy's hair and pulled his head back so the gun pressed into the bone. Keenan glanced over at the other one, saw his body tense, listening.

La última posibilidad, Machito.

¡No sé!

He pulled the trigger. A dull click as the gun jammed. Machito screamed, kicked out at him. Keenan brought the gun down on his head, slammed his face into the floor. The other one was on his knees now, lunging for the door. The kid, surprised, brought the gun up just as the man barreled into him, driving a shoulder into his gut. They went down in a heap, the kid gasping for breath. Keenan dropped the .45, drew the Glock from the shoulder holster as the man scrambled to his feet. He shot him, once, at the door.

He got to his feet, thinking. Machito was moaning, both arms wrapped around his head. The one in the door was still breathing—a thick, bubbling sound. Chest wound. He'd be dead in a few minutes. The kid lay beside the table, coughing.

Keenan sighed. He got the fat one by the hair, pulled him up to sitting position, leaned him against one of the cots. His head lolled back. Keenan slapped him, twice. His eyes opened.

Keenan let go, stepped over to the partner, got a handful of his shirt and flipped him over. He put the gun under his chin, looked up at Machito, who was shaking his head, raising one hand. Keenan pulled the trigger. A moment later, as Machito screamed, slapping bits of bone and brain off his face, Keenan realized that he'd been pointing.

He turned, saw a large freezer in the front room. As he started for it, Machito pushed up off the cot, his eyes wild, lurching toward him. Keenan spun, shot him through the throat. Machito hit the floor and skidded, catching the edge of a display case with his shoulder. Glass showered over him. He flipped onto his back, his feet trying to get a grip on the floor. Keenan walked around the display case, leaned over, and put a round through the side of his head.

He found the cocaine, packed in plastic, in the bottom of the freezer, under a thick layer of ice. He retrieved the .45 and got the kid to his feet. The kid leaned against the door, coughing. Then he straightened, shook his head.

"Shit."

They dragged the bodies to the edge of the dock and tumbled them into the harbor.

Four days had passed before the bodies washed up. Kee-

nan forced himself to let a week more go by before he reached for the phone, dialed the ballistics lab.

"You got anything on a couple of floaters Area B pulled outta the harbor," he asked the lab clerk.

The clerk punched it up on his computer, the keys clicking softly. He shifted some papers around, punched the keys again, then put Keenan on hold. When he came back, his voice was apologetic. The bullets were missing. Just misplaced, probably. Try back in a few days.

Fine, he'd thought, smiling to himself. *Trust the lab to fuck it up.*

The bait shop had remained closed for a week. A fire, the sign said. When it reopened, there was new glass in the display case, a fresh coat of paint on the walls. A bit of plaster, he thought, over the hole where they'd dug the bullet out.

Now, in the harsh yellow light of the warehouse office, he watched Sagria carefully, waiting for the pitch. If they wanted something, why set up the hit? Was he just stalling, giving the *mestizo* a chance at a clean shot? Or did he really want to talk? *Slow down,* he thought. *Feel it out.*

Sagria spread his hands.

"Your mistake, of course, was you became greedy."

Keenan watched him. His head was sweating. And the accent was slipping, not so smooth as before.

"I wonder about this two years ago," he continued. "When does he become greedy? For two years, you arrest my couriers, take a little off the top before you make your report. A bit here, a bit there. This I can accept. Your salary, I understand, is not large. For two years, you take your little bites. I admire your restraint. 'A disciplined man,' I think. I try to find your source, but you I do not confront."

He smiles, shrugs.

"A businessman, he must pay the tax."

Then, leaning forward, his face stern.

"But when you take my people, you do not make the arrest, I read in the papers that they float in the harbor, I think maybe it's time we talk."

"You want the bag. I want the money and the bullets. What's to talk about?"

Sagria cocked his head, looked at him with curiosity. *Bullets?*

"Alas, it is not so simple. There is still the matter of my men, the ones who could not swim."

Keenan shrugged.

"No papers, no prints. They don't exist."

Sagria tapped his forehead with one long finger.

"At first, I think the same. But then, I think this is wrong. These men, maybe they are more real now than they were in life."

He picked up the bullet, holding it gently.

"Such men are tools, like this bullet. Barrio rats, we call them. They are nothing until I put them to use. But now, like this bullet, they become interesting. Your homicide detectives, they ask themselves, 'Who are these men? Where do they come from? Who kills them?' "

Keenan watched his fingers toy with the bullet, making it vanish and reappear, the light shining on the dull metal.

"What do you want?"

"Ah, you see? We have something to talk about after all."

His hand disappeared into his pocket again, emerging with a small key, which he laid on the table.

"Open the briefcase."

Keenan picked up the key, unlocked the briefcase and

popped the latches. The money—ten stacks of twenties— was wrapped in thin paper bands. He picked up a stack and ran his thumbnail over the edge of the bills. He stopped counting at a hundred.

"A good feeling, yes?"

Keenan dropped the money into the briefcase, closed it. *Take your time*, he thought. *Don't rush.*

"I'm listening," he said.

Sagria smiled, returned the bullet to his pocket.

"I have an associate, a man with whom I am doing business. He wants some information that I want to give him. A gift to my friend. I think of you. An easy task."

"What kind of information?"

He took a paper from his pocket, slid it across the table.

"A name, nothing more."

Keenan glanced at the paper. A single page of an FBI informant's report, the speaker identified only by his six-digit identification number. Large sections of the page were blacked out with a thick marker.

"An informant," Sagria said quietly. "A man who speaks when he should be silent. You have access to such information, do you not?"

Keenan tossed the paper on the table.

"You got this, why do you need me?"

Sagria gave a sad smile.

"Alas, that is all we have been given. An appetizer, offered by a man we do not trust."

Keenan thought about it, then pushed the briefcase across the table.

"Keep your money," he said.

"A point of honor, Lieutenant?"

"It's not my line."

"He is an informant, Lieutenant. A man of no honor. But like Machito and Garvas, my poor swimmers, he may have great worth as a corpse."

"To who?"

Sagria smiled.

"That is my business."

Keenan shook his head.

"You want me to make it my business. I like to know who I'm working for."

Sagria considered for a moment, nodded.

"Our friend of the angels."

Keenan hesitated, shook his head. He gestured to the bag.

"Check your merchandise. I'll take the bullets."

Sagria gazed at him, thoughtful. Again, *bullets*. He glanced at the bag.

"A poor bargain, don't you think?"

"As you said, I made a mistake."

"I did not mean for you. My poor Machito, he had a family."

"Spare me."

Sagria looked at him from under his heavy brows, frowning.

"That I cannot do."

Cocky son of a bitch, Keenan thought. *Ready to give the signal if I walk out.* He glanced down at the bullet in the middle of the table. *Still. You listen, you learn.*

He waved a hand at the canvas bag.

"Check it," he said.

Sagria shrugged, unzipped the bag. He took out a plastic packet, unwrapped one corner and touched his finger to the powder. As he raised the finger to his lips, Keenan took the .45 from his pocket, swung it up with both hands, and shot

him, twice, in the chest. The packet exploded in a white cloud. Sagria tumbled back off the chair. Keenan came around the table and shot him again, once in each eye.

He bent over the body, ran his hands through Sagria's pockets. He found the bullet, slipped it into his pocket. But when he searched for the remaining bullets, he came up empty. He felt the panic rise within him. *Where were the other bullets?* He squatted beside the body, thinking about it. Sagria had the bullet from the wall. If the others had vanished from the ballistics lab . . .

A memory tugged at him. He ran his hand across his face. The realization straightened him up. He took a step back, slapped his forehead.

"Ah, shit."

He picked up the briefcase, glanced around. The cocaine had settled in a white mist over the table and floor.

"Shots fired."

Eddie Shea pressed against the wall of the narrow hall, drew the hammer on his service revolver back with both thumbs. He edged toward the glass door, which was propped open a crack with a strip of cardboard. A pale light shone from the warehouse floor beyond.

He could hear his partner's breathing behind him. His palms were sweating. He paused, rubbed his right hand along the side of his pants, shifted the gun. He reached for the door, jerked it open.

He went through the door, moving fast. He split to the left, found cover behind a stack of crates. He got the gun up on top of the crates, hoping it wasn't paper towels inside, and did a quick scan of the warehouse floor. Empty. Then he

saw the office off to one side, the lights on. A figure moved past the window.

Breden came through the door, split right, and ducked behind another pile of crates. A stack of iron rods leaning against the wall behind him toppled with a crash. In the office, the figure froze, ducked out of sight.

"Police," Shea shouted. "Toss out your weapon!"

For a moment, nothing happened. Then a sudden movement, a crash of breaking glass, and the figure darted past the window, heading away from the door.

Shea edged around the side of the crates, then went left for the wall. He heard footsteps, off to his right, knowing it was Breden. He came up on the office from the back, away from the windows. He peered around the corner to the door, which was closed. Two steps up, back to the wall, a quick glance through the window. A body lay in a snowfall, arms outflung. The face was coated with blood. Otherwise, the office was empty. A window on the opposite wall had been shattered, the glass pushed out. A shuffle of footprints in the dust.

He stepped down, went around the office, keeping it between him and the open warehouse floor. Under the window, the footprints led off toward a door, with a stair beyond. Breden came up from behind a forklift and swung his gun up to cover the doorway, waving him forward. He followed the footprints, which trailed off before they reached the door.

Not enough for a trail, Shea thought. *But he's got it on his shoes.*

Breden came up behind him, and they eased into the stairway. Metal steps, two flights for a floor. If he was on the stairs, they'd hear his footsteps. Three floors above them, a

bare bulb hanging at each landing, a dark basement below. You could see between the steps all the way to the top. He could be waiting in the doorway to pick them off as they came. Or in the basement . . . He didn't even want to think about that.

"Where's our backup," he whispered.

Breden shrugged. He was sweating hard, the drops trailing down the side of his face.

Shea swallowed, waved Breden up the stairs.

He went down.

Keenan heard the cop ease into the basement, feeling his way in the dark, not wanting to use his flashlight. He ducked out of the aisle, then kept still for a moment. There was a lot of basement between him and the window, where a thin strip of moonlight fell across the back wall. He'd have to drag a packing case over to climb out. If the cop heard him, he'd get him hanging from the window frame, put a bullet in his leg in case he managed to pull free. That's what he'd do. Weird to be on the other side, listening to the cop move through the darkness, trying to figure a way out. His heart was pounding. Not the high he got on a bust, but scared. He wanted the whole thing over—Sagria dead, the .45 under thirty feet of water, the money tucked away in a safe-deposit box in a bank down in Providence, even a bit of information he would find a use for, soon.

It was close; until the cop stepped into the basement, quicker than he expected, he was sure he'd make it. Now he could hear sirens in the distance, could feel it slipping away from him. The cop moved into the long aisle, moving slow, keeping to the right. Without thinking, Keenan stepped

clear, brought the .45 down, and emptied the magazine down the length of the aisle.

The first three rounds caught the cop, spinning him around. His hand grabbed at a crate, and a whole stack crashed down on him. Silence.

Keenan stood for a moment, uncertain. Footsteps echoed on the metal steps.

Get out! Now!

He ran down the aisle to the window, dragged a crate over and clambered up. He tossed the briefcase through, hooked the window frame with his fingers, and heaved. He hung for a moment, his arms trembling with the strain, then got a knee into one corner, wedged a shoulder through, and he was out. He grabbed the briefcase and ran for the fence.

It was snowing. The air tasted like freedom.

8

Riccioli was in a foul mood. The newspapers were playing the cop's shooting at full volume—two photographs and a thick headline: "Cop Clings to Life!" A major cocaine distributor had been killed, execution style, and the crime scene —the tiny office, the table and two chairs—suggested a negotiation gone awry. A third body, an unidentified male Hispanic, had been found at the scene, armed with a rifle but killed with a knife.

Riccioli shook his head. It didn't make sense. A meeting, that much was clear. The killer was expected, even trusted.

He cuts the bodyguard's throat, then strolls down to his meeting, where he pulls a .45 and blows away a ranking Colombian, then pauses to gun down a cop on his way out the door. Any way you look at it, a serious breach of good business practices.

Riccioli tossed the newspaper aside. The locals would claim jurisdiction, because of the cop. But a deal gone this sour might leave bodies strewn across the countryside for months. Sagria's murder left a hole in the distribution network, and a lot of angry Colombians. His people would have to work their files hard in the next few weeks, trying to keep up. Nothing like a gang war to fuck up the files.

A folder on his desk held the night's surveillance reports. He flipped through them quickly, pulled out the D'Angelo transcripts. He skimmed them, making notes with his red marker in the margins. An hour in the parking garage below the courthouse, forty minutes parked on a side street in Medford, the last stop of the night. Starting to get impatient.

Riccioli smiled. He was feeling better now.

The last transcript was from the team in Athol. His eye ran down the page, paused. He started again, reading with a growing sense of alarm.

"Shit!" He hit the switch on the intercom. "Joan, get Haggerty in here. Now!"

He got up and paced. When he heard the outer office door close, he went to the window, stood looking out. The door opened behind him. He didn't turn.

"You wanted me."

"Sit."

He watched the traffic on Congress moving past Post Office Square toward Faneuil Hall. A week ago, he had left the office early on a Saturday afternoon to meet his wife there.

While the girls scrambled through the cobbled plaza, they sat on a bench, eating frozen yogurt, Caroline telling him, quietly, the reasons why she wanted a divorce.

He turned to face Haggerty. He had caught her early, still wearing her sneakers. Her suit was expensive, tailored to show off her figure. He remembered, too clearly, the days of living on an Assistant U.S. Attorney's salary, crammed into a tiny apartment, buying a few good things for the office while your jeans split at the knee. Not so long ago, even now. Looking at her, he felt a burst of envy, and with it, a sudden awareness of desire. She was a stunning woman, her face delicately carved, her figure taut from exercise. The kind of woman, he thought, who can shut down street comments with a cool look. A woman that men stare after in restaurants. A type that exists only in fantasy, until she passes you on the sidewalk, stealing your complacency, making you despair at your life.

He cleared his throat.

"You went out to Athol," he said. He picked up the transcript and dropped it in front of her.

She glanced down at the transcript, then back up at him. Registering the fact of the tapes, her eyes narrowing. He turned back to the window.

"I don't encourage contact with the subject of an ongoing investigation. In fact, I require that any such communications take place only with my authorization."

"I needed information."

"On what?"

"The file seemed incomplete."

He was quiet for a moment, considering.

"What did you learn?"

"I'm not sure. Walsh is a bitter man. He filed a grievance

after his partner's death, then withdrew it. Now he talks like a man who's learned a few things the hard way."

"Could be guilt."

She shook her head.

"That's what I thought at first. I went out there to see if I could shake his story. He's not a man who shakes easily."

"As I recall, we're talking about a guy who spent a few years as a drunk."

"That's just it. You look at this guy now, he's a man waiting to die. But he's looking it in the eye. It would take a lot to turn this guy into a drunk. He's like a man who lost his faith. Now he doesn't need it. He's got D'Angelo."

Riccioli smiled.

"The Church of Johnny."

"He's a quiet guy, Walsh. Not much interested in telling his side of the story. Makes you work it out for yourself. He knows more than he's saying."

"All right." Riccioli turned, perched on the window ledge, his legs stretched out in front of him. "Let's suppose, for a moment, that you're onto something with this. Walsh has a past. He's seen too much, lost his illusions."

He flicked a speck of lint off his pants, ran one finger along the edge of the crease.

"How does that help us with D'Angelo?"

Haggerty glanced down at the legal pad on her lap, the page still blank.

"He claims there's no connection."

"But you disagree."

"It's just an instinct."

"The trouble with instincts," Riccioli said, "is they make what's simple seem complex. This guy, he's got no friends left. Lots of enemies. He doesn't sleep too well at night. You

come along, trying to get his side of the story, he's gonna grab onto you like a drowning man. He'll pull you into the middle of this, and we lose our shot at D'Angelo."

"That's not what happened out there."

"I know what happened. I read the transcript. I'm telling you this as a warning. Stay clear of this guy. We didn't create the situation. It landed in our lap. I give you credit for that. Our job now is to make the best of it. D'Angelo's starting to get itchy. Let's not blow it now."

Haggerty nodded, silent. He watched her for a moment, looking down at the blank pad in her lap, thinking about it.

When he stood, she closed the pad. She got up, smoothing her skirt.

"Everything okay, otherwise?"

She looked up at him, surprised.

"Life treating you okay?"

"Sure. Fine."

Riccioli smiled, wanting to say more, but feeling awkward now. He stuffed his hands in the pockets of his coat.

"This place can eat you up. No one knows that better than me."

She smiled, looking away.

"It's a lot of work, but I don't mind. It's exciting."

"Just don't forget to have a life."

They stood in silence for a moment, embarrassed. Riccioli glanced down at some papers on his desk.

"Could you ask Joan to step in here on your way out?"

"Tony."

Keenan stood on the porch, smiling at her through the screen door. Sunglasses folded in his hand. T-shirt and jeans neatly pressed under the leather jacket.

"I was out here running errands. Figured I'd stop by, see how things are going."

She pushed the door open.

"The kids are at school. I was just straightening up. Danny'll be sorry he missed you."

She stood in the middle of the kitchen, looking at the dishes in the sink. She must look terrible, her eyes tired. Dressed for housework. She smiled.

"Can I offer you some coffee?"

"Thanks, Anne. That'd be nice."

Walsh had six boxes of wood screws on the counter next to the register, sorting them by size.

"A couple of weeks of farmers digging through 'em, they get all mixed up," Jerry had said, dropping the boxes on the counter. "We get complaints. Some guy tries to use a half-inch screw on quarter-inch plywood, he brings 'em both back. I don't give him his money, I lose a customer."

A guy was looking at pipe wrenches in aisle two. A woman by the window was examining prices on the snow shovels, frowning. Ted, the stockboy, had walked down the street to meet his girlfriend for lunch. Jerry was back in the office with the blinds down, doing the bills.

Walsh took a sip of coffee, watched the girl coming across the square, all bundled up in a parka. Watched her stop on the sidewalk, the traffic passing, then come on across, pausing under the awning to push the hood back. The bell on the door gave its dull jingle.

It was the haircut, Jack figured, that drew the eye. He watched her as she walked back into electrical, across to aisle four, and back up to where the wood screws should have been. The woman by the window looked up at her as

she went past, shaking her head, going back to her shovels. He'd seen women with shorter hair in Harvard Square, maybe Jamaica Plain, even bald in recent years. Holding hands, dressed in those T-shirts with Spanish slogans, a *campesino* waving a rifle in the air, a little pin in the shape of a triangle up by the shoulder. When he was in uniform, they'd give him hostile looks, waiting for him to make a comment. A lot of cops did. Or just a grin, nudging your partner, making little kissing sounds as they walked past. He'd just shrugged. No stranger than being a cop, walking the streets in a uniform all summer, fifteen pounds of gun belt dragging at your hip.

Harder, maybe. All the stares.

She was coming up the aisle toward the counter now, smiling at him. Her hair was like the crewcuts they used to give kids, but soft, so you want to run your hand over it. Pretty when you looked at it up close. Dark, with little streaks of silver, showing off her long neck. Her eyes looking at you, amused, telling you she didn't care what you thought.

"You got 'em," she said, shaking her head. She pointed at the wood screws. Unzipping the parka, shrugging out of it. And there it was, the Spanish, the *campesino*, stretched tight across her breasts. No pin.

He smiled.

"Customer service."

"I know you," she said. "You're up the road from me. I see you getting on the bus."

"You're in the red house. With a porch."

"That's it. How's your leg."

He shrugged.

"How'd you hurt it."

"I got stupid."

"Never hurt me." She smiled again, her eyes wrinkling slightly. "I lied. I know about your leg."

"Yeah?"

"Small town."

"Funny I haven't seen you around."

"I hang around the house, mostly. I'm a potter. Got a wheel set up in the living room. I get a lot of orders this time of year, for Christmas. I get going, I can be in there for days."

"But you hear the rumors."

She shrugged.

"People talk. You're a tragic figure, you know?"

"That's what they tell me."

She looked down at the box of screws, dipped her hand in the pocket of her jeans and came out with a three-quarter-inch. She grinned, shook her head.

"I'm not sure how to ask for this . . ."

"Let's skip it. It's too easy."

"I need about ten of these."

He counted them out, snapped a tiny paper bag open with a flick of his wrist, dropped them in.

"That's fifty-four cents, with tax."

"I love these little bags," she said. "Only place you get 'em."

"That's why we're here."

She stuffed the bag into the pocket of the parka before putting it on. She zipped it up, raised the hood.

"Stop by some time. I'll show you my wheel."

He shook his head, smiling to himself, as she crossed the street.

Takes all kinds.

* * *

"You hear from Jack?"

Anne shrugged.

"His lawyer talks to my lawyer."

She was wearing an old gray tank top, tied in a knot under her breasts. When she reached for her coffee, Keenan could see her nipples outlined against the cloth. Her hair was pulled back in a ponytail, no makeup, a pair of old sweatpants on her legs. She was beautiful.

"What about the kids?"

"Danny writes to him. I let Becky scribble on the paper with a crayon. He calls once in a while, talks to Danny about the Celtics."

"They still got him under wraps?"

"Pretty much. He won't give us his address. Says it's better we don't know."

"How do you send the letters?"

"There's a post office box out in Worcester. Someone forwards it."

He took a sip of his coffee.

"That's tough," he said.

"Danny took it hard. He's had some trouble in school."

"You want me to talk to him?"

"It's nice of you to offer. He looks up to you. His father used to talk about you."

"I'll stop by some time when he's home."

"Come for dinner."

He smiled.

"How can I refuse?"

And suddenly, she was crying. The tears ran down her cheek. She wiped at them with the back of her hand. Smiling at him, sadly. Shaking her head.

He reached out, took her hand. She squeezed it, hung on. He stood, came around the table to where she was sitting, taking both hands now, raising her out of her chair. He put his arms around her, pulling her to him. She buried her face in the hollow of his neck, sobbing now. His hand drifted across the bare skin of her lower back, gently.

"Tell me," he whispered.

9

"There's the bus," Harmon said. He dropped the newspaper next to his chair, went over to the window. He checked his watch. "Six-seventeen. Running late."

Cardoza came out of the kitchen, wiping his hands on a dish towel.

"All the traffic down at the Food King. This morning, a lady down there asked me to thump her cantaloupe. She's got this melon in her hands, smiling at me. She says, 'I can never tell with these things. I want a ripe one.' You believe that? Thump my melon, she says."

Harmon watched through the binoculars as two women and an old man got off the bus. Then Brodie, heading off down the road, carrying a lunch bucket. Walsh came last, taking his time on the steps, getting the cane out first. He hesitated for a moment, looking up the road.

"Looks like something caught his eye."

He scanned up the road a second. Nothing. He brought the binoculars back to the bus stop. Walsh was gone.

"Shit. Where'd he go?"

He swept the glasses along the strip of road down to his driveway, all the way to the house. Then back along the road in the other direction. He caught a glimpse of movement among the trees on the far side of the road.

"Got him. He's heading up the drive to the red house."

Cardoza picked up the pen, made a note in the log.

"Ever been there before?"

"Not since we've been here."

He was standing on the porch, looking away from the door, like he was having second thoughts, getting ready to leave. The door swung open.

"Well, whad'ya know."

"What?"

"Lady friend."

The door closed behind him. Harmon ran the glasses over to the side of the house, where the old pickup was parked.

"I got a blue Ford half-ton. License 413 DYZ."

"House number?"

Back to the door.

"Two twenty-one."

"Phone wires?"

"Southeast corner, to a pole on the next lot."

"I'll call Fowler. Get a truck out tonight."

* * *

She kept the place hot. A wood-burning stove in the kitchen, glowing red. Electric space heaters plugged in everywhere. She comes in a room, the first thing she does is turn up the heat. There's an inch of snow on the ground, wind bending the trees back, and she answers the door in her underwear. Smiling at him.

"I'm glad you came."

Little panties and the *campesino* shirt. Clay on her arms, the insides of her thighs. Grabbing his arm, pulling him in.

"Don't let the cold in."

Photographs on all the walls, black-and-white prints taped to the paneling. Old women on a hotel porch in Miami. Farm workers in a field, squinting against the sun. A stripper on a stage, a snake draped across her shoulders.

"So tell me," she called from the kitchen. "You were really a cop?"

"Seven years."

"You like it?"

"For a while."

He crossed the room, paused in front of a row of pots on a shelf. Navajo designs, mostly. A few in bright pastels, modern patterns.

"Are these yours?"

"You see it, I made it."

"Nice work."

"I'm having tea. You want some?"

"Sure, thanks."

"You want mint, chamomile, or Sleepy Time?"

"Anything."

Beyond the shelf were more photographs. Three kids sitting on a sofa in a vacant lot, a burned-out building at the

rear. A couple of guys in drag, blowing kisses. An Elvis impersonator, his gut sticking out of a silk jumpsuit, signing autographs for two women with hair piled high on their heads, their faces serious.

"I like your pictures."

"My true love. I'm not that good, really. It's the people you look at, not the shot."

She came out of the kitchen, carrying two cups. She handed him one, sat down at her wheel. A mound of clay was piled on the plate, shapeless.

"Maybe I'll take you. Behind the counter at the hardware store, you know? Get that look you have."

"What look?"

"Cop look. Watchful."

He sipped the tea. Mint.

"You always walk around in your underwear?"

"I got tired of washing the clay off my clothes. Does it bother you?"

He looked at her long, slim legs, the lean angle of her hip, her small breasts under the T-shirt. She smiled at him, set her cup down on the floor, pulled the low bench up close to the wheel. She turned it on, the mound of clay spinning.

"Your customers mind?"

"They're mostly women. Housewives. They look at the pots. Once in a while, one of them gets interested."

"Yeah?"

She shrugged.

"It's a small town."

"You always live here?"

"I moved out from Cambridge last year."

He smiled, sipped his tea.

"I grew up in upstate New York. Got tired of the noise in

the city. Somebody heard about this place. It was cheap. How 'bout you?"

She pressed her hands in the clay, shaping it. Digging her thumbs in to make a ridge.

"I grew up here."

"No kidding. And you came back anyway?"

"Not much choice."

"Alaska. California, a lot of people go there."

"I got kids. I hope to see 'em again, one day."

She was silent, a line of clay spilling over the top of her hand. She broke it off with the tip of her thumb, and it dropped to the floor.

"What do you do when they get interested," he asked.

She looked up at him.

"Depends," she said.

He got his hands under her knees, eased in slow. Her heat surrounded him. She turned her face away, her breath quickening as he found the rhythm.

"Wait," she whispered, and her hand came across her forehead, trembling.

He went in harder, making it happen. Bent down to get her nipple between his teeth, tugging at it gently.

"No! Tony, wait."

She put her hand against his chest, pushing him back. He stopped, looked down at her.

"I'm sorry. I just . . ."

The hand moved across her mouth, and she shook her head. He eased his weight off her, settled beside her on the bed.

"It's okay," he said. "I understand."

She looked away. His hand settled over hers on the bed.

"You want me to go?"

For a moment, she lay still. Then she nodded. He found his pants on the floor, the shirt a few feet away. She watched him dress, not saying anything. He came around the bed, sat on the edge to tie his shoes. When he finished, he leaned over, kissed her on the forehead.

"I'll call you."

She shook her head.

"In a few days, maybe?"

"I'm sorry, Tony."

He left her there, the sheet pulled up under her chin. At the bottom of the stairs, next to the phone, he found her address book. It was under Jack, nothing else. A P.O. box in Worcester. He dropped the book, went out through the kitchen, closing the door softly.

"Coming out."

Harmon lowered the glasses, checked his watch.

"Twenty-two minutes."

Cardoza came over to the window. Brodie was coming up the drive, rubbing his hands against the cold.

"Quickie?"

Harmon shrugged, making a note in the log.

The sun was setting over the trees. Cardoza squinted, shielded his eyes with one hand.

"What's he got in his hands?"

Harmon raised the glasses, tracking him down the drive to the road.

"Looks like a pot."

10

Frankie Defeo paused on the steps, yawned, rolling his shoulders like a boxer stepping into the ring. Behind him, the lawyer stopped short, halfway through the glass doors, waiting.

"Look't him," Johnny said, laughing. "Been on vacation."

Russo looked up at him in the rearview, leaning out the window of the Cadillac to wave the kid over.

"He a right kid, Johnny."

"He's a clown." Johnny tossed the butt of his cigar out the window. "I had a circus, this guy'd fit right in."

He was coming over now, the lawyer right behind him, looking nervous. Johnny pushed the door open, slid over on the seat.

"Get rid of the lawyer."

Russo got out of the car, walked around the front, caught the lawyer's arm just as Frankie was getting in the car. He stuffed a twenty in his breast pocket.

"Get a cab," he said.

He walked back around the car, got in.

"We set?" he asked the rearview.

"Let's go."

The lawyer looked relieved as they pulled away from the curb.

"I hate them fuckin' guys," Frankie said. "This one, he tells me he's gonna talk to the judge, get me declared indigent. I say, what the fuck? *Indigent*. I got a job. He says, 'What's your job?' I say, you're lookin' at it. This, right here. This is my job. He's lookin' around. I say, you go to court, *I* go to court. He's like . . . *Wha?* I say, Where you live? Newton. All right, I say, I'll come to your house in a year, I'll buy it. Give you cash, in your hand. Who's fuckin' indigent?"

"Shut up, Frankie."

"It's just, what am I, a bum here?" Frankie leaned forward, tapped Russo on the shoulder. "Hey, Tommy. Could we swing by the T&D, let me get my car?"

Frankie stared at him.

"You hear me? Did I say something?"

Russo got on the Southeast Expressway, the traffic slowing to a stop at the top of the ramp. Brake lights flared. When they crawled into the South Station tunnel, Johnny

100

cracked the window, lit a cigar. He sat in silence for a moment, his face flushed. Then he sighed, shook his head.

"First rule, Frankie," he said. "You talk, they hear you. A car's easy. They got transmitters the size of your fingernail. You gotta pick your spots. The tunnel's good. Underground parking garage. There's days I gotta talk to someone, it's raining, I spend the whole day goin' back and forth, through the tunnels, out to the airport, whatever."

"Hey, that's smart, Johnny."

"It's basic. Survival. You think this is smart, they'll have your ass in Lewisburg before you can say 'I married money.' Smart is figuring out what you *want* them to hear, gettin' something on the tapes so you can use it in court. That's strategy. Now, you tell me, what'd they ask you in there?"

"I don't know. It was a load of shit, you know?"

"Did I ask for your opinion? You were there, you tell me."

"Where was I, who was I with, what'd we do. Bullshit questions. I told 'em, 'Heh, I'm gettin' married soon, you know? Where'd you be?' They just look at me."

"Who was it?"

"Assistant D.A. Little guy, Schumann. Guy taking notes, didn't get his name. And some guy sat in the corner, didn't say nothing. Just watching. Gotta tan, nice suit."

"*E italiano?*"

"*Non lo so. Forse.*"

"Riccioli, the U.S. Attorney. Him, you don't fuck around with, you got it?"

Frankie shrugged.

"They ask you anything else?"

"When's the wedding."

* * *

101

"You know these movie stars, can't take a crap without someone's watching them? That's us. Only we got a bunch 'a guys, their whole job is to screw us. The D.A., the federals, the fuckin' IRS. Like dogs, sniffin' around us, just waiting their chance."

Johnny waved the waiter over, an old Chinese guy in a white jacket. He took the chopsticks off the napkin, held them up.

"You wanna bring me a fork? I can't eat with these fuckin' sticks."

"Me too," Russo said. "You all right, Frankie?"

"I'm okay."

"You got the fried noodles with the hot sauce?" Johnny asked the waiter. "Last time I was here you put 'em on the table."

"Dinner only," the waiter said. "Not lunch."

Johnny looked around the empty restaurant.

"You too busy, or what? Bring us the noodles. You come back, we're gonna order."

The waiter went back to the kitchen.

"I gotta look at the menu," Frankie said. "What's good here?"

Johnny leaned across the table, grabbed the menu out of his hands, slapped it on the table.

"Nothing's good here. It's a crappy place."

He put his finger against Frankie's forehead, poked at him, twice.

"You hear okay, Frankie? I been talkin' here. You eat the same place every day, you get what Jackie got. Or some guy from the U.S. Attorney's office gets smart, puts a wire under the table. You're just gonna eat, fine. Go where you want, let 'em listen to you chewing. But you wanna talk business, you

don't go there. You pick a place you ain't been in a while, the food's lousy, no reason in the world you should go there. What're they gonna do? Someone comes in here now, sits down, we just shut up, eat our food."

The waiter came out of the kitchen with a basket of fried noodles, a bowl of sweet and sour. Johnny handed him the menus.

"You got specials today?"

"Specials, yes. We got—"

Johnny raised his hand, stopped him.

"Whatever. I don't care, all right? Just bring us the specials. Put 'em in the middle of the table, we'll take what we want. Okay?"

The waiter ducked his head, disappeared.

"All right," Johnny said, turning to Frankie. "So you walked on the Mullen thing. They got nothing but Jackie griping 'bout you on the tapes, and the judge cut you bail. Means they got no case. What're they gonna do? Look for a witness, maybe. Hope the gun turns up. They'll try to push it to trial, 'cause that's what they get paid for. We go in there, say you were at the house, planning the wedding, right? The whole thing's gonna stink, the jury'll be holding their noses."

"So I'm clean."

"They're just goin' through the motions. Anybody else, they would'a dropped the case. But we're having this wedding here, you're joining the family, they figure they'll get an early start on you."

"No hurry," Frankie said. "I'll be here. I'm not going anywheres."

Johnny picked up his fork, drawing lines on the table-

cloth. Russo watched him, a long, curving trail of lines like a rake would leave in the lawn. Watching his face now.

"You did okay," Johnny said, not looking up.

"Glad to help, Johnny."

He looked up, frowning.

"Help what? Did I need help?"

Frankie hesitated, caught off guard.

"What I meant was . . ."

"I didn't have no problem with Jackie Mullen. That was your mess. You clean it up before you come into the family."

Frankie was silent. This wasn't going as he figured, sitting in his cell, keeping his mouth shut. Doing it for the family. A ritual, just the same as the wedding. And when he walked, Johnny was there in the Cadillac, waving him over. Taking him out to celebrate, right? So he brings him to this dink place, no one in it, starts givin' him a lecture about keeping his mouth shut. Like he doesn't *know*? What's he been doing in there for two days, jerkin' off? He's gotta sit there, nodding. *Good idea, Johnny. I'll keep that in mind.* Telling him now the whole thing was his screwup, like he had debts or something. Some kinda bum, getting Johnny to pay to keep the shame off his daughter.

Johnny pointed the fork at him, said:

"You gotta stop thinkin' like a punk. This thing we got, it's a serious business. We got subsidiaries, partners in every city in the country. Most of what we earn is clean, from investments. People come to me, they need help, I say, 'Fine.' I help 'em out. I take an interest in their affairs. They see the value in this, so they give me an interest in their business."

He picked up his water glass, swirled it so the ice clinked softly.

"I sit in my office, people bring me my envelopes. Maybe that impresses you. But you think I get to keep it? We got stockholders, just like a company. Every guy that works for me, he's a stockholder in this thing. I gotta give him his share. You wanna know, I spend most of my time figurin' out the percentages."

He looked over at Russo, grinned.

"Used to be, ten years back when Jerry A. was running things, we had to send half down to Providence."

"Good old days," Russo said, smiling.

"What was good? I spent half my time sitting in a café on Hanover Street, trying to do business on a fuckin' pay phone."

"Coffee was good."

"I drank so much coffee, I could'a floated home. You get nervous, start looking for cops on your way to the bathroom."

He shook his head.

"Day I moved my operation down to Southie, that was the day I started to get things under control. People from the neighborhood, they can't just stop by, ask you to solve their personal problems. They got business, they gotta get in their car, drive down there. By the time they get to my office, I know they're serious."

"I always wondered why you moved down there," Frankie said. "These ain't our people down there. Fuckin' Irish."

Johnny turned, looked at him.

"See, that's the point. You think like a punk from the neighborhood. I'm a businessman, that's where I run my business." He took a cigar from his coat, lit it. "Anyway, I made a point movin' down there. The Irish, they had to

come to terms with me, show some respect. So I moved in, made sure they had to look at me every day. They didn't like it. Week after I bought the building, some kid tried to burn it down."

Frankie grinned.

"Yeah? What happened to the kid?"

Johnny puffed his cigar, shook the match out, tossed it on the table.

"You go to church, you can light a candle." The tip of his cigar glowed. "Now, I own half the buildings on the street. The Irish want something, they come to me. We do business."

"Like Fat Jackie."

Johnny considered him for a moment.

"Yeah, Jackie and me, we did business."

"I don't know," Frankie said. "You see 'em down there on St. Patrick's Day? Drinkin' that green beer? End of the day, half of 'em can't stand up. You're gonna do business with these guys?"

"You think I got a choice?"

Frankie shrugged. Johnny looked at Russo, shook his head.

"Tell him."

Russo took out his wallet, slipped out a dollar, held it up.

"What's that?"

Frankie looked at him, grinned.

"What'ya mean? It's a dollar."

"No, you're wrong." Russo laid the dollar on the table, took a red pen from his inner pocket. "It's a suit."

"A suit."

"That's what I said. A suit." He uncapped the pen. "You

go to the tailor, you buy a suit, you ever think where it comes from?''

"Kinda suits I buy?" Frankie laughed. "Hong Kong, probably. You guys get yours custom, right?''

"Any suit, same thing. Whether the guy makes it there, or he gets it shipped in from Mongolia, he's gotta pay for it the same.''

Russo drew a line across the dollar near one end.

"The guy who sells the suit, that's his cut. He's gotta pay for the materials, that's about the same.''

He drew another line, a short distance from the first.

"Shipping, tax, rent, all that stuff, same thing." He drew a third line, looked up. "Now it gets complicated.''

"Yeah? We get a piece of that?''

"Sure, we get a piece of everything. Direct, if we got a deal on the guy, or else we get it from the shipping company, the unions, lotsa places. But it's not just us." He drew a line of boxes across the top half of the bill. "The suit's stitched in New York, then the Gambinos get a share. It gets shipped outta a warehouse in Hartford, Ray takes his piece. Garment workers are all Chinese now, so we slip a little to the chinks. The tailor's a Jew, I don't know, maybe he pays something to the rabbi. You get the picture?''

"Not much left.''

"Hey, we're just getting started here. Now you got the guys work for us, they get their share. Those garment workers, they're up on the third floor, you pay one guy. Four floors up, it's a different guy. South end of the building, they both get a share. It's all negotiated, so nobody gets pissed off, wants to tear up the suit.''

"Tommy's amazing," Johnny said. "Keeps all that shit in

his head. I just spread it around the way he says, everybody's happy."

Frankie laughed.

"Except the guy who buys the suit, right?"

"He don't know, won't hurt him." Johnny reached over, took the dollar from Russo. He folded it, tucked it in Frankie's pocket. "This shit's important. The whole business, it's right there on that dollar."

Frankie patted his pocket.

"Yeah? Then I'm a rich man."

Johnny looked over at Russo. He puffed his cigar, shook his head.

"You're easy," he said to Frankie. "Like reading the fuckin' newspaper." He leaned forward, jabbed Frankie's forehead with one finger. "It's all right here. Anyone who wants to can read it."

Johnny leaned back. He stuck the cigar in the corner of his mouth.

"Tell me something. Whatcha want?"

"Me?"

"You go to sleep, what'ya dream about?"

Frankie grinned. "Besides women?"

"I look like I'm jokin' here?"

"I wanna be rich."

"That's it?"

"Hey, I'll take it."

Johnny glanced over at Russo.

"He wants to be rich."

"I heard."

Johnny shook his head.

"You gotta think about it, work it out in your head. What you want, the thing you gotta have, that's your weakness.

Your problem is you got no idea what you should want, so you say, 'I wanna be rich.' Any idiot can say that." He puffed his cigar. "You ever go fishing?"

"Yeah. I been fishing."

"How do you catch a fish?"

Frankie grinned at Russo, shrugged.

"I dunno. Stick a worm on a hook."

"You find something it wants, stick it right in its face. They used to hunt wolves, they'd tie a goat to a stake. The goat cries all night; it's scared. The wolf hears it, knows it's weak, so it comes along, gonna take a bite. But it gets there, starts eating the goat, some guy jumps outta the bushes, jabs it with a spear. The wolf, he's strong, but *desire* makes him weak. You get what I'm saying?"

Frankie shrugged.

"Still wanna be rich."

Johnny looked at him, thoughtful.

"Desire," he said, touching Frankie's forearm lightly with the tip of the fork. "That's what'll kill ya."

And then, the waiter comes over, piling dishes in the middle of the table. Johnny smiling, tucking the napkin in his collar. Frankie looked down at his arm.

Four little dents in the skin.

Keenan watched them come out of the restaurant, Defeo pausing on the sidewalk to chew a toothpick, looking up at the sky. When he glanced down, Johnny was climbing into the Cadillac, vanishing behind the tinted windows, pulling the door closed. The car glided out of the parking lot. Defeo sighed, crossed the street, stopped beside a new Saab, dug in his pocket for the keys. He got in, taking a moment to

check himself out in the rearview, run a hand through his hair. Then he reached for the keys.

He looked up, surprised, as Keenan rapped on the window, flashed his badge. Keenan smiled, seeing his eyes go blank, his expression shift from momentary panic to the dull gaze of a street punk, going dumb at the sight of a badge. Then the kid's eyes slid up to Keenan's face, flickered briefly with relief, then disdain. Defeo shook his head, started the car.

Keenan drew his gun, laid the butt against the glass.

"Knock, knock," he said. "Don't make me break your pretty windows."

Defeo hesitated, glared at him. Slowly, he reached across to the passenger side, popped the lock. Keenan strolled around the front of the car, one hand trailing along the bright hood. He climbed in, ran his hand across the upholstery, shook his head.

"You've been a good boy? Got yourself a toy?"

Defeo scowled, keeping his eyes straight ahead.

"You're gonna fuck me up, man. People see me sitting here with you, they're gonna lose all respect for me."

"Yeah?" Keenan glanced around at the neighborhood, grinned. "Same old story. Guy makes it big, he don't remember his old friends. We go back a long way, Frankie."

He reached into his coat, drew out a pack of cigarettes, shook one loose. Frankie reached across, snatched the pack away.

"I don't like people smoking in the car."

Keenan looked at him, surprised. Defeo hit a button, and the window descended. He tossed the cigarettes onto the street. Keenan flushed. His hands became very still. He glanced around the car.

"This thing set you back . . . what? Like twenty thousand?"

Defeo looked out the window, watching a truck roll over the crumpled cigarette pack.

"Something like that."

Keenan nodded, his hand moving across the dash, pausing on the gleaming Blaupunkt stereo.

"You get the off-the-lot discount on it, or you go straight?"

Defeo glared at him.

"Hey, this is for my bride. You think I'm gonna give her a stolen car?"

Keenan shrugged.

"You're a punk, Frankie." His hand caressed the buttons on the stereo. "You know how you can tell a punk? Expensive shoes and a stolen jacket. Hangs a little long in the sleeves, you know? Shoes you gotta buy, 'cause if they don't fit, you get blisters."

He twisted a knob, and it popped off in his hands.

"Oops." He tossed it into Defeo's lap. "You're gonna have to get that fixed."

Defeo looked down at it. He picked it up, fitted it back onto the pin in the front of the radio.

"Get out."

"Ah, Frankie. Now you're pissed. And we were havin' such a nice talk."

Defeo leaned across him, opened the door.

"I said get out."

Keenan sighed.

"You wanna do this the hard way? Maybe you're dirty, got a little coke in the glove box? I could impound the car,

pull you in on suspicion of being a punk with a short memory."

Defeo was silent, his eyes fixed on the steering wheel. Keenan popped the glove box open, glanced at the title, peered under the warranty book.

"You ever watch the guys at the police garage take a car apart? They have a great time. Tear up the carpet, cut the upholstery open, yank the engine out. They get finished, there's always a couple parts lying there on the floor of the garage. You ask 'em about it, they're like, 'Hey, we got most of 'em back in there.' "

Defeo put the car in gear, glanced in the rearview, eased out into traffic. Silent, he headed up a ramp onto the highway, got in line for the toll at the tunnel.

"You wanna talk to me," he said. "You got till we get outta the tunnel. That's where you get out."

"What's the hurry?" Keenan yanked the handle next to his seat, laid it back. "We'll talk about old times."

Defeo looked at him. His eyes narrowed.

"You lookin' for money?" He yanked his wallet out of his back pocket, tossed it into Keenan's lap. "Here, this is it. That's what I got."

Keenan picked up the wallet, grinned. He slipped a thin wad of bills out, fanned them—a pair of twenties, a few singles.

"What, you're gonna buy me off with forty-four bucks?"

He glanced through the wallet, found a folded bill stuffed in the credit card pocket. He unfolded it, smoothed it against his wrist. One side was marked with red lines, squares. He glanced at the back. Nothing. He added it to the pile. Defeo was watching his rearview, easing into the next lane.

"I got a bank card now. I want cash, I go to the machine."

"Like a normal guy."

Ahead of them, a car pulled up to the toll. Defeo glanced over at the money in Keenan's hand.

"You wanna give me a couple of those, we can pay the toll?"

Keenan raised his eyebrows.

"Yeah? They make you pay now? I thought you had a friend used to wave you right through."

"Yeah, well, I had a lot of friends. I gotta be more careful now."

"Important guy."

"Just gimme the fuckin' money."

Keenan peeled off a pair of ones, passed them over. Defeo lowered his window, started to hand them to the attendant, then snatched them back. He shook his head, separated the top bill, shoved it back at Keenan.

"Christ, not this one! Gimme another."

Keenan looked down at it—marked in red. He smiled. He peeled off another bill, passed it to Defeo.

"Sentimental value?"

Defeo snatched the money from his hand, stuffed it back in the wallet.

"None of your fuckin' business."

A horn sounded behind them. Defeo flicked the finger at the driver out his window, put the car in gear, and headed into the tunnel. He looked shook, like he knew he'd slipped up. Keenan caught a glimpse of the marked bill as he tucked it into his pocket. Defeo fixed his eyes on the road.

"You wanted to talk to me?"

Keenan drew a bullet from his pocket, held it up.

"How's your memory, Frankie?"

11

Frankie found a spot near the entrance to the parking garage. He let the engine idle for a minute, enjoying the way it growled. Black Camaro, the windows tinted dark. He'd picked it up in the South End during the morning rush. Just like when he was a kid. Waited outside a package store, like he's talking on the pay phone, while a guy runs in for cigarettes on his way to work. Leaves the keys in the ignition. The guy standing at the counter, watching as Frankie walks over, jumps in. Mouth hanging open, he can't believe it.

He turned the engine off, but left the key in it, flipped

through the radio dial, looking for a station that would come in underground. Static, all the way down the dial.

"Yo, Johnny. Okay to talk here." He grinned, shook his head.

There was a box of tapes on the floor of the backseat, and he dug through it, found some old J. Geils, put it on low. He sat back to watch the dashboard clock tick up toward five, keeping an eye on the people trickling out through the glass doors, sneaking out early.

At about ten past, he saw her through the doors, stopping to talk to the security guard in the green jacket. Old black guy, reading his newspaper the whole time. Never even spotted him sitting there, what? Half an hour, at least.

The girl came out, carrying a backpack. She had it open, taking her helmet out. Blond hair, little round glasses. Stopping next to the only bike in the place to roll up her jeans. Frankie flicked his cigarette out the window, started the engine.

She rode up the ramp, waving to the guy in the booth. Frankie tossed the guy a five with the ticket, watching her turn left, heading for the river. He lost her for a few minutes in traffic, picked her up again on the bridge, coming up behind her, watching her ass as she pedaled, then going on past, getting a good look at her face. He got caught at the light in Cambridge, third car back, watched her come up on him in the rearview. She stopped at the front of the line, one foot down for balance, watching for an opening in the traffic.

When the light changed, he started up slow, ignoring the horns behind him, letting her stay ahead, get a little speed up. She turned east out of Kendall Square, heading up Archbishop Medeiros past the warehouses. He checked the mir-

116

ror, saw a Federal Express van turning into the street, moving slow.

"Shit."

He hit the clutch for a second, popped it, making the car jump, losing speed. Put the emergency flashers on and edged over onto the shoulder, letting the van go past. He watched it get on up the block, past the girl, make a right into an alley. A glance in the rearview. The road was clear, both ways.

He dropped down a gear, hearing the engine wind up, saw the girl look back as he came up on her. Made a big show of swinging wide around her, then, as he pulled even, cut the wheel hard, getting her with the edge of the bumper. She was thrown over to the right, bounced off a parked car, and came back across the hood of the car, her face going hard off the windshield. He punched the brakes, and she slid off.

He gave the rearview a quick look. Nothing. He jumped out, trotted around to the front of the car.

She lay in a heap, one arm twisted under her. He saw her glasses, shattered, a few feet away. He picked them up, stuffed them in the pocket of his jacket. Straightening, he saw a woman watching from the door of a warehouse, her eyes wide. He pointed at the girl.

"Call an ambulance, for Christ's sake!"

The woman vanished into the warehouse. He walked back to the car, backed it up, and swung wide around the girl. Taking it easy up the street, around the corner, down two blocks to the Galleria beside the river. He turned into the underground lot, took a ticket, and went down two levels. He left the keys in the car and rode the elevator up, stripping off his leather jacket. Walked into Banana Republic

and laid down a hundred-eighty dollars in cash for a tan bomber jacket, all kinda stupid patches on the sleeves, looked like a fuckin' boy scout. He stuffed the other jacket in the bag and walked down the escalator, out through the flickering TVs in Lechmere to the street, where he got a cab.

"Southie," he told the driver.

And two minutes later, they were on the expressway, heading over the bridge.

Easy.

12

"Tony. Phone."

Keenan waved from across the squad room, picked up a phone on the nearest desk, punched the flashing button.

"Narcotics. Keenan."

"Tony, this is Anne Walsh."

"Anne."

He settled into the beat-up swivel chair and propped his feet on a radiator, where a pair of gloves steamed.

"I'm sorry to bother you at work."

"Please. I've been trying to get up the courage to call you for four days."

"Something's happened, Tony. I wasn't sure who else to call."

He sat forward, pulled the phone across the desk.

"Are you okay?"

"I'm fine. The kids are fine. It's nothing like that, exactly. At least, I don't think so." She hesitated. He could hear the children in the background.

"Do you think you could come by, Tony?"

He checked his watch.

"I'm off in an hour."

"It might be nothing."

"Don't apologize. I'm glad you thought of me."

He sat for a moment, staring out the window, the dial tone buzzing in his ear. The P.O. box was a dead end. A remailing service in Worcester, whose clients ran to young couples with bad debts, telephone sales outfits, a few men with exotic tastes in entertainment which they kept hidden from their wives. The owner, unimpressed by his badge, had chewed his cigar, silent, while Keenan hinted at grand jury interest, eyeing the pair of file cabinets that stood against the wall. The man flicked the ash from his cigar into a filthy coffee cup, blew smoke at the ceiling, where a fan turned lazily.

"You're outta your jurisdiction here," he said. He leaned forward, thrust the cigar at Keenan. "Without confidentiality, I got nothing here. My customers, they want to be left alone. That's what they pay me for. You want to look at my files, go get a court order."

Driving back to Boston on the Pike, Keenan figured he might take the guy's advice. Wrap a quarter key and drop it

in the mail, put in a call to the local police. They bust the place open, box up all the files on suspicion. He drops by the next day, asks to sort through the files, looking for evidence on a distribution ring. Let the fucker chew on that for six months, waiting for it to get to trial.

Only problem was it put him a little too close to the action. Better to stay clear of it—get Robbie Lucas to make the call, send him down there with a list of box numbers, tell him to get the files on all of 'em. Walsh turns up, you make it a joke, say, "This a coincidence, or what?" Put the file aside, spend a little time digging in the others, then drop the whole thing. Just another weak tip.

He pushed up out of the chair. Forty minutes left in his shift. Not much reason to hang around. He'd swing by Anne's, put it down as talking to an informant.

He smiled.

In a way, it was true.

"I felt stupid after I called you. I mean, it's probably nothing. I tried to catch you, but they said you already left."

"It's no trouble."

He'd tried to kiss her at the door, feeling her draw back slightly. She led him into the kitchen, pointed to the table.

"This came in the mail today."

It was a small box, like the kind a dentist would use to ship plates to the lab. Or bullets, when you get them mail order. She'd opened it, left the tape folded back so Keenan could see the edge of an envelope. He bent over it to look at the wrapping, not touching it. Her name and address had been printed with a red marker.

"No return address," he noted.

"I figured it was something I ordered from a catalog. For the kids."

"Then you'd get a return. A company logo, maybe. They figure it's advertising, you know?" He looked up at her. "This pretty much how you found it?"

She nodded. He took a paper towel from over the sink, slid the envelope out of the box. It was a plain white envelope. Bulky, creased along a hard edge when it was stuffed into the box. Scrawled on the envelope in the same red ink were the words "Jack Walsh, Free Man." The envelope had been torn open at one end. He tipped the contents into his hand. Bits of glass. A pair of wire frames, the lenses gone. Little round glasses, like the hippies used to wear.

He looked up at her.

"You got any idea what this means?"

She shook her head.

"Know anybody who wears these?"

"Nobody I can remember."

He looked at the envelope.

"Probably a joke," he said. "Somebody Jack knows. Maybe one of the guys in the department. Cops have a weird sense of humor. I get some kinda stupid thing in my box in the squad room about once a month."

"Don't lie to me, Tony," she said. "One of his friends would've called me for his address. Maybe asked me to send it on. Whoever sent this, they wanted me to open it. I'm supposed to get scared, tell Jack so he comes running back here to protect us."

He looked down at the glasses in his hand.

"Pretty obscure for a threat."

"They figure Jack'll get it."

He sighed, slid the glasses back into the envelope, stuffed it back in the box.

"You want, I can ask the guys at the lab to run prints. But there's not much we can do about it, even if we get a positive. Whoever sent this was pretty careful. You gotta have an explicit threat to get someone for this, and then it's a federal case. I'd have to pass it on to the FBI guys."

She stood leaning against the counter, rubbing her cheek with the back of one hand. He realized it was a gesture he'd seen her make at parties, when her mind drifted, nodding at some bit of gossip.

"Maybe I could have a talk with Jack." He shrugged. "See what he makes of it."

She considered him for a moment, then looked out the window. The kids were playing in the side yard.

"He's got a brother out in Athol," she said. "That's where Jack grew up. His family had a hardware store out there. The last time I saw him, when he was still in prison, he talked about going back there."

Keenan nodded.

Sometimes you get lucky.

"The first week this guy worked narco, we're talkin' six years ago maybe, they raided a house over in Dorchester used by some wholesalers. Bars on all the windows, iron door with a little peephole, and this little boy—had to be, what? Six, seven? Hangin' out on the street with a cellular phone dangling from his belt. Walsh, he's the buy, got hair down to his shoulders, one of those mustaches so thick you can't see his mouth. Goes up to this kid, like, *Say, young fella, shouldn't you be in school?* And he grabs the phone off the kid's belt, so he can't warn the guys in the house. This kid—

looked like he coulda been on Sesame Street, right? Sticks his hand down in his sock, comes out with a .38. I'm not kidding! A Saturday Night Special, had it strapped to his ankle with duct tape. Walsh is like, *Ah, shit.* I mean, the expression on his face, he's disappointed in this kid. You can see it, he's diving behind this Chevy, the kid's blasting away with this little gun, and he's got this look on his face, like, *What's the world coming to?* The cops are all jumpin' outta their cars, this kid, he's following Walsh around the Chevy, shooting at him. *Ping! Pang!* Bullets bouncing off the sidewalk, off the cars. Keeps missing him. The gun's too big for him, he can't keep it pointed straight. Walsh dives under the car, the kid bends down, *Bam!* Shoots him right in the ass. Kid pulls the trigger again, but the gun's empty, he's fired six shots comin' around the front of the car. The cops get to him, the kid's taking a speed loader out of his pocket, gonna try again. Cops pull Walsh out from under the car, he's like, *Am I bleeding?* They look him over, nothing! Pulls his wallet outta his pocket, the whole front of the wallet's torn away, opens it up, his badge is all mangled. The bullet hit his wallet, bounced right off his shield. We find it down the street, next to a streetlight. You believe that?"

Cardoza shook his head, *No shit.* He peeled a strip of tape off a new reel, threaded it through the heads, and wound it onto the empty reel. Punched the record switch, let the tape wind out a couple inches, then hit "pause."

"They ever hit the house?"

Harmon lowered the camera, let the curtain fall back.

"You kidding? Time they got round to it, the house was cleaned out. Guy opens the door in a bathrobe. *Yes, officers? Come right in.* I thought Walsh was gonna deck him."

He slipped the lens cap on, set the camera on the table.

"Anyway, we had the place wired up, took it to trial on conspiracy. Got some good pictures of that kid, though. I gave one to Walsh, from just before he went under the car. The kid's got the gun aimed right between his legs, little puff of smoke coming out of the barrel, and Walsh is hanging onto his balls with both hands, looking like he's tryin' to jump over the bullet. I heard he hung it over his desk."

Cardoza had the new tape set up. He switched it to sound activated, then went back to the kitchen to finish the *ziti*.

"So you knew this guy?" He dipped his finger in the sauce to taste it.

"I knew all those cops, the narco guys. Used to work the same cases, until someone decided whether they wanted to go local or federal."

Across the field, he could just see Walsh in his green bathrobe through the bedroom window, hanging from the door frame by his fingertips, doing pullups.

"Weird to be watching him now."

"This ain't weird. This is boring. Weird would be nice. I could use a little weird."

The front door opened, and they could hear Brodie stripping off his coat, giving a little groan as he bent down to change his boots for a pair of sneakers. He came into the living room, headed straight for the heat vent in the floor.

"Man, I hate standing around in those trees."

He stood astride the vent, hands in his pockets, shivering. Every morning, he waited for Walsh at the bus stop, rode into town a few seats behind him, and spent the day in a small office above the barber shop, across the square from the hardware store. Coming home, he got off the bus and walked a few hundred yards up the road to a grove of trees, where he waited for twenty minutes after Walsh had gone

into his house, coming up the drive like he'd gotten off the next bus.

"What's happening," he asked.

"Workout."

He came over to the window.

"Left the blinds up again."

"You think he's getting careless?"

Brodie shrugged. He took his hands out of his pockets, blew into his cupped palms.

"We've been at this awhile. Not much to stay tense about."

"You don't have his troubles."

The tape machine clicked on. Cardoza came out of the kitchen, picked up the headphones, listened.

"Making dinner."

Brodie grinned at him.

"Hey, Cardoza. Whad'ya get when you cook with Mexican jumping beans?"

Cardoza shrugged.

"Hopalong *Quesadilla.*"

"You pick that up in town?"

"Guy in the barbershop."

"Figures." He tossed the headphones on his chair. "Harmon tell you he knows this guy?"

"No kidding," Brodie said. "He always this quiet?"

"I say we call this guy up," Cardoza said. "Cut all this shit and get him over here for *ziti.*"

"He can bring the bald lady."

Cardoza laughed.

"Get some straight answers. Just, you know, we been sitting over here wondering when the show starts. He got any plans when these Italian gentlemen show up?"

Harmon smiled, taking it.

"See if he wants pictures."

He was out of breath. He had to stop cutting an onion, put the knife down, sit for a second. He was pushing it lately, raising the numbers in his workout, feeling the muscles get hard. Thirty pull-ups, a long series of leg stretches that made sweat bead on his forehead, then sit-ups on a board tilted on an angle off the bed. It left him breathless and dizzy, but he needed it. The strain on his muscles eased the stress in his mind.

He kept remembering an old man, a mugging victim, his face bloody, who'd staggered into the station house during his shift one night, when he was still new to the job. He'd taken his story, let him look through the books of mug shots, then driven him home to a tiny apartment in a bad part of Dorchester. The old guy had invited him in for coffee, and he'd declined, telling him he'd stop by in a few days. It was a couple of weeks later before he remembered, and he swung by at the end of his shift one night, found the old guy sitting in his front window, a shotgun across his lap, watching the street.

"You can't be too careful," the old man told him. He showed Walsh the bolo shells he got through a mail-order house out in Idaho—two little silver balls connected by a half inch of copper wire.

"Tears 'em up," he said, his eyes bright. "Get one of 'em in the gut, that wire slices right through. Even cuts the spine, if you're close enough."

A few weeks later, the calls started coming in from his neighbors, complaining that he'd taken to pointing that shotgun out the window, sighting on people on the side-

walk as they walked past. When the beat cop knocked on the old man's door and told him to lower the gun out the window by the barrel, the old guy sat down in his chair, tucked the shotgun under his chin, and pressed the trigger with his toe.

Now, as his breath grew even and he went back to chopping the onion, the .25 tugging at the pocket of his bathrobe, Walsh caught himself thinking of the old man again. Making dinner in his tiny apartment, the shotgun leaning against the chair by the window. In recent weeks, as he sat in front of the television at night, he imagined the old man sighting down the barrel at a world full of muggers, unwilling, in the end, to surrender his fear. When the thoughts came, Walsh pushed up out of his chair, got down on the floor and did sit-ups.

It eats you up, he thought. *Till the waiting is worse than what you're waiting for.* He tried not to imagine how many weeks would pass before he took to sitting at the window, the shotgun in his lap. And how many beyond that until he put it in his mouth.

It didn't help, those guys sitting in that house across the field, watching him. He'd picked up the tail a few days back, the night he'd walked across the highway to Terry's. Coming back, that little pot in his hands, taking it slow because he couldn't use the cane, he spotted a man coming out of the trees a couple hundred yards down the road, not seeing him as he headed up the drive to the next house. Weird. He started watching the house, caught the flash of a lens in the window facing him, reflecting the setting sun. The next morning, there's a phone truck outside Terry's house.

Three years in narco, he can't spot a surveillance? He'd been worried, until he saw the truck, with its government

license plate. Same way the dealers used to spot 'em. Calling out as they walk down the street, *Hey, home! Looks like you got trouble on the line!*

Feds, most likely. But why were they watching him? He thought about it during his workout, and the question made him nervous. He added on twenty more sit-ups, until his stomach twitched with the strain. Two guys minimum—one for the tail, another for the wire. Just sitting over there, for weeks maybe. A lot of money, just to baby-sit an ex-cop. Unless they expected trouble. Figure they can set up their cameras over there, get the whole hit on film. Get D'Angelo in court, watch him squirm when they run the tape for the jury. Couple of his guys taking out a cop. A prosecutor's wet dream.

They had D'Angelo wired up for years, didn't get shit. Must figure this for a sure thing. Let the cop sit over there, worrying. Drop a few hints in the North End where he's hiding, sit back and get it all for the movies. Maybe even send in an undercover guy to finger him for D'Angelo, make sure they get it on tape so they can make the connection in court.

The woman, Haggerty. Came all the way out here to ask him about Jerry, like anybody cared about something went down almost five years ago. Gave him an uneasy feeling at the time, but he couldn't put his finger on it.

He put the knife down, dug through a kitchen drawer until he found her card—*Katherine Haggerty, Assistant U.S. Attorney.* Call me, she said, you ever want to talk. He'd stuffed the card in a drawer, thrown his coat on, walked three miles around the lake, until his leg throbbed. Remembering, now, how strange it was that he saw another guy out there, walking along the far side of the lake by the old

pumping station, the weather down in the low twenties. Same guy rode the bus with him every day, got off up at the highway, walked up the road and into the trees.

What's he gonna do, Walsh wondered, *if one of these days there's a car waiting at the bus stop, a bunch of guys from Boston watching me get off the bus with my cane?*

Walk on down the road and into the trees, if he's smart.

These guys, he wondered, *have they been told to get involved, or just let it go down for the cameras? Are they cops, or just spectators?*

He looked out the window. The lights were going on now in the house across the field. Thing to do, if he wanted to know, was to walk on over there and ask. Get out the window on the far side of the house, over into the trees by the lake, then circle back where they wouldn't be watching for him. See the look on their faces when he knocks on the door. *Hi, neighbor.*

Maybe let them come over, have a look at the place, work out the best camera angles. You want me to die in the living room? Light's better in the kitchen, you say? No, really, whatever's best for you.

He grinned, shook his head. Who was he kidding. These guys, they'd been over this place already, got wires in all the rooms. Even got Terry's place wired up now, because he stopped in there once after work. Very thorough, these guys.

Terry. Giving him that little smile, like she knew what he was asking but was gonna make him work for the answer. He's wondering about these housewives, coming to look at the pots, but as they walk around the living room, starting to sneak looks at those muscular thighs gripping the wheel, her long fingers in the clay, the way she smiles at you, like she's got something she's not saying . . .

"You like pots?"

And suddenly, she's selling him a pot. Coming over to the shelf, taking one down.

"You like this one?"

"Yeah, it's nice."

Embarrassed, like she caught him with his pants down. She's smiling at him, getting him to smile, too, as he realizes the trick. Reaching for his wallet, anyway. Thirty-five bucks, a nice pot—deep red, an Anastazi pattern, she called it—but what's he need with a pot?

It sits on his kitchen table, a couple pencils stuck in it until he can think what to do with it. And he's still curious, imagining the scene. Thinking about stopping by again some evening, see if he can get an answer.

He smiled to himself.

Probably walk out with another pot.

13

First, they make a wrong turn coming off Route 2, swing around the traffic circle, under the highway, heading south. Middle of the night, no lights anywhere, forget trying to find a road sign. They're just driving along this empty road, nothing but trees on either side of them, Frankie says:

"This ain't right. Town's right there next to the highway on the map."

Richie's driving real slow now, looking for a street sign on all these dirt roads going off into the trees, like he's back in Charlestown, shaking his head.

"You see a town back there?"

"You went round that traffic circle so fast, who's gonna see anything?"

"We woulda saw some lights."

"These fuckin' windows, you could drive up Mass Ave, think you're in the country."

Little red Toyota that Richie picked up from an auto body shop in East Cambridge, the windows tinted so dark that when they pulled up at Frankie's place around eleven o'clock, he can't see who it is, squinting at them under the streetlight. Richie reaches across, opens the door, he's like, *What the fuck's this?* Pair of fuzzy dice hanging from the rearview, salsa tapes in the glove box, seats covered with white fur. Richie, he thinks it's funny, he pulls out a pair of sunglasses, pops 'em on.

"Hey, Frankie. We cool."

A little ride up to the country, four guys squeezed into this little car, eating pizza outta a box. *Like the old days,* Frankie thought, the four of them boosting a car on a Saturday night just to get out of town for a couple hours, have a little fun. Richie Locasto and the Florio brothers, guys he grew up with. Help them out a little, get them in with Johnny. And, anyway, it's about time to get some guys in there *he* can trust, someone to back him up if it ever gets nasty.

Only now they're lost, and he's starting to get a bad feeling. Jimmy's got the map open in the backseat, holding a penlight between his teeth. The backseat's so small, he's trying to shove the shotgun out of the way for a second so he can get the map spread out, getting the barrel over in his brother's face. Pauli shoves it back at him, getting pissed.

134

"Hey! Whatcha doing with this thing? We hit a bump, I'm gonna lose my face here!"

"Just hold it, will ya? This fuckin' map's folded all wrong."

"You're on the wrong side. That's Boston. You gotta turn it over."

Jimmy turns the map over, gets it folded. Richie slowing down to a crawl now, coming to a stop, right there in the middle of the road. Reaches over to turn the heater up.

Jimmy puts his finger on the map, talking around the penlight in his teeth.

"All right, I got it. Here's the town. Right up here, north of the highway. We're on this road here, going south. We passed this lake here a couple miles ago. So we gotta get turned around, head back into town."

"How come we gotta go all the way back," Pauli asks. "Frankie said the guy lives south of town, by the lake. Could be right in here."

"Yeah, but he said it's a little road runs outta the town square. Am I right, Frankie?"

"That's what the guy told me."

"This road, it's a highway," Jimmy said. "Besides, there wasn't no houses by the lake."

"So we turn around?" Richie had the car in gear, waiting.

"I guess so."

Richie eased over to the side of the road, cut the wheel and swung around. He thought about backing it up, keeping it on the pavement, but the shoulder looked okay, just a little icy, so when he got to the edge of the road, he kept going, bringing it around slow. It felt all right until the rear wheels hit the shoulder and he cut the wheel back to straighten out. He felt the car start to slide, cut the wheel

135

back again to catch it, but his foot slipped off the clutch, and the front tires grabbed.

"Aw, fuck," he said as the car kept sliding, off the road now, the back end coming all the way around so they were looking back down the highway when they hit the ditch. The car dipped, gave a choking sound, and then died. The headlights lit up the trees.

"That's good," Frankie said, looking at him. "Someone teach you that, or you pick it up yourself?"

"Shit, Frankie. It didn't look that slick."

"Hey, you're right. But we look pretty slick sittin' here in this fuckin' ditch, don't we?"

Pauli leaned forward, grabbing the seats.

"So whatta we do now?"

"Can you start it?"

Richie hit the ignition. It gave a whine, coughed, then nothing. He shook his head.

"Maybe up on the road."

"So we gotta push."

Jimmy shoved his door open and put a foot down.

"There's water in this ditch."

"No shit."

"It's cold out there, man. We're gonna get soaked."

"So you get a cold. We do this thing, you go see a doctor."

"Get a nurse to sit by your bed."

"Hey, I know a couple nurses, they'll sit *in* your bed."

"What's her name, Danny Allmaro's sister. She's a nurse."

"Yeah? Well, she can sit on my face."

"We gonna do this thing, or what?"

They got out, wedged a couple of branches under the wheels, tried to get a footing on the slope, and pushed. The

car moved a few inches, slid back. They leaned on it for a minute, their breath like smoke in the cold air.

"We had a rope," Pauli said, "we could pull it out from the road."

"You got a rope?"

"Maybe there's one in the trunk."

"Look't this car. You think the guy owns this gonna carry rope in his trunk?"

"Maybe."

Frankie got hold of the window rim, pulled himself up to Richie's door.

"Gimme the keys," he said. "We're gonna look in the trunk."

On his way down, he slipped, landed on his ass, and slid down into the water.

"Well, shit."

Richie stuck his head out the window.

"Hey, Frankie. Someone teach you that, or you pick it up yourself?"

He got up, the three of them busting a gut.

"I'm glad you're laughing, assholes," he said. " 'Cause I dropped the keys."

That shut them up. Got Richie out of the fuckin' car, all of them down on their hands and knees in the freezing mud, feeling around for the keys.

It was then that the cop showed up.

Deputy Sheriff Andy Parker, taking his time, heading home from a swing shift he'd spent up on the median strip east of the Phillipston exit. Coming around the bend, car in the ditch, four guys scrambling around in the mud like they've lost something. He hits the brakes, pulls it over right

there in front of them, gets out. They're looking up at him, getting up real slow, their clothes all covered with mud.

"Looks like you boys got a problem."

None of them smiling, watching him. He pulls the flashlight from his belt, starting to sense there's something wrong, when one of them grins, shrugs.

"Hit a patch of ice."

The one next to the car starts climbing up the slope, so he puts the light on him, reaches down with his other hand to pop the snap on his holster.

"Maybe you want to stay right there, son."

The guy straightens up, standing there beside the passenger door, hands on his hips.

"We could use a tow," he says.

For a moment, everything is very still. Then, just as he flashes the light into the open window of the car, spots the shotgun leaning against the seat, one of the guys at the bottom takes off, splashing away down the ditch toward a bunch of trees. As he draws his gun, he sees the others start moving, two of them diving behind the car. The one by the door leans into the backseat, his hand closing around the shotgun, then just keeps going, rolling behind the bucket seats, the shotgun coming up. Parker gets the .38 up in front of him, stepping back, and puts a round through the windshield. A moment later, the glass explodes from within, and he hears the pump on the shotgun, sees a smoking shell tumble into the mud. He takes two quick steps to his right, getting the patrol car in front of him, and sees one of the guys in the ditch pop up from behind the trunk, a little snubnose .38 in his hand.

Sweet Jesus.

He puts a round into the trunk about an inch from the

guy's face, watches him give a little grunt and drop out of sight. Then the shotgun roars, and he hears a sound like a handful of rocks hitting the side of the cruiser. He squats down, moves toward the front of the car, hearing footsteps splashing away in the ditch. And suddenly, he's thinking about his daughter, asleep in her crib, even as he steps around the front of the cruiser, sees the guy coming out of the car, raising the shotgun until it's pointed right at him, pulling the trigger . . .

Frankie pumped the shotgun, shot him again, watching his body give a little jerk as the round caught him above the hip. He stepped toward him, keeping his eye on the gun lying there next to his hand, kicked it a few feet away. He put the barrel of the shotgun under the cop's chin, bent down to feel for a pulse. Nothing. He turned, saw Jimmy watching him over the trunk of the Toyota, his face red in the glow of the taillights.

"You wanna call those guys back," he asked, "we can get the fuck outta here?"

He was opening up the store, rolling the security grate on the front window up into the awning. Sonny, the morning cook over at Frank's, was sitting on a crate in the alley, cooling down, having a cigarette.

"You hear what happened?"

Jack locked the grate into place, walked over.

"What's that?"

"Sheriff's deputy was killed out on the highway last night. Found him in a ditch next to a stolen car. Someone got him with a shotgun, took off in his car."

Jack stood for a moment, thinking about it.

139

"Took the sheriff's car?"

"Yep. I hear they found it in Springfield this morning."
He shook his head. "Kinda thing don't happen much out
here."

Jack nodded. His stomach was beginning to tighten up.

"Where'd you say it happened?"

"Over on 202, a couple miles south of town. Out past the
lake."

"Stolen car?"

"That's what the cops said that came in for breakfast this
morning."

"They know where it was stolen?"

Sonny shrugged, flicked his cigarette down the alley.

"I guess not." He dropped his hands on his knees, got up
with a sigh. "Gotta get back, cook all those eggs 'fore they
start hatching."

It was late when they got back to Boston, coming up the
Southeast Expressway from Providence, where they'd
switched cars the second time. Richie finally starting to get
calmed down when they passed the storage tanks by the
harbor and swung off the highway down into the Callahan
Tunnel, heading into East Boston.

"Oh man, oh man," he kept saying. "A fuckin' cop."

"Hey, forget it," Jimmy told him. "Best thing is just forget
it happened. They can't trace the car. The guns are buried in
the woods down in Rhode Island. None of us says something stupid, they got no evidence."

Frankie was silent, staring out the window.

"These things happen, you gotta just cut your losses. Cop
pulled up, what were we gonna do, sittin' there with a
stolen car, bunch of hot guns? Guy pulled up so fast, didn't

touch the radio, just got out of the car. It was an opportunity, is all."

Frankie shook his head. No way to put it, it didn't look like a major fuckup, a bunch of guys didn't know how to do a simple job. It was a bad way to get started. He was gonna have to put these guys on ice for awhile, get 'em some money, tell 'em to keep their heads down.

Thinking as they turned north out of the tunnel, going to pick up Jimmy's car before they dumped the stolen one in Dorchester, this one's gonna stick to me. I'll be forty, sitting up in Johnny's office makin' phone calls, anyone sees me with these guys, they'll say—*watch that ice, now!* Keep Jimmy maybe. Stayed cool, ready to shoot that cop when he came round the car.

And now they were pulling up outside Jimmy's house, easing around the corner before they let him out so his mother wouldn't see them, watching him trot back to his car. Frankie opened the door, got out.

"You guys do the car," he said to Pauli. "I got some things to do."

He waved to Jimmy, walked back to his car. Thinking about it, as he drove back through the tunnel, down the expressway to Broadway, across the bridge into Southie. He felt himself getting nervous as he parked, walked across the street to the warehouse, seeing the Cadillac parked out front. Johnny watched from the second-floor window as he came up the street.

14

The sheriff sat behind a green metal desk, like they use in welfare offices. He hunched over a file, a pair of reading glasses perched on his broad nose. His lips moved slightly as he read.

Jack's leg hurt. He had started leaving the cane behind the counter at the store for short walks around the square, trying to walk through the pain, to make the steps flow like a stream tumbling over rocks. The physical therapist in the hospital had urged him to meditate on that image, picture the water swirling around all obstructions, finding the easi-

est path. Muscles working together, the joints rolling his weight forward smoothly, a leaf flowing downstream.

Only, with every step, there was a grating sensation, like a car with a bad transmission, the gears chewing at a weak spot. The pain kept flaring in his hip and knee. After a few minutes, he dropped onto a bench at the edge of the square, one hand massaging his knee. The cold made it worse, getting into his bones, making the sidewalks treacherous.

Maybe Terry was right. California.

He looked up to see the deputy getting out of his car, hitching his gunbelt, coming his way. Stopping right in front of him, hands on his hips.

"You Walsh?"

He nodded, expecting it.

"Sheriff wants to talk to you."

He got up, walked back to the car with the deputy, started to climb in the front.

"Backseat," the deputy said, grabbing his arm just above the elbow, like they teach you to do when a guy's cuffed, helping him into the car behind the wire mesh.

"Am I under arrest?"

"Beats me." The deputy started the car. "You done anything I should arrest you for?"

The sheriff grunted, closed the file. He laid his glasses on the desk, looked up.

"Can't say I'd want to be in your shoes, son."

He sat back, folded his arms.

"Seems to me you might have paid me a call when you moved back to town, Jack. Let me know what to expect."

"The fewer people know, the safer I feel."

The sheriff's eyes narrowed. He leaned forward again, the chair squeaking beneath his bulk.

"You figure maybe I'm on D'Angelo's payroll?"

"I didn't say that."

He slapped the desk, the pens jumping.

"C'mon, Jack! I've got a deputy shot dead three miles south of town. Quarter mile from your place. I got no leads, no evidence. Some guy from the U.S. Attorney's office in Boston calls me up, tells me I got a prime mob target living right here, I don't even know it. Hour later, I get this file by courier, all the way from Boston, tells me how you smeared Johnny D'Angelo's son all over a street in the North End. You thought maybe it wasn't important?"

He paused, giving Jack a chance to answer. Then he shook his head, disgusted.

"That car we found in the ditch, we got a make on it about an hour ago. Registered in Somerville. That's across the river from Boston, my memory serves. Someone walked into a repair shop, took the keys off the peg on the wall, drove it away. They didn't even have to break into the place. Opened the door with a key, drove out with the car."

"You get the name of the shop?"

"That matter?"

"Could."

"Well, the state police didn't give me that piece of information. Fact is, we got four sets of footprints in the ditch. None of 'em match my deputy. You want to speculate what brings four guys out from Boston in a stolen car, armed like they're gonna hit the beach at Anzio, they end up in a ditch less than a mile from your place?"

Jack shrugged.

"I guess they made a wrong turn."

145

No smile. Looking at him, sucking at the corner of his lip. Finally, turning in his chair to look out the window.

"You got lucky last night, Jack. But your luck, it could change any time. You don't seek police help, means you thinking 'bout protecting yourself. You got guns up at that house, Jack? As I remember the law, a man just outta prison, like yourself, he's lost his right to bear arms. Thing like that could send you back to prison, Jack."

"What is it you want?"

The sheriff turned back to him, smiling now.

"I hate to be rude, Jack. But I want you gone."

"So where you gonna go?"

Terry had two pots in the oven, and she kept the little light on in there, bending down to look in at 'em every few minutes.

"I don't know. Maybe California, like you said."

"You might like it. Stay up north. Everything south of Santa Barbara's just Hollywood. Except, there's this little town in the mountains up north of L.A., what's the name. Ojai. I know some people love it there."

Jack shook his head, laughed. Artists, maybe a couple of psychics. My kinda town.

"Hard to imagine. Get a job as a security guard, maybe. Spend the rest of my life wondering when I'm gonna see my kids."

"You got a choice?"

"Not that I can see."

"So go. Start over. Send me a postcard."

"Fact is, I can't even do that. I'm on parole, can't leave the state. Gotta report in once a week to a lady in Boston. They

cut me some slack, let me do it by phone. Special circumstances."

She leaned against the top of the stove, letting the heat
from the oven warm her bare legs. He could see a red mark,
like a fresh bruise, on the inside of her thigh, way up high.
When she bent down to look at the pots, he got a good look.
Teeth marks.

"So pick a town," she said, straightening. "Someplace
here in the state, nobody knows you. Get a job."

"You tried getting a job in these little towns, the economy
like it is? Try it with prison as the last entry on your re-
sume." He was looking at her legs, wondering. "Anyway, if
they found me this time . . ." He shrugged.

"Anyone you can talk to about this?"

"I'm talking to you."

She smiled at that. Hitched her butt up on the edge of the
stove, pressing the soles of her feet against the oven door.

"In fact," he said, "I'm thinking hard about staying here."

"Yeah?"

"This thing with the deputy, it's got everyone on edge.
Sheriff's threatening me, but he's gonna be watching out for
these guys now. Might be the best place for me now."

"You really got guns over there?"

He smiled, gave a cough.

"Doesn't matter, really. Sheriff wants me gone, he can
search the place, get one of his guys to drop one in a closet.
Not much to stop him, unless someone tells him to back
off."

He gave another little cough, marking it on the tape.
When the surveillance guy runs it back for his boss, he'll just
have to watch for the needle to jump, find the spot.

"He starts harassing me," he went on, "I'll just have to pack up in the middle of the night, take off."

In other words, *If you want me where you can see me, lean on the sheriff*. He wondered if he should repeat it, drive the point home. But Terry was looking at him funny, giving him a little smile.

"I hope you stay," she said.

And she put her feet down, had a look at her pots. Giving him another glance at the mark on her leg.

No question. It was teeth.

15

He figured he got off easy. Johnny sitting there behind the desk, talking into the phone. Not even looking at him. Making him sweat, wondering what he's heard. Then, finally, hanging up, rubbing at his face like he's tired. He sighs, pushes the phone across the desk at him.

"You call up Maria, tell her you takin' her to lunch. Get her outta the house, her mother can get something done for once."

So Frankie picks her up. They drive around, trying to decide where they're gonna have lunch, they feel like fish, or burgers, or what? Finally, Maria looks at him, she says:

"I'm not hungry. Let's go fuck."

Twenty minutes later, they're at his apartment, she tells him to sit on the couch, puts on some music, makes him sit there watching while she takes her clothes off, slowly, running her hands over her body. When he can't take it anymore, he grabs her, bends her across the coffee table, and . . .

The way he figures, it all came out right in the end.

Haggerty glanced up from her desk, saw Riccioli standing in the door to her office, looking at her Chagall poster, the ficus tree in the corner, the Navajo blanket on her chair.

"You made it nice in here."

He gestured toward the empty chair beside her desk.

"Got a minute?"

She closed the file she'd been reading, shoved it aside.

"Please."

The old swivel chair groaned, tilted back as he settled into it. He caught himself, gave a slight smile.

"My first office, when I started over at Flynn & Ransom, it had this heating duct that went right across the ceiling. In the summer, it used to drip right over my desk. I called the building people, they couldn't figure out where the water was coming from. The office was too small to move the desk, so I had to keep a bucket on the desk. Every couple days, my secretary used to dump it in a plant. I always suspected she made the coffee with it."

She smiled back at him. He shifted his gaze to the file cabinet beside her.

"Have you been keeping up with the updates on the D'Angelo file?"

"I was just looking at the surveillance transcripts."

"Any impressions."

She hesitated a moment.

"He's spotted the surveillance."

He nodded.

"I'm afraid I agree."

"Is that a problem?"

"Hard to say. He's trying to send a message, telling us he knows we're watching. At least he's not running."

He leaned back in the chair, ran his hand through his hair. His eyes were on the Chagall poster—a pair of angels hovering over a ghetto.

"Tell me," he said. "What would you do in his position."

"Run."

He smiled, glanced over at her.

"So would I," he admitted. "This guy, he refuses to make any serious efforts to hide. He gets out of prison, he moves back to the one town where people know him."

"Have you ever lived in a small town," she asked.

He looked at her, surprised.

"Me? No. I grew up here in Boston."

"In a way, it's more anonymous than a city. Everyone knows your business, but no one would admit to an outsider they've ever heard of you."

He reached over, caught a leaf on the ficus, feeling the gloss with the tip of his thumb.

"I've never been able to keep one of these things alive."

"Too much water," she said. "They like to be dry."

He nodded, let the leaf swing back. He turned to look at her.

"You think you understand this guy," he said.

"I wouldn't say that."

"What would you say?"

151

"He's bitter. He's looking for a way out, but he won't run. If he's spotted the surveillance, maybe he figures he's safe. If he just sits tight, waits it out, the cavalry will show up when he needs them."

"You think he'd be receptive to an offer?"

She thought about it, remembering the contempt in his voice when he mentioned Riccioli's role in the drug sweeps, his anger at a betrayal she could hardly imagine.

She shrugged.

"He needs a friend."

"I'm taking lunch."

Jack handed his brother the register keys and put the cash drawer on the edge of his desk. Larry dropped the keys in the pocket of his cardigan, his eyes on the old manual typewriter on which he pecked out his letters.

"Flip the sign on your way out," he said, two fingers hovering above the keyboard.

At the door, Jack lifted the OPEN sign off its hook on the door, turned it over to show a little clock, a smiling store clerk, his hand raised, saying, WE'LL BE BACK! He set the cardboard hands on the clock for two o'clock, pulled the door shut behind him.

Most days, he ate in the store, ordering a sandwich from Frank's, black coffee in a cardboard cup. If it was slow, he might walk down the block, take a seat at the counter, get a bowl of soup. But today, he had business. He crossed the square, walked down the block past the barbershop, turned left, heading out toward the Food King. He cut across the elementary school parking lot, taking it slow because of the ice. Just beyond was a strip mall, the storefronts empty. On the windows, a hockey player slapped at a puck. Above his

head were the words WALT'S SPORTING GOODS and TOP GUN SHOOT-
ING SUPPLIES. Jack walked around back, knocked at a metal fire
door next to a Dumpster. He waited a minute, then knocked
again.

He heard footsteps, the door swung open. Lou Walt, a
burly man with a beard, his long brown hair pulled back in
a ponytail, stepped back to let him in. He wiped his mouth
with a paper napkin.

"I was eating lunch. I figured you weren't coming."

"Got held up at the store." Jack glanced around at the
dusty boxes scattered across the floor. "You get it?"

Walt grinned, stuffed the napkin in the back pocket of his
jeans.

"I got it. It's a beauty."

He turned, walked over to a rusty metal cabinet, pulling
out a ring of keys. He unlocked the padlock, swung the
doors open, and lifted a metal case down from the top shelf.

"Let's go over here, in the light."

He led Jack over to the window, laid the case on an over-
turned crate, and flipped the latches.

"Heckler & Koch MP5, with a retractable tube stock." He
lifted the gun out, snapping the stock into place. "Thirty
rounds of nine-millimeter Parabellum, muzzle velocity of a
thousand feet per second, rate of fire six hundred per minute."

He grinned, held the gun out to Jack.

"Course, you gotta reload."

Jack raised the gun to eye level, sighted down the short
barrel.

"Numbers?"

"It's clean." Walt turned back to the case, pulled out a

153

pair of short tubes. "You got your telescopic and night sights, optional. Cost you another hundred and eighty."

"I'll take 'em."

"Smart man."

Jack handed him the gun.

"Wrap it up."

16

Keenan drove past the hardware store, closed for the night. He swung out along the road to Walsh's house, cruising past without slowing down. A couple lights showed in the windows. He found a driveway, got turned around, and headed back to town. Then south on the highway past the lake, looking for the spot where the deputy was killed, trying to imagine how Frankie could have missed the turn coming off the highway, ended up on the wrong side of the lake.

On a straight section of road, he saw two deep grooves in the shoulder, pulled over. He got out, crossed the highway,

stood looking down into the ditch. There were bits of red glass stuck in the mud. From the taillights, he figured. Tire tracks in the grass led down into the ditch. Lots of footprints, left by the cops, searching for spent shells, bloodstains, anything that might look like evidence.

Only once, during his years in uniform, had he felt it come close enough that, later, lying in bed, he could imagine himself sprawled on a dirty floor, a bunch of cops standing around, shaking their heads. It happened on a domestic-abuse call in the Mission Hill project. He had knocked on the door of a third-floor apartment, heard gunshots, and kicked the door in. He went in low, leading with the gun, saw a woman lying on the floor of the living room next to a couch, bleeding from a hole in her chest. His partner edged into the narrow hall, throwing doors open on either side. Keenan bent to check the woman's pulse, felt an unsteady flutter beneath his fingers. Looking up, he saw a man, his dark face gleaming with sweat, huddled behind the couch. He held a blunt .38 out before him, his hands shaking violently. The gun was pointed at Keenan's face.

"Easy," Keenan said, his voice quiet.

The man drew the hammer back with his thumbs, making a whistling sound with his throat. At that moment, Keenan's partner stepped out of the hall. The man looked up, and Keenan raised his service revolver, shot him in the head.

And suddenly, Keenan remembered the cop in the warehouse. Falling, as if in slow motion, the crates tumbling around him. Sheer luck that he'd survived. He was sitting up in bed now, the papers said, greeting visitors. When he got out, they'd give him a medal.

Keenan walked back across the road, got in the car. No

use putting it off any longer. He swung it around, staying off the shoulder, and headed back to town.

"We got company."

Brodie had the television on, a preacher with a pile of silver hair waving his hands, shouting about salvation. He looked up, saw Harmon raise the binoculars.

"Car coming up the driveway. Looks like a Ford Fairlane. Driver's a white male."

Brodie pushed out of the chair, snapped the television off, went over to the foot of the stairs.

"Cardoza!"

He came back to the window.

"You got a tag number?"

Harmon shook his head.

"No front plate."

Brodie sighed, reached for his coat.

"Guess I'll take a little walk."

It took him a minute. Staring out the window, watching the guy come up the steps, a little box in his hands. When the face registered, he let the curtain fall, took a quick step backwards.

"Shit!"

He pulled the .25 from the waistband of his pants, racked the slide. When the knock came, he yanked the door open, put the gun about an inch from Keenan's nose.

He didn't even flinch.

"Hi, Jack. You gonna let me in?"

"You picked a stupid place to hide."

Keenan set the box on the kitchen table, looking around.

"Who's hiding?"

The gun dangled from Walsh's hand. He waved it at Keenan's coat.

"You wanna open up, let me see if you're carrying?"

Keenan smiled, unzipped his heavy coat, held it open for him to check. Walsh nodded.

"Seems to me you used to keep a little one in your boot."

Keenan lifted the cuff of his pants. Sneakers and tube socks. Walsh stuffed the gun in his waistband.

"Kinda jumpy," Keenan said.

"I got a good reason."

"No argument." Keenan moved to the window, looked out at the fields, the woods beyond. "You get lonely here?"

"I talk to the walls."

Keenan laughed, giving him a funny look.

"That a warning?"

"You worried?"

"I sleep okay."

Walsh looked at the box.

"You come all the way out here to bring me this?"

"That, maybe have a little talk."

" 'Bout what?"

"Anne."

Walsh was silent for a moment. He reached over and picked up the box, reading the address on the label.

"She give you this?"

"It came in the mail. She called me up, told me about it. I told her I'd take care of it."

Walsh opened the box, took out the envelope.

"Jack Walsh, Free Man."

"You feel free, Jack?"

He tipped the envelope, and the glasses slid into his hand,

little bits of glass slipping between his fingers, scattering across the kitchen floor.

"Ah, damn."

"I guess you know what that means."

Walsh shook his head.

"Chris. The girl who was with me on the night of the accident. She wore these."

They looked down at the shattered glasses in his hand.

"I get back to town," Keenan said, "I'll ask a few questions. See what I can find out."

Walsh dropped the glasses on the table. His face was flushed, his jaw tight.

"They sent this to Anne?"

"You figure it's a threat?"

He raised his eyes to the ceiling for a moment, getting his anger under control. Looked around at the walls, picturing a man wearing headphones, hunched over as he strained to catch every word.

"Let's take a walk," he said.

They headed out along the road toward the lake. Keenan noted how, as they left the house, Walsh kept his hand in his coat pocket, curled around the gun.

"We get a couple hundred yards up the road," Walsh said, his voice quiet, "a guy'll come outta that house back there, the brown one. He'll stay back a way, keep us in sight until we get out to the lake. I don't think he's got a field mike. At least, I've never seen one. Don't get many visitors."

Keenan glanced back at the brown house, thinking of the gun taped to his back, under his shirt. *Rules that out.*

"You know who they are?"

"Feds, I guess. I saw one of 'em get in a car the other

morning, looked like a guy worked on the heroin raids in Dorchester a couple years back. Takes pictures."

"Yeah?"

"They probably got you when you drove up. Some guy in the federal building will spend a couple days figuring out who you are. Won't take long, since you rode up in a department car. They'll call you in for questions, mark you down as a player."

"Thanks for the warning."

Walsh pointed to a path that split off from the road, leading off through the trees.

"We turn here."

They walked in silence on the narrow path. Keenan going over it in his mind, looking for an angle. Ahead, he could see the moonlight shining on the water. The path widened as it came up on the lake, and Walsh dropped back so they were walking side by side. He looked off across the water.

"You and Anne seeing each other?"

Keenan shrugged.

"Not really. Maybe."

Walsh was silent. They walked on. Across the lake, the pumping station stood in shadows, the chain link fence that surrounded it pulled down in several places. The kind of place, Keenan thought, where teenagers come to party in the summer, put their boomboxes on the top of one of the buildings, pile their clothes on a rock, and jump in the water naked. Boys grabbing at the girls, pulling them under, splashing to the surface close together, feeling each other's bodies up close, wet and cool. He smiled, then saw Walsh looking at him.

"You spend much time with the kids?"

"Not really. I just stopped by a couple times, is all. Anne

says to tell you they're fine. She wanted to send some pictures for you, but she forgot."

Walsh stopped, turned to look off at the trees. Keenan wondered if he was going to cry. But Walsh turned to face him, his eyes hard.

"This thing, the glasses, I'm supposed to take it as a threat. Like they wanna remind me they know where my family is."

"That's what it looks like."

"You still got contacts in the North End?"

Keenan hesitated for a moment, wary.

"I know some people."

"I want you to do me a favor. You put word out, they touch my family, I'm gonna pay 'em a visit." He paused, glanced around him. "The way my life is now, I'd have nothing to lose."

And suddenly, he stepped in close to Keenan, making him take a step back, his hand coming up between them to touch Walsh's chest, hold him back.

"You and me, we got history," Walsh said, softly. "I saw you standing there on my porch, I thought, oh, my my. Maybe we'll get some answers."

"What're you talking about?"

"You come out here, delivering a message that's got nothing to do with you. I ask myself, why? Maybe you're doing it for Anne, like you said. But the way I see it, that still makes you an errand boy for a guy who wants to threaten my family."

Keenan dropped his hand, stared back.

"You really wanna make another enemy, Jack?"

But Walsh was looking away, over his shoulder, jerking his chin to make him look.

"Back there, in the trees."

Keenan looked, but all he saw was trees.

"Guy's pretty good on city streets," Walsh said, "but out here in the woods, he moves like a guy sneaking in late. More he tries to hide, the easier he is to see."

And now Keenan could make out a shape among the shadows, crouched down, watching them look at him.

"You always had a good eye," Keenan said.

"Just knowing what to watch for."

Walsh turned, headed back up the path.

Angie D'Angelo was angry. She sat with her arms crossed, glaring at the manager of the Ritz Carlton, listening to him explain, carefully, just how the problem happened.

"You see, it was a mix-up. You made your reservation with Mr. Simons . . ."

He gestured to the Director of Special Events, a small man who was trying his best to vanish into a corner.

"And the film company had made its arrangements with me directly, because they plan to use a variety of locations throughout the hotel, including some that have the potential to be quite disruptive. I'm sure you can see how the problem came about."

She stared at him.

"Of course," he went on quickly, "the ballroom will be in some disrepair, what with the lights, the cables, and what have you. I understand they will be shooting in the kitchen, as well."

In the corner, Simons flinched. *God, don't say shooting!*

"Needless to say," the manager smiled, spread his hands, "we intend to return your deposit in full."

Angie gave him her sweetest smile.

"That won't be necessary," she said.

His eyebrows went up.

"Oh?"

"This film company, they won't need your ballroom."

He sighed. With a practiced flip of his wrist, he opened a brown leather reservation book, turned it to show her the calendar, the days marked in red.

"Well, I'm sorry to differ with you," he said. "But as you can see . . ."

She leaned forward, closed the book. He looked up, startled.

"I don't know who called you," she said. "The D.A., the U.S. Attorney. You wanna know, I don't care. I have a contract, and my daughter's wedding reception isn't moving. You can tell your movie people to reschedule. If they don't like it, you tell 'em my husband has some influence in the transportation unions in this city. They'll find their equipment dumped in a parking lot up in Maine."

She sat back, smiled.

"As for you gentlemen, I suggest you supervise our party personally. My husband can be very . . ."

She paused, considering. The manager had begun to sweat. Simons looked like he might cry.

She turned to him with the word, offering it to him slowly, like a gift.

"Precise."

Janice Sidney, the file clerk in the U.S. Attorney's office, hated dealing with attorneys. Secretaries knew the importance of keeping things in order—not dumping a file on your desk when you read it, but flipping the pages back against the manila cover, moving back through time with

each page you turned. Or, at least you could train a secretary. You see them bring the files back. If the proper procedures aren't followed, you speak to them.

With the lawyers, though, it was best not to expect much. And the young ones were the worst. Most of the senior attorneys had learned to stay in their offices, let their secretaries fetch the files. But the young ones . . .

She sighed. Eight o'clock in the morning, and she finds Haggerty waiting at the door, still wearing her sneakers beneath her power suit, asking her as she fishes her keys out of her purse to pull almost thirty inches of files on Operation Clean Sweep, a series of drug raids that took place six years ago. Just looking at her, Mrs. Sidney could imagine how the files would come back: pages dog-eared and torn, shifted out of order, even moved between folders. It would take her hours to put them in order.

She scowled as she loaded the folders on a library cart. Sneakers, with a pinstripe suit.

What struck Haggerty, after plowing through a foot of paper, was that a drug sweep was good for business. The police move in, bust half the dealers, and the other half raise the prices through the roof. With each arrest report came a press release that listed the quantity of drugs seized and an estimated street value. By the time she'd reached the third week of such reports, the price had shot up, making each raid seem more impressive, and—as the press releases hinted—putting a financial burden on both dealers and users as the supply dried up.

She glanced over at the row of untouched folders on the cart, wondering what the price would be when she reached the last files. It would be interesting, if you had a few days,

to track the rate of property crimes during the same period —stolen cars, televisions, welfare checks. Would the rate of muggings and liquor store holdups climb with the street prices that the press releases boasted? Were there more shootings, more wives beaten, as the junkies grew desperate, watching the cost of a fix soar out of reach? Did anyone gain by this operation but the politicians who posed before piles of seized drugs for the television news?

The answer to that one, of course, was yes. A few dealers, who had the luck—or information—to avoid the raids, watched the news reports with broad smiles. A few people grew very rich, very fast.

Glancing back over the arrest records, she found blacks, Hispanics, few older than their mid-twenties. Clearly, the ones who suffered were the street dealers, the kids who stood in the rain for hours, watching the cars cruise past, waiting for a bullet or a sale. The arrests ran as high as the bottom-rung distributors, working out of apartments with armored doors and bars on the windows. The Uzi types, with their constant fear of a raid—not by the cops, but by other dealers looking for a score.

The guys at the top, they sat in their North Shore mansions, watching the whole thing on television. As the price rose, the remaining dealers on the street would begin calling, their voices urgent, looking to buy. When the sweeps ended, and life went back to normal, the ones who'd been busted came dragging back to their street corners, willing to pay any price to restock the inventory before their customers drifted away.

And what if, Haggerty thought, you knew someone inside? A cop, probably. Or a prosecutor. Someone who could warn you where the raids were coming, maybe steer the

whole operation away from a small group of dealers. Someone like that could make a fortune overnight. And he could
seize control: put the competition out of business for a few
weeks, make everyone come to him. Looking at it that way,
the money to be made during the raids seemed small. The
real score was market share.

It was an interesting idea. But all she had was the word of
an angry cop. A hint that a tip-off had blown a raid. Could
she trust him? An alcoholic, trying to save his own skin,
Riccioli had said, dropping hints, hoping to get her interested. Maybe sneak into the Federal Witness Protection Program, get set up with a new name, a job, a house in some
little town in Indiana where D'Angelo would never find
him.

It made sense. Until you drove out and talked to the guy,
saw the anger in his eyes. Anger mostly at himself, for blowing it, letting the betrayal he'd seen make him a drunk, a
bad cop, a man whose children would learn to forget him.
Sitting there in that little house, waiting to die.

Haggerty trusted her eyes. What she'd seen, what she'd
sensed in his voice, was enough to make her pull the files,
looking for a lead. Now even Riccioli was stopping by her
office, talking about offering him a deal. She had nodded,
agreed. But in the back of her mind, she thought, what do
we really have to offer him? He didn't want their protection,
saw no value in it unless they let D'Angelo take his shot for
the cameras. But if she could ease the pain in his eyes, show
him that she took his betrayal seriously, he might go along.
An even trade: help us get D'Angelo, we'll find the guy who
got Jerry Friar killed.

She lifted the next file from the cart, thinking, *If you make
it.*

17

When Angie told her husband how she handled that little confusion at the Ritz, he laughed so hard he choked on his pot roast.

"You're a pisser," he said. He grabbed her around the waist, pulled her onto his lap. "These guys, they think we're gonna come in shooting. Machine-gun wedding."

"We'll get you a ring," she told him. "They can kiss it."

"I gotta learn to mumble. Stick my lip out, like this." He did his Brando. "I'm gonna make you an offer . . ."

"You never could do that."

"Hey," he said, offended. "I get in the papers. That's not good enough for you? Marry a famous man?"

"I married you, you were a punk. That's what my dad said."

"Your dad! He's out here the day we moved into this house, asking me what I paid for it, did I get a loan. I told him, I don't *need* a loan. I pay cash."

"I think I heard this before."

"Like I heard I'm a punk." He slapped his forehead. "Geez, I forgot."

"What?"

"I gotta go steal a tux for the wedding."

She shoved him.

"Stop it."

"You want me to look nice, right?"

She pushed up off his lap, went over to the counter. She picked up a knife, started cutting up the chicken.

"You talk to Frankie yet?"

"Talk about what?"

"The future."

"I'm supposed to know about the future? I keep today under control, I'm doing good."

"You know what I mean."

Johnny sipped his beer.

"I got plans for him."

"He's gonna be family, Johnny. Not just one of your employees. It's important to Maria."

He frowned, watched her hack at the chicken with the blade.

"She's marrying the guy," he said, "I'm supposed to make him *capo di regime*?"

And suddenly, she was crying, her shoulders shaking.

She put the knife down, brought her hands up to wipe her face, but they were covered with grease. Johnny got up, went over to her, tore a paper towel off the roll. She pressed it to her face, shook her head. He put his arms around her.

"She's our daughter, Johnny. She's all we got, since Vinnie . . ."

She bit her lip. The tears gleamed on her face.

"Sometimes, I wake up in the morning, I don't think about him. I'm making breakfast, and I realize it. Like I forget we had a son. I swore I wouldn't forget him, Johnny."

"Time passes, baby. You get over it."

She shook her head, pushed him away.

"I don't wanna get over it!" She turned to the counter, snatched up the knife. She hacked at the chicken, her hands trembling. "I want my son back."

Walsh looked up. Larry was standing beside him, one hand rubbing at the edge of the counter, his face flushed.

"I was in yesterday," he said. "Working on the accounts."

"Yeah?"

"I came over to the register for the charge receipts, and I dropped my pencil."

Jack rubbed a hand over his face. It was early.

"Sorry to hear it."

"When I bent down to get it, I happened to glance under the counter."

Jack nodded, wearily.

"Yeah, I figured."

"You wanna tell me what that is under there?"

"Remington .410 pump, pistol grip."

"You got a permit for it?"

"No, Larry. No permit."

"I want it out of here today."

Jack looked at him. He was wearing a blue shirt and a red bow tie. He had a pencil holder in the pocket of the shirt, embossed with the Ace Hardware logo and the words *Hi! I'm Larry.*

"I wish you'd reconsider," Jack said.

"It's my store, Jack. I'm trying to do you a favor here. But I don't want guns in my store. It's bad enough we've got this guy."

And he jerked a thumb toward the front window. The brown-and-white sheriff's car had pulled up in the loading zone in front of the store first thing on Monday morning, the deputy just sitting there behind the wheel. At first, Walsh figured it meant they were finally going to take this thing seriously, pull a unit off traffic duty and assign him to watch out for trouble. But after an hour or two, he realized the guy wasn't watching the street, or the customers. He was sitting in his patrol car, staring through the display window at the counter. Watching *him.* If three guys from Boston walked through the door and started shooting, he thought, the guy'd probably arrest him. Charge him with creating a disturbance.

"All right," he said. "You're the boss."

Thinking about where else he could hide it, out of Larry's sight, but within reach if something happens. Maybe loosen a board in the plank floor under the counter, slip it in. Might have to trim the barrel a bit more, but he meant to do that anyway.

Larry nodded, looking like he wanted to say something else. Instead, he turned and walked back to his office. Closed the door, pulled the shade down.

18

"You sure that's the house?"

Frankie peered through the windshield, nodded.

"Yeah, that's it." He pointed. "No car, see? This guy don't drive."

Jimmy shook his head, doubtful.

"I wish they had numbers out here."

"We're in the fuckin' country. You want numbers, go back to the North End." Frankie glanced at the dashboard clock. "That thing right?"

Jimmy looked at his watch.

"Two forty-five."

"All right, park it. I'm sick'a waiting."

Jimmy eased over onto the shoulder, slowly. He felt the gravel crunch under the wheels, no ice this time. He killed the engine, left the keys in it. Frankie reached up, popped the plastic cover on the dome light, unscrewed the bulb. He looked over at Jimmy, grinned.

"Learned that from a cop," he said. "They don't see ya when the door opens."

They got out, stretching their legs in the cold. Jimmy hit the latch for the trunk, and it opened silently.

"I like this car. Got a lotta nice stuff on it."

It was a gray Acura, stolen off a lot in Framingham. Smelled like money. The cops they'd passed on the way out had ignored them.

"It gets us home, that's all I want."

The shotguns were wrapped in a blanket. Frankie unfolded it, lifted the guns out. A twelve-gauge pump, and a street sweeper they'd picked up in Roxbury, the pistol grip wrapped in black electrical tape. He spilled a box of shells onto the blanket, and they loaded the guns. Across the fields, the houses were dark.

Frankie pulled two bandanas out of his pocket, handed one to Jimmy.

"What's this?"

"I always wanted to be a *bandito*. Like in the westerns."

He tied it across his face, swung the twelve-gauge up to firing position.

"Hey, Meester. Hands up!"

Jimmy shook his head.

"Maria know you act like this?"

"She thinks I'm cute."

172

"Cute little *bandito.*"

He leaned the shotgun against the side of the car, tied the bandana over his face.

"You ready?"

Frankie looked up at the sky.

"Wait'll these clouds pass over. Make it darker."

They crossed the field, the shotguns cradled in their arms. The frozen ground crunched under their feet. As they came up on the house, Frankie held up a hand. He squatted, pointed at the back of the house.

"You get in close, there. Get an angle on those windows, you can get a shot at him, if he jumps out. Don't be shooting through any windows, though. Could be me."

Jimmy squinted at the house, trying to imagine the layout.

"You're goin' in there?"

Frankie shrugged.

"'Less you can think of a way to get him to come out."

Jimmy thought about it.

"How do I know it's you coming out?"

"I'll wave my banana."

"You'll do what?"

"What'd I say?"

"You're gonna wave your banana."

"I said that?"

"Just now."

"I meant my *bandana.*"

"Right." Jimmy raised his shotgun. "I'll tell ya, I don't know how Maria feels, but you go wavin' that thing at me, I'll shoot it off."

Frankie stood up, shucked the pump to chamber a round.

"Let's just do this thing, okay?"

* * *

Walsh was awake, staring at the ceiling, his mind trying to hold on to an image of Anne on their wedding day, smiling, when he heard the faint sound of glass breaking in the hall. He slipped out of bed, his hand finding the shotgun clipped to the bedframe. He pumped it, crossed to the window. He got his back to the wall, took a quick glance. The front yard was empty, the gravel driveway pale in the moonlight. He thought he saw a car parked out on the road, partly hidden by a cluster of trees. He glanced over at the house beyond the field, where the surveillance crew was set up. The windows were dark. Had they seen them coming in? *This is it, guys,* he thought. *What you've been waiting for.* In his mind, he imagined a man dozing at the window, his head snapping up as the tapes started to roll. *Now get on the phone!*

He heard bits of glass hitting the floor. Someone trying to get a hand through the narrow window next to the door, reaching for the dead bolt. Walsh slipped out of the bedroom, across the dark hall into the kitchen. He stayed away from the window, edging along the wall past the refrigerator. He could see a man crouched in the yard, the moonlight glinting off his gun. So two of them, at least. Probably more, a couple to cover the windows, one to stay with the car.

In the hall, the latch clicked. He heard the door pushed open, felt a chill as the cold air rushed in. One guy he could take, but if there were more? He thought of the cocaine muscle he'd seen down in Dorchester, with their MAC 10s and Uzi's.

He opened the basement door silently, edged down the stairs, pulling the door shut behind him. At the bottom of the stairs, he found the fuse box, flipped the circuit breaker to cut off the power. He wanted it dark.

It was the basement that had first attracted him to the

house. *The Bunker*, he called it. He'd spent two days bolting strips of sheet metal across the inside of the door, then installed a security bar that slid into a housing on a beam to the left of the door. He bricked up the narrow windows at the top of two walls, then spent an afternoon moving a cord of knotty pine stacked in front of the coal chute. In the old days, the coal truck would pull up in the driveway, pop a hatch at the side of the house, and dump the coal into the corner of the basement. When the owners switched to oil, they'd stuck an oil tank under the basement stairs and covered the hatch with sod. Walsh, poking around in the basement while his brother haggled with the rental agent upstairs, had noticed the chute. A few nights after he moved in, he paced off the side of the house, poking at the dirt with a kitchen knife until he'd found the hatch. He borrowed a hoe from his brother and broke the sod around the edges of the hatch. Carefully, he'd lifted the circle of sod away, then cleared the last dirt from the hatch. He snapped the rusted hinge off with a hammer, so that—by grabbing the handle— he could lift the hatch free. He replaced it, laid the piece of sod back over it, pausing to satisfy himself that a quick glance would miss it.

Returning to the basement, he'd cut a series of notches into the wooden chute, then nailed strips of wood beside the notches as steps. At the top, he strained against the hatch, managing to push it up with his shoulder and heave it aside.

Now, moving through the darkness, he found the MP5 mounted on the wall to the left of the chute, three clips taped to an old leather belt hanging from a nail. A hundred and twenty rounds, counting the clip in the magazine. He laid the shotgun on a crate, slipped the ammunition belt over his head. The concrete floor was cold, and his bare feet

ached. But the weight of the gun in his hands, the night scope illuminating the basement with a strange green light, gave him confidence. If they wanted him, they'd have to make it down the narrow stairs, find him behind the stack of crates.

Or maybe siphon some gasoline out of their car, pour it down the steps, toss in a match. He heard footsteps over his head, moving through the house. A hand tried the latch on the basement door. There was a pause, then a loud thud as the man stepped back and kicked it. The door held. After a moment, the footsteps moved away, across the kitchen, paused at the door, then out onto the back porch.

"Hey, Poncho!" The voice was faint, but he thought he could hear a flat East Boston accent. "There's nobody home."

Walsh heard a second pair of steps on the back porch. A low murmur of voices, then the sound of drawers being yanked open, their contents spilled onto the floor. The footsteps moved from room to room, as they dug through closets, tipped over furniture, shattered the tube on the television. Finally, the sounds grew sporadic, then stopped. He heard the footsteps move out onto the back porch, down the stairs into the yard. His grip on the gun eased, and he felt the tension in his neck. He arched his shoulders, wishing he'd grabbed his shoes from beside the bed.

The roar of the shotguns took him by surprise. He heard glass breaking, realized they were shooting out the windows along the back of the house. He shook his head in disbelief. This was the best D'Angelo could send?

The shooting lasted less than a minute. When it ended, he heard laughter. He imagined them walking away, joking about it, and suddenly, he was angry. He was hiding in the

176

basement from these guys? He eased up the stairs, listened at the door, then slipped the bolt and edged into the kitchen, keeping a light tension on the trigger of the MP5. The house was empty. Shards of glass and shotgun pellets were strewn across the kitchen floor, the dishes on the counter. Part of a cabinet had been blown away, and a shelf of glasses. The light fixture over the table was gone.

He went into the hall, looked through the front window. Two men were walking up the driveway toward the road. Lights had come on in a few houses nearby, but the road was deserted. For a moment, he was tempted to stick the MP5 through the broken window, cut 'em down. But they'd be useless to him dead. D'Angelo could find other killers.

He was sure now there was a car parked out on the road. He grabbed his coat from the rack, found his shoes in the bedroom. He slipped out the back door, cut across the field behind his house to the ditch. Staying low, he followed it to the trees, climbed over a wire fence, and crossed a field to the road. He came out near the bridge, a few hundred yards beyond the car. The bridge crossed a narrow stream, a path beneath it worn by generations of kids taking a short-cut to the lake. He slipped under the bridge, came up on the car in the trees on the opposite side of the road. His breath came in harsh gasps, and his leg ached. He found a spot behind a fallen tree, rested the gun in the angle of a branch.

The two men were carrying their shotguns over their shoulders, like hunters. He could hear them laughing as they walked up the road, taking their time. Strolling back to their car, enjoying their bravado. *Any moment, one of 'em will stop to light a cigarette, maybe take a piss—show how cool he is.* Relaxed, knowing the cops would have to make the drive out from town.

He put the night scope on them, taking a good look at them, like ghosts in the unearthly green light. They wore bandanas over their faces. *So much for pictures,* Walsh thought. He wondered if the surveillance guys were watching now, their telephotos scanning the trees. He smiled, imagining them crowding to the windows as the shotguns roared, cameras clicking away.

He shifted the scope over to the car. *Might as well give 'em a thrill.*

Jimmy lowered the shotgun, slipped a hand into his pocket as they approached the car, then remembered he'd left the keys. Fucking little town, you could leave an expensive car sitting by the road, nobody'd touch it. He was turning to tell Frankie, grinning, when the car exploded.

"Jesus!"

Frankie dropped onto the road, rolled into the ditch. Jimmy could hear the gun now, chattering, the high-pitched whine of the bullets coming out of the trees. The car rocked slightly, glass flying in all directions. Jimmy took two steps, jumped into the ditch, landing on top of Frankie. Bits of glass rained down on them.

Frankie shoved him off, digging in his coat pocket for shotgun shells, stuffing them into the gun.

"You see that shit?"

"Fucker coulda killed us, easy."

"What is that thing?"

"Uzi, maybe."

Frankie pumped the shotgun, got to his feet. He ran down the ditch, staying low, until he found a good spot, then popped up, leveled the gun, and fired three quick rounds, pumping fast. He ducked as a hail of bullets slammed into

the trees above his head, bringing a branch down on top of him.

"You see him?"

"I see the gun flashing. Over there, in the trees."

The gun opened up on the car again, tearing it up. Frankie pointed down the ditch.

"You go down there, we can get a cross fire on him."

"Fuck that! Let's get outta here! There's gonna be cops all over this place any minute. We gotta find another car."

Frankie thought for a moment.

"Shit!"

He got to his feet, fired twice more into the trees, dropped back. The stream of bullets skittered down the road from the car, danced above their heads for a moment. The car was burning now. They could smell burning oil, gas fumes.

"Which way?"

Jimmy pointed toward the bridge.

"Looks like a river over there. Take us back off the road."

Frankie squinted toward the bridge, nodded.

"Get around behind him, maybe."

"C'mon, Frankie! Let's go, all right? We'll come back for this guy."

The car exploded. The roar was deafening, and a fireball rose into the treetops. They ran for the bridge as a shower of metal descended on them.

Terry peered through the curtain, then unlocked the door.

"Christ," she said. "What the hell is going on over there?"

Walsh pushed past her, swung the door closed. She looked at the gun in his hands, her eyes wary.

"I need your help."

She looked at his eyes, saw the calm there. She nodded.
"How?"

"So let me get this straight."

The sheriff stood looking down the road toward Walsh's house, his thumbs hooked in his gunbelt. Behind him, a man hooked a chain to the scorched car frame, preparing to winch it up onto a flatbed. Deputies paced through the nearby trees, collecting shell casings, spent bullets, bits of metal from the car. The sheriff looked at Walsh.

"You were spending the evening at this lady's house. You woke up at the sound of gunfire, and remained in the house until you saw the first patrol car arrive."

Walsh nodded. "That's right."

"You've got no idea what all the shooting was about?"

"None."

"Why somebody shot out your windows?"

"Sorry."

"And that pair of shotguns in your house?"

Walsh shrugged.

"Maybe they dropped 'em on the way out."

The sheriff sighed, turned away. He watched the car being dragged up the truck's ramp to the sound of screeching metal.

"I guess we'll find this one's stolen, too."

"Could be."

He gave Walsh a hard stare.

"You're proving to be real uncooperative," he said. "I get your prints off those shotguns, I could pull you in on a weapons charge."

Walsh nodded, pulling his coat tighter around him. He

wished he'd thought to grab a pair of warmer pants on his way out of the house.

"You could, but you wouldn't know anything you don't know now. And, if my guess is right, you'd find the U.S. Attorney's office leaning on you awful hard."

The sheriff rubbed the back of his neck.

"It's tempting," he said. "Just to change your attitude."

Walsh was silent. The sheriff looked around at the shards of glass covering the road. He smiled thinly.

"What kind of gun would you say might do this to a car?"

Walsh looked around, pursed his lips.

"Expensive one, I'd say."

19

Riccioli paged through the surveillance photos slowly. Haggerty watched as he frowned, rubbed his jaw, then, reaching the end of the sequence, broke into a grudging smile. He shook his head.

"Seems your boy's got a sense of humor." He closed the file, slid it across the desk to her. "So you figure he was in the basement?"

"The surveillance guys were watching the gunmen, so they missed him coming out of the house. But the tapes picked him up in the kitchen after the first shots. They figure

he must have slipped out the back, come up to the road through the trees."

Riccioli picked up a pencil, made a note on a legal pad. He glanced up at her, nodded.

"I'm listening."

Haggerty consulted her notes.

"No clear ID on the gunmen, because of the masks. The car was stolen, nothing left to print. A deputy brought his hunting dogs out to the scene. He was able to track them through the woods for a mile or so, but that's all. There was a car reported stolen this morning not far from there, so it looks like they got away clean."

"Any chance Walsh is dirty on this?"

She shrugged.

"Looks like he had a clear shot at them in the pictures."

"So, what? He's got a thing about Japanese cars?"

"Maybe he wanted to slow them down. Mess their car up so they couldn't use it, then let the local cops pick them up."

"What's the sheriff think?"

"Walsh has an alibi. The woman across the road, the potter, claims he was with her all night."

Riccioli smiled.

"Breathing life unto the clay."

"So it seems."

"And the gun?"

"He probably stashed it in the woman's house. We could try for a warrant if you want, but . . ."

He waved her off.

"Just curious." He gave it some thought, rubbing two fingers along the edge of his desk. She noticed that the wood was dull in that spot. "Comments?"

She shrugged.

"Strike two."

Frankie told Jimmy Florio to meet him at the T&D about ten o'clock, and by the time he got there, ordered his coffee and eggs, Frankie had told him how they were gonna do it.

"The guy works at a store, right?"

Jimmy shrugged, chewing.

"So we both hit stores before. That's how we do it. Just walk in, pull a gun from under your coat and start shooting. Maybe hit the cash register, make it look like a holdup."

Jimmy thought about it. He shook his head.

"It's a hardware store, right?"

"A store's a store."

"They close up at, what? Five? Means we have to do it during the day. Could be a problem."

"That's the thing." Frankie was leaning forward on the table, his voice excited. "This is a little town. How many cops you think they have? First thing we do, we get to town, is stop at a pay phone, call the cops. We tell 'em there's a guy shooting up a gas station way the other side of town. They all go screaming over there, we do the guy, take off."

Jimmy held his coffee cup right up in front of his face, so the steam made him squint.

"You think we shouldn't tell Johnny till after?"

"Hey, we screwed it up. We're just finishing the job. I don't want none of those guys thinking I do things half-assed, you know? We're taking care of business here."

Jimmy wiped up the eggs with his toast.

"When you want to do this thing?"

"Now. Today."

"I can't today. I gotta go to the dentist."

Frankie looked at him.

"You gotta what?"

"I told you 'bout my tooth, Frankie. I eat something cold, it kills me. This one, here."

He stuck his finger in his mouth, way in the back.

"I had this appointment for three months."

Frankie sighed.

"Jimmy," he said. "It's January. You're gonna be eating ice cream?"

Johnny looked up at his watch. Two minutes to seven. He got up from the table, dropped his napkin on his chair. Russo looked up from his egg drop.

"Phone," Johnny said.

He walked back past the swinging door to the kitchen, the waiter nodding and smiling, went down the narrow steps to the bathrooms. A pay phone hung on the wall between the two doors. At seven, the phone rang. He picked it up.

"Yeah?"

"It's me."

"Go on."

"You got lucky."

"No kidding."

"Your boys hadn't screwed it up, you'd be sitting in a courtroom in a couple months, watching it on TV. The whole place is wired up, they got surveillance crews watching the house, a guy who tails him when he goes out. Anything happens to this guy, they get it on film."

Johnny was silent for a moment. When he spoke, his voice was quiet.

"How's he look?"

"He opens the door, sticks a gun in my face. The guy's scared."

"Good."

"But I'll tell ya, the guys you sent out there last time, you stand a better chance the guy gets hit by lightning."

"Like you said, I'm lucky."

"He wanted me to give you a message."

"What?"

"That package to his wife, he didn't like it. Happens again, he's gonna come after you."

"He's coming after *me*?"

"That's what he said."

"I love this guy! What's he think, we're playin' around here?"

"Well, on the evidence . . ."

Johnny hung up the phone. Son of a bitch! The guy's sitting out there in a fuckin' hardware store, he's making threats? For a moment, Johnny wanted to get in the car, drive out there, see this guy himself. Then, as he calmed down, he started thinking about it, seeing the threat for what it was.

An opportunity.

When he came back to the table, Russo looked up. Johnny was smiling.

Anne thought about it, but she couldn't see a problem. In fact, it was kind of amazing. How often do you win anything? Danny hanging on her sleeve as she listens to some guy at the Police Benevolent Association, assuring her that, yes, Danny's won two Celtics tickets for the Golden State game. Seats at half-court, third row. Pick up the tickets at the box office.

After she hung up, she thought to wonder why, two years after Jack left the force, they still had Danny on their list. But then, she figured, what the hell, it's a benevolent association. Let them be benevolent.

"Yes!" Danny stuck a fist in the air, pumped it, like the players did on television when the ball soared into the net. Becky giggled.

"There's still homework," Anne reminded him. "No homework, no game."

"Ah, Mom."

Anne called her mother, arranged to drop off Becky at five o'clock, then they'd head over to the Garden, leave some extra time to pick up the tickets, let Danny get a T-shirt or something.

She wished she'd watched a game on television before, hoped she could figure it out.

"So?"

Terry's boots made a crunching sound in the snow. She wore her parka, with a heavy sweater under it. Her head was bare. She stopped to look out over the lake, shivered. The late afternoon sunlight dappled the water. On the far side of the lake, a group of teenage boys were tossing rocks at the pumping station. She took Walsh's arm, and they walked on. His leg was hurting, so they went slowly. He leaned on his cane.

"You're just gonna wait for them to kill you?"

"I didn't say that."

"You sound resigned to it."

"I just said I'm not going to run from 'em."

"So you just sit here."

"I've got a life to lead."

"Working in your brother's store? Sitting over there in your little house, watching TV? That's a life?"

They were coming around the narrow end of the lake, and Walsh could see the boys on the trail now, four of them, flinging rocks at each other.

"I'm one of those people, I have to get off by myself, work things out in my head. When I'm clear on what I have to do, I do it."

"So that's what you're doing?"

"I guess."

They walked in silence. They could hear shouts from the boys echoing in the trees.

"It's better this way," he said. "I've done things I'm not proud of. Drank too much. Hurt people."

She looked at him, nodded.

"My dad was an alcoholic," she said.

"Yeah?"

"He used to come home, maybe twice a week, and beat up my mother. When I was sixteen . . ."

She looked out over the lake, her lips tight. After a minute, she shook her head.

"I never could figure him out. How he lived with what he did. He loved us, you know?"

Walsh was quiet for a moment. When he spoke, his voice was so soft she had to strain to hear it.

"Some things, you can't think about. So you drink, and when you're drinking you do other things. Then you gotta drink some more." He smiled, sadly. "In a way, I got lucky. At least I went down fast. Now, the last thing I'm thinking about is getting drunk."

They walked on, coming up on the boys. Three of them

189

were trying to push the smallest one into the water, but he was quick, and stayed on his feet.

"I'm sorry about your father," Walsh said.

"Me too. I haven't seen him in twelve years."

"How about your mother?"

"It's a package deal."

When they got up to the boys, Walsh slowed to let her go ahead, switching his cane into his left hand as he moved to the edge of the path. One of the boys, the one they'd been pushing around, turned to look at Terry as she passed.

"Yo," he said. "Nice haircut."

That got them laughing, and Terry shot him a sarcastic look. He reached out and caught her arm.

"Hey, you a man or a woman?"

Walsh got a hand on his wrist, dug his thumb into the tendons at the base of the palm, breaking his grip. He could smell beer on the kid's breath.

"Take it easy," he said, his voice quiet.

The kid jerked his hand away, rubbed at the wrist.

"What's wrong with you, man? I'm just talking to the lady." He flashed a grin at his buddies. "The *lady*."

"Jack," Terry said. "Let's go."

Walsh felt a hand grab his shoulder. A football type, with a thick neck and a letter jacket. Leaning in close, giving him a hard stare.

"You got a problem, buddy?" He'd practiced the line, getting a snarl into the last word.

Walsh shook his hand off.

"You're making a big mistake."

The little one's eyes got big, and he put a hand over his mouth, looked at his friends in panic. A comedian. The big

one moved a step closer to Walsh, put a hand on his chest, gave him a little shove.

"Yeah? I'll break your other leg, dad."

The small one darted forward, kicked at his cane. Walsh heard it crack. He looked down. It was split six inches above the tip, the wood splintered at a sharp angle. The big guy was laughing.

"Hey, looks like you're fucked, dad."

Walsh put his foot on the tip and snapped it off. Then he swung the cane in a sharp arc, driving it into the big kid's stomach. He doubled over, gasping. Walsh shifted his weight, turning, and drove an elbow into the base of the small one's jaw. The kid stumbled over some rocks, went down. Walsh turned, saw the big one start to straighten. The cane swished in his hand, whistling down on the back of his shoulders, knocking him to the ground.

He turned to the other two, the cane raised.

"Well?"

"Jesus! You trying to kill 'em?"

"You want a turn?"

They backed away. Walsh turned and flung the cane into the trees. He cursed under his breath, angry at himself for losing his cool. He gestured to the big kid, on his knees now, one hand holding his neck, where the edge of the cane had raised a welt. There were tears on his face.

"Get him out of here."

He limped up the path to Terry, took her arm, and moved her away. They walked in silence, taking the path back to the road. She didn't look at him.

"I'm sorry," he said, finally. "It got away from me."

She kept her eyes on the ground.

"It's not worth that. I hear it a lot."

"And you don't get angry?"

"At what? Stupidity? I'd be angry all the time."

The sun was low, and the shadows of the pines fell across the path. He realized that she was looking at him.

"It comes easy to you, doesn't it? What you did back there. You're a violent man."

He didn't answer. As they reached the road, he glanced back, saw the tail emerging from the trees. He wondered if he'd passed the kids on the trail.

"It scares me," Terry said.

He nodded. It scared him too. He thought about another kid, a lifetime ago, stretched out on the floor of an empty apartment, his eyes fixed on the ceiling.

His leg ached.

"I'll walk you home."

The phone rang as they were headed out the door. Anne hesitated, then picked it up.

"Anne? It's Tony Keenan."

"Tony." Danny was standing beside the door in his Celtics T-shirt, his coat halfway zipped. He gave her a look.

"C'mon!"

She waved him out to the car, shifted Becky on her hip.

"I can't talk, Tony. We're headed out the door."

"Okay. I just wanted to let you know that I saw Jack."

"You did?"

"I showed him the glasses. He figured same as me, a prank. Nothing to worry about. But he said to tell you that you were right to ask."

"I'm glad he approves." Her voice was icy. "Can we talk another time, Tony?"

"Any time you want."

"I'll call you," she told him, wondering as she hung up if it was true. Maybe. In a while.

She carried Becky out to the car, strapped her into the car seat. Danny fidgeted in the front seat.

"We're gonna be late," he complained.

"There's plenty of time," she said. "We just have to drop Becky on the way to the highway, and then it's ten minutes into the city. Twenty, if we hit traffic. We'll be the first ones there."

He scowled at her. She sighed. How could something he wanted so badly make him so unhappy? He seemed to think it wasn't real, like he couldn't trust her to make it happen. Maybe if his father were here . . .

She pushed the thought aside.

"Buckle up," she told him, backing out of the drive.

At the box office, the girl handed Anne an envelope marked "Walsh."

"These are already paid for," the girl said. "Take a left, down to the season-ticketholder's gate. You're in the third row, center court. Great seats."

Anne took the envelope, wondering why the PBA had to pay for the tickets. Most places around the city, they got donations. Businessmen were only too happy to make a big show of their generosity, hoping for a bit more protection in return. Even the crooks had PBA stickers on their cars, trying to avoid parking tickets.

She looked down at the envelope in her hand. For a moment, she thought of the envelope with the glasses—"Jack Walsh, Free Man."

Danny was tugging at her hand.

"Come on!"

He pulled her toward a souvenir stand, his eye on a full-size poster of Larry Bird. *What an ugly man,* Anne thought as she reached for her wallet.

They found their seats, settled in. The stadium was filling up, the crowd cheering as the teams came out for warm-up, tossing dozens of balls at the baskets, running a few passes. The players paid no attention to the noise, caught up in the casual grace of their own bodies. Anne watched them, fascinated. Getting rich by throwing a ball at a hoop.

They were in the middle of a row, and the seats were tight, but Danny didn't seem to notice. He watched with his mouth open as Bird flicked ball after ball into the net. Anne tried to find a comfortable place for her knees. Behind them, two men pushed their way along the row. She leaned forward to let them pass, but they settled into the seats directly behind her.

When the players drifted out, she watched a television news crew setting up at one end of the court, the sportscaster grinning under the bright lights. A photographer came along the bench, stood with his back to them for a moment, looking out at the empty court. Then he turned, looked up at them. He smiled at her, raised his camera, snapped a shot. He gave a little wave, wandered away.

An announcer came on, working the crowd up for the introduction of the teams. Danny gripped her arm, rigid with excitement. Anne settled back.

Funny how the guy chose them to photograph in the crowd. She raised a hand to her hair. Smiling at her.

20

The deputy pulled up in the loading zone about four-thirty, sitting in his car for a few moments, staring in at Jack, who ignored him, going back to the receipts spread on the counter. For three days, they'd been driving up, sitting there maybe forty minutes, one of them using the time to eat his lunch. Then they'd start up, make a U-turn across both lanes, and take off.

Only this time, Jack caught movement from the corner of his eye. He looked up to see the deputy getting out of the car, taking a moment to put on his hat, and walk around the

car toward the door. The bell rang as he came in, headed for the counter.

Jack heard Larry open the door to his office. *Fine, let him handle it.* He went back to his receipts, letting them talk over him.

"Can I help you, Dave?"

"Larry. How you?"

"I'm good. What's up?"

"Sheriff wants to have a talk with your brother. Hope it won't leave you short."

Larry glanced up at the official Ace wall clock over the counter, a picture of John Madden smiling, waving at you, on the face.

"Well, it's just about closing. I guess I can spare him."

He laughed, laid a hand on Jack's shoulder. Jack looked up at him, and he pulled it off, quick.

Jack left the receipts on the counter, followed the deputy out to the car.

"I know you."

The deputy pulled out into traffic, glanced up at him in the rearview.

"I was two years behind you out at the high school."

"You ran track."

"Yeah, the four-forty. You were a miler, right?"

"Didn't have the kick for the shorter stuff."

"You still run?"

"Used to, before I hurt my leg. Even ran the Boston Marathon once."

"Yeah?"

"Finished under three hours."

The deputy nodded, turning up past the square toward the courthouse.

"I were you," he said, "I'd be running right now."

Larry was getting ready to lock the door when they pulled up out front, two guys in a battered green Ford. One of them jumped out, grabbed the door and yanked it open, grinning at Larry standing there with the key out.

"We're closing up," he said.

The other guy got out slowly, came around the car, flipping the keys on his finger.

"Ah, man." The one at the door threw up his hands. "I got a burst pipe out at the house. I don't get a pipe wrench, my wife'll kill me. Just take a second."

Larry scowled, glanced up at the clock. Then he stepped back. It was a sale.

"Hurry up," he said and went back to the counter.

The first one, dark, with his hair cut short, trotted back toward the plumbing supplies, while the other waited by the door. But then, they were both dark, dressed nice, wearing sport jackets, good pants. Shoes shined. Larry looked again, frowned. Odd, they weren't wet.

The guy was coming up aisle three, carrying a wrench. Larry put the key in the register, rang in his code. When he looked up, the guy was at the counter, holding out the wrench. He reached out to take it from the guy.

The wrench came across his knuckles, flicking his hand away. Larry gasped, looked up. It wasn't a wrench. The guy was grinning at him.

"You Walsh?"

Larry nodded. His hand was bleeding. He raised it to his mouth.

197

"This is for Vinnie," the guy said.

Then he raised the gun and shot him.

The radio squawked.

The car lurched over to the curb. The deputy jumped out, opened the back door.

"Change of plan," he said. "You're walking."

"What's going on?"

"Out! You walk on up the street and see the sheriff. You know where he is, right?"

He jumped back into the car without waiting for an answer, pulled a U-turn, smoking his tires.

Frankie bent over the guy, sprawled across the floor behind the counter, got the knife under his ear and flicked his wrist. Blood spurted over the back of his hand.

"Ah, shit."

He looked around for something to wipe his hand on, then wiped it on the guy's pants. Jimmy was leaning over the counter, watching him.

"Frankie."

"What?"

"The guy Johnny told you about, what'd you say his name was?"

Frankie looked down at the pencil holder in the guy's shirt pocket: *Hi! My name is Larry.*

"Walsh," he said.

"You get his first name?"

Frankie shrugged. Jimmy rubbed his chin, looked at him.

"Any chance it was Larry?"

21

The body was on a metal table in the back room of Herrick's Funeral Home. Jack saw three entrance wounds in the chest, bunched close together. Three quick shots. One ear was missing.

The sheriff was watching his face. Behind him, the coroner was standing over a tray of surgical instruments, pulling on a pair of latex gloves.

"That's my brother."

The sheriff nodded.

"I'm sorry. We all knew Larry. It's a formality, we have to do it."

Walsh didn't say anything. He looked down at the body. Thinking about the deputy coming into the store, walking toward the counter, hitching his gun belt, Larry coming out of his office, nodding. *I guess I can spare him.* The deputy dropped him by the side of the road, letting him walk up the block to the sheriff's office to find out from the dispatcher that everyone was out at a shooting. Sitting there in a green plastic bucket chair almost an hour before the Sheriff comes back, tells him to come on out for a ride, he's got something he's gotta ask him to look at. Thinking now about the shotgun he carried home in a garbage bag the night before, wondering if Larry had reached for it, his fingers touching the empty clips under the counter as the killer raised his gun.

No, Larry would have reached for the phone, running his finger down the pad, looking for the number of the sheriff's office as the guy shot him.

"Come on, Jack." The sheriff took his arm. "Time we had that talk."

"So, don't tell him."

Frankie nodded. They were coming into Cambridge on Highway 2, heading past the Alewife T station and up over a railroad bridge toward Boston. Driving Jimmy's car now, the stolen Ford dumped back in the woods outside the town, left for the cops, give them something to do.

"I mean," Jimmy was saying, "it's the wrong guy, we just shrug, you know? Hey, weird coincidence. Too bad it wasn't his brother. Turns out it was the right guy, you tell him, give him the ear."

"Swing by my apartment," Frankie said. "I got it written down somewhere."

* * *

200

Walsh sat at a long, oak conference table in the courthouse, looking out the window at the falling snow as the sheriff briefed Kate Haggerty, the woman from the U.S. Attorney's office, and a small, balding man, who introduced himself as Jim Rickman, the local district attorney.

"The car's clean," the sheriff told them, consulting a yellow legal pad on the table. "Same deal as last time. Stolen in the metro Boston area. No prints. Same thing in the store. Lots of prints on the counter, but nothing clean enough to get an ID. Ballistics gave us a preliminary. It's a .38, and they got a nice pattern on the bullet, so if we ever find the gun, it should be easy to match."

"So what you're saying," the D.A. interrupted, "is we have no physical evidence."

"That's about the size of it."

"Witnesses?"

"A couple who saw the car pull up, but nothing you'd call solid."

Haggerty cleared her throat.

"Actually, there is a witness," she said.

The sheriff frowned, flipped through his notes.

"I don't see any report of . . ."

"Your people didn't interview him," Haggerty said. "He's a federal law enforcement officer, on loan to my office from the DEA. He was assigned to surveillance of Mr. Walsh."

She glanced at Walsh. Their eyes met, and she looked away. The sheriff glared at her.

"You want to explain why I wasn't told about this?"

"It was strictly need-to-know. I didn't even know until a few days ago. We have a Title 3 wire surveillance on the crime scene, as well, but . . ."

"So you got it on tape?"

"Well, no. When our man saw Mr. Walsh leave the store in your car, he assumed that your people would drive him home, so he started shutting down for the day. He was changing the tape reels when the suspects drove up."

"He *assumed* he could shut down?" The sheriff was enjoying this, drawing the word out with a slight smile.

"However," she went on, staring back at him, "he did get a look at the driver. We've had him looking at the books most of the night. He's made a tentative identification."

"Who?"

They all turned to look at Walsh as he spoke. Haggerty hesitated. She glanced at the D.A., who shrugged.

"His name's Jimmy Florio," she said. "He's an associate of Frankie Defeo."

"And who's that?"

She looked at him, surprised by how little he knew of the events that were shaping his life.

"D'Angelo's son-in-law. Or will be."

Walsh leaned forward, his knuckles white against the edge of the table.

"So you've got him."

Hoping. Haggerty shook her head.

"I wish it were that easy. Without some hard physical evidence, we don't have much of a case. We could pull the kid in, try to scare him, see if he'll roll. But he's been through it before, got an acquittal on auto theft a couple years back. He's gonna sit tight, make his name with the family. He'll figure out pretty soon that if he goes to trial, we've got a driver but no killer. His lawyer lays into our witness on cross—how far away were you, did you see the crime take place, all that stuff—it just won't fly. The kid'll know he's gonna walk."

Walsh looked down at the table.

"You've been running this surveillance how long?"

"I haven't run anything."

"Your people, then."

"Since you got out."

He sat back, his fingers tapping lightly.

"So my brother's dead, the deputy out on the highway, and we've still got nothing. That a fair appraisal?"

"It's fair to say that, yes."

He was silent for a moment.

"So, what? We wait for them to take their next shot? See if they kill somebody else?"

Haggerty closed her file, clipped her pen to the top of the folder. She looked up at him.

"That's what I asked you here to discuss."

Carlos Diaz lay on a bed in Room 721 of the Holiday Inn on Cambridge Street, watching a television that flickered without sound. Arturo, his bodyguard, sat by the window smoking, his feet propped up on a chair. A nine-millimeter automatic lay on the table beside his arm.

The phone rang. Diaz picked it up, listened for a moment. "Send him up."

He hung up, lay back on the bed, his forearm across his eyes. When the knock came, Arturo heaved himself out of his chair, picked up the gun and crossed the room. He opened the door a crack, the gun held flat against the door jamb. Then he nodded, stepped back, holding the door open. D'Angelo stepped past him, glanced over at Diaz, motionless on the bed. He turned to Arturo, raised an eyebrow.

"He alive?"

Diaz sighed, heaved himself up on one elbow.

"Johnny," he said. His words were heavily accented. He gestured toward the chair. "Please, come in."

Johnny glanced at Arturo. Diaz gave a flick of his fingers, and Arturo stepped out, closing the door behind him. Johnny crossed to the television. *I Dream of Jeannie.* He turned the sound up, settled into his chair.

"What'sa matter," he said. "You're not sleeping good?"

Diaz patted his broad belly.

"My digestion is poor. The doctors tell me I must eat less." He shrugged. "I get hungry. I eat. I suffer."

Johnny nodded. His own stomach had been acting up lately, forcing him to cut back on the rich foods he loved.

"You know you got a tail?"

"He's down in the lobby, yes?"

"Blond guy, looks like a football player."

"One of my friends at the DEA. He thinks I come to visit a woman. We hire a prostitute to come in with us. Perhaps, when we are done . . ." He smiled. "Tell me, please, how did you know?"

"Tommy Russo watched you come in."

"Of course."

Johnny looked over at the television. The blond girl with the ponytail, wearing that little harem outfit, disappeared in a cloud of purple smoke. The cloud spun into the air and was sucked into a bottle. A guy in a uniform popped a cork in the bottle.

"I always loved this show," he said. "Guy keeps a woman in a bottle. Friday night, maybe he invites his friends over, puts the bottle in the middle of the table. Have some."

Diaz sat up, swung his legs off the side of the bed. He rubbed his face with one broad hand.

"My friend," he said. "Three of my people are dead. A

large quantity of merchandise has been lost. The police, they say we are fighting among ourselves. Are we fighting, Johnny?"

"I got no argument with you."

"That's what I tell myself. I think, Johnny, he knows his business. What does he gain by killing my couriers, or my cousin, Sagria. Johnny does not like this kind of business, this killing, shooting in the eyes. This is not Johnny."

Johnny was silent, watching on the television as the guy in uniform dangled from a window, his feet kicking.

"But then, I ask myself, who? This man who kills my people, does he work alone? Or does someone help him?"

"He's a cop," Johnny said. "He thinks he's got a right."

"And yet, it was you who suggested we might use this man."

Johnny sat back, smoothed his tie.

"Guy like him, he's never more than a disposable asset. You follow me? He's got something you want, okay. But you gotta remember what he is, always."

Diaz smiled.

"You are telling me, Johnny, that you have no more interest in this asset?"

"Let's say I understand your distress."

"You would have no objection if I took measures . . . How shall I say? To minimize my exposure?"

Johnny got up, walked to the mirror. He ran the back of his hand over his chin.

"We're done here, I'm gonna get a shave."

"Do my words offend you, Johnny?"

"Nah," he said. "But look at it this way. You fly up here from Miami to take care of a problem. When it's fixed, you

fly back. I gotta live here, and this guy has my prints all over him. You take him out, the cops come looking for me."

Diaz nodded, thoughtful.

"A difficult problem."

Johnny turned, smiled at him.

"Trust me," he said. "It's under control."

22

"What's in it for me?"

Walsh had hung back all day, listening to her, thinking his own thoughts. Finally, as the setting sun cut through the snow sky, setting the burnished wood of the conference table afire, she offered to buy him dinner. They rode over to Brook's Steak House in her car, asked for a table in a corner. Walsh leaned forward, blew out the candle on their table.

Sitting over their menus, she told him she needed an answer to take back to Boston. If he had a question, now was

the time to ask it. And, sure enough, he hit her with the tough one.

"I mean," he went on, "you want to put a wire on me, send me in there so D'Angelo gets fired up, starts to act unruly. That's fine for you. You get a gunshot, it makes your case. But I'm still dead."

"We wouldn't let it get that far."

He looked skeptical.

"How can you tell, sitting out in a van in the street some-place, when it's coming? My experience, these things get moving, they pick up speed pretty quick."

"All I can say is that we've done this before. We don't need a gunshot, only an expression of intent. You meet him in a public place. If they make an explicit threat, or take any steps to isolate you, we got conspiracy and kidnapping. That ought to do it." She leaned forward, her voice growing softer. "As for what's in it for you, I can't make any prom-ises. But I've been looking back at the records on your part-ner's death. On the basis of the information you provided, I think I can get authorization to reopen the investigation."

He thought about it. The waitress came for their order. They both ordered fish, broiled dry. Two salads, spring wa-ter. A smile passed between them.

"Clean living," Walsh said.

"I need an answer."

Walsh glanced around at the other diners, chatting over their meals. Maybe they worry about money, their jobs, the tension in their marriage. One of them, looking over at him sitting here with Haggerty, might think he was just a guy having dinner with a beautiful woman.

A beautiful woman with a tough mind. He tried to imag-ine her listening to the tape, in a room full of lawyers, taking

care not to flinch at the sound of the gunshots. Looking over the pictures, him sprawled in a gutter, blood leaking out of his nose. Maybe they'd get it on video, crowding around a television set to watch the gun come up, the muzzle flash, his head jerk back. She would be professional about it, he thought. Nothing showing in her face. Just examining the evidence.

"I'll have to sleep on it," he told her.

"I've seen the reports. You don't sleep well."

He looked at her.

"There anything those reports don't tell you?"

"Not much."

He nodded, trying to imagine how he must look to this woman, with her high-powered job, her tailored clothes, her apartment in the city. A man who spends his nights pacing the floors in a tattered bathrobe, watching old movies on television, getting down on the floor to strain his muscles until he collapsed. A man at the end of his road. She might wonder what he had to lose.

"What happens to the store," she asked him.

"I called Larry's wife. She takes the kids down to Florida to stay with her mother in the winter. She's flying back to talk to the lawyers. You want my guess, she'll sell it, move back down there. She never liked the cold up here."

"So you're out of work."

He smiled.

"I'd say that's the least of my worries."

He sat back as the waitress brought their salads, watched Haggerty spoon a tiny amount of dressing onto the edge of her plate. She was a slow eater, taking the smallest of bites onto her fork, chewing pensively.

"People like you drove me crazy when I was a cop," he

told her. "When you're on duty, you have to eat fast. It gets to be a habit. Then you meet a woman, you take her out to dinner, you're through with your meal and she's still working on her salad."

She laughed.

"In law school, I studied all the time. On weekends, I used to make these big meals—salad, vegetable, my own bread. Not because I loved to cook, but just to get away from the books. Then I'd sit down at the table, the book would be lying there next to my plate. So you read while you eat, right? I'd make myself cover so much material with each bite. Read a little, take a bite. Like a reward. It drove my boyfriend crazy, too."

Walsh kept his eyes on his salad.

"What's your boyfriend do?"

"Now? He's a tax accountant out in Los Angeles. When I knew him, he was a social worker."

"That's a change."

"I thought so, too."

They ate in silence for a moment. Then, not looking up, she said:

"So how about you?"

"What?"

"Any habits that annoy your loved ones?"

He looked up at her.

"You mean besides fucking up their lives?"

It was late when she drove him home. He made her let him out on the road, near the end of his drive.

"It gets icy," he told her. He pointed to a gravel turn-out just beyond the drive. "Best thing is to pull up right there."

She watched as he limped up the drive to the dark house.

210

He walked slowly, she noticed, his head turning from side to side. Scanning for movement. Like you'd see in the old news clips of soldiers on patrol in Vietnam. As he stepped onto the porch, she put the car in gear, then hesitated as she saw him bend, pick something up off the top step. He stood there, looking at it, his back to her.

A perfect target, she thought. After two minutes, she put the Volvo in reverse, backed onto the road, the gears whining as she swung past the drive. She shifted into first and turned in. As she drove up to the house, he turned to look at her, his face calm in the headlights.

He stepped down off the porch, walked over to her window, leaned in.

"I'll do it," he said.

She looked down at his hands. He was holding an envelope, torn open. She reached out, took it from his hand. She flicked on the dome light.

The envelope had no address. Inside, there was a photograph—two men in stadium seats glaring at the camera; in the row below them, a woman and young boy. She looked up at him.

He reached in, laid his finger on the woman.

"That's Anne. This is Danny with her, my son."

His finger moved up to the two men.

"I don't know the guy on the left. But this one, in the fancy suit, that's . . ."

She nodded.

"I know who it is."

211

23

"D'Angelo has season tickets."

Riccioli looked across his desk at Walsh, taking his measure. His coat and tie were wrinkled, but his face was still, showing nothing.

"Four seats, third and fourth rows, center court. We've known about it for some time. He uses them, or he gives them to business associates, guys he wants to reward, kids in the neighborhood. It's good public relations."

He glanced down at the photograph.

"I can see why you view this as a threat."

Haggerty shifted in her seat. She sensed hostility in Walsh's silence. Sitting next to him, she could see Riccioli as he did. He seemed too smooth, a politician in his Armani suit and muted tie, every hair in place. For a moment, she imagined how he might have looked to a cop, appearing on the nightly news with the mayor to claim credit for a massive drug bust.

"The key problem," Riccioli went on, "is entrapment. If you taunt him or in any way incite him to . . ."

Walsh leaned forward, laid one finger on the corner of the desk.

"Wait a minute," he said.

Riccioli paused, looking at him.

"Entrapment, that's *your* problem. The way I see it, the key problem is I walk in there, the guy pulls out a gun and kills me. That's the *key problem.*"

Haggerty winced. She wondered for a moment if she should interrupt, but Riccioli nodded, smiled.

"Of course," he said smoothly. "My apologies. I'm used to thinking about operations only from a legal standpoint. It's an old habit."

"And I'm used to thinking about getting my ass shot off." Walsh sat back, tugged at his jacket. It buckled slightly across the back of his broad shoulders, Haggerty noticed. "It's a new habit. You might even call it a way of life."

Riccioli smiled some more.

"You choose your backup," he said expansively. "Anyone. Your own guys, feds, whatever. You set the terms. When and where, how you make the approach, how long you want to talk before you break it off. Nobody will fault you for getting out if it gets tight. You let us worry about the tapes."

"Frankly," Walsh said, "that was my intention."

"And that's fine. I just want to make sure you know, for your own information, the kind of thing that could blow the case."

"You really think I'm gonna *taunt* the guy?"

"No, of course not." Riccioli picked up the photograph, tossed it across the desk. "But I look at this, I think you might want to threaten him."

Walsh was silent for a moment, then he smiled.

"I might."

Haggerty gave a sigh. The tension eased, as Riccioli sat back in his leather chair, rocking slightly.

"My guess, looking at this picture," he said, "is that's what he has in mind. Turn it around on you. Get you to make a threat against him, so that when he kills you, he can play it as self-defense. Make you out as some kind of nut who kills his kid and then goes after him. If he's clever, he might plant some dirt on you, make it look like you're on the payroll. Everybody hates a crooked cop."

"Wonderful."

Riccioli leaned back, propped his feet on the edge of his desk. Italian loafers, Haggerty noted, with nylon socks.

"Johnny's a smart man," she said, leaning forward. "It would be a mistake not to foresee some surprises here. If he's expecting Jack—ah, Mr. Walsh—then it won't seem quite as much a setup. If he showed up out of nowhere, Johnny'd smell a wire in a second."

"You might be right," Riccioli conceded, giving her a hard look. *Jack?*

"There's something that confuses me," Walsh said.

"Shoot."

"Well, why now?"

"I'm sorry?"

"This picture, it seems kind of an afterthought. They just killed my brother, they don't need to convince me to come after 'em."

Riccioli glanced over at Haggerty, then remembered she had been out of the office for two days. No chance to look at the transcripts. He chose his words with care.

"I've been looking at the surveillance reports for the last couple days. It's my suspicion—and it's only a suspicion, mind you—that D'Angelo didn't authorize this last attempt. Defeo's been keeping out of sight. He called the daughter, told her he has the flu. Otherwise, there's no sense of urgency, no crisis talk. Nothing like you'd expect to get after a botched hit. Even when they're talking for the tape, you can usually pick up if they're nervous."

He gave a thin smile.

"I think our friend Johnny may have a loose cannon on his hands."

Walsh frowned, shook his head.

"I find that hard to believe."

"It might explain the timing," Haggerty commented. "Someone's not with the program."

"If we assume that Defeo screwed it up," Riccioli added. "Killing that deputy, for example. Then it begins to add up. He goes out there trying to win back the old man's respect, and meantime Johnny's not telling him about the real plan because he's a fuckup."

He glanced over at Haggerty.

"Excuse me."

She nodded.

"Defeo's the type," he went on. "We've been hearing about him for a while now, but his record's pretty clean. His

216

only arrest was for beating up a kid outside a bar up in Revere. He took a baseball bat to the kid's head." Riccioli grinned. "I hear some guys down at the D.A.'s office wanted to call it assault with intent to distribute."

Walsh sat back, ran a hand across his face.

"All right. Where does this leave me?"

The impatience was back in his voice. Try listening to someone tell you your brother's dead because of a screwup, Haggerty thought. And then, from nowhere, came the certainty: *they weren't close.* She glanced over at him, tried to imagine his emotions.

"Well," Riccioli was saying, "pretty much where we started. If you're willing to take the risk, I think we've got a shot."

"So to speak."

Riccioli smiled.

"Sorry. My point is, if you agree . . ."

"I've already told her I'd do it."

"All right, then. Haggerty will take you down to the surveillance boys, get you fitted up for a wire. They'll need some time to work up the best rig. Then you come back up here, and we talk about where and when."

Walsh nodded, getting up. Riccioli rose, came around the desk. He put his hand out.

"My pleasure, Mr. Walsh."

Walsh smiled.

"I think that's fair."

Walsh chose a spot mike stitched into the collar of a sport shirt. He brushed aside the technician's suggestion of a crotch rig.

"What I want," he told the guy, "is for a guy who's gonna

217

get right in my face, tell me what he thinks. I meet a guy who wants to talk to my crotch, I'll let you know."

Haggerty tried not to smile.

"I worked narco. First thing a guy does if he gets suspicious is grab your balls. A gun or a wire, that's where most people hide it."

The technician shrugged, laid the tiny microphone aside.

"I'll need one of your shirts," he said. "You be wearing body armor?"

Walsh hesitated, then shook his head.

"Too obvious."

"We got some new stuff that's pretty thin."

Walsh glanced over at Haggerty. She shrugged. He thought about it for a moment, then shook his head.

"This guy, he's gonna be looking for it."

"They'll probably go for a head shot, anyway," the technician said. He made a note. "Weapons?"

Walsh smiled.

"Just the wire."

On the elevator, Haggerty turned to him.

"You don't have a lot of faith in this, do you?"

Walsh watched the numbers lighting up above the door.

"D'Angelo's a smart guy," he said. "It's too easy, I just show up. He's gonna be looking for a wire."

"Then why are you doing it?"

He shrugged.

"Can't think of anything else."

The doors opened, and a cluster of secretaries got on. They rode in silence to their floor.

"You want a cup of coffee or something," Haggerty asked as they got off. "I keep a pot in my office."

"Riccioli waiting for us?"

"I'd like to talk to you alone first."

"Then I'll take that coffee."

They walked down the narrow hall, past the secretaries' stations to a row of small offices. She opened her door, flicked on the light, watched him take in the Chagall poster, the plants, the Navajo blanket on her chair.

"You live here, right?"

"Just about."

"Got a little apartment, you go there to sleep."

"Please. It's too depressing."

She crossed to the desk, pulled a bag of coffee out of a drawer, spooned some into a paper filter.

"So why do you do it?"

She poured water into the pot from a plastic jug.

"I ask myself that a lot lately," she said. "What else should I do? Get a job at a big firm, work the same hours for more money? Get married and have kids?"

He settled into the chair across from her.

"No dreams?"

She looked at him, amused.

"You really want to hear about *me*?"

He nodded, smiled. She dropped into her chair, kicked off her shoes, scratching the soles of her feet against the edge of a bottom drawer.

"I wanted to do environmental work. Spend a couple years in a firm, then do legal work for the Sierra Club. Live in Denver or Seattle, spend a lot of time outside. But in law school, I got interested in some constitutional issues surrounding RICO. You know, what's it mean to convict a guy for talking to somebody else. That kind of stuff. Wrote an article about the Commissions case. So I ended up in crimi-

219

nal work, listening to tapes of guys like D'Angelo talking to their buddies." She smiled. "What about you? Why'd you become a cop?"

"My dad was a cop. My uncle. It's sort of in the genes."

"I've never understood that."

"What?"

"How a job like that, no regular hours, bad food, low pay, can run in a family. Seems like the kids would want to do anything but be a cop."

Walsh shrugged.

"You gotta live it, that's all I can say. You're a kid, your dad comes home in his uniform, it's like he's *special*. A hero, even if all you see him do is sit in front of the TV with a beer. You figure he's seen it all. Out catching the bad guys, like on TV. Then you get on the job yourself, you find out your dad's been sitting behind a desk the last ten years, the whole squad knows he keeps a bottle in his drawer. Some hero. By that time, it's too late. You don't know anything else, all your friends are cops, and you're still dreaming you'll do it right, be a hero for real."

"Is that why you went into narco? To be a hero?"

He laughed.

"You remember those TV shows back in the seventies? What's that guy's name? Beretta. He lives in a rathole apartment with a parrot, but when he's on the street, he's a master of disguise. Dresses up like a preacher, a bum, a Chinese guy. That was gonna be me. Make it a game, catching 'em with their pants down. Make the buy, then go busting into their house like Superman. That, to me, was real cop."

"But it went bad."

He looked over at the Chagall. Haggerty followed his

eyes. Some nights, the angels soared, airy and delicate, through Haggerty's dreams.

"You have to trust your partners," he said. "You get like brothers, so you know what they're thinking before they do. You know what they want, what scares them. You know how they're weak. And, the way they treat you, you know a couple of those things about yourself. It's like looking in a mirror, you know?"

She nodded.

"Working undercover, it's weird, because you start to see how close it is between cops and the bad guys. Not the street dealers so much, that's mostly project kids. But I got Mafia guys living in my neighborhood, up in Medford. It's like, the only difference in those neighborhoods is if you're Irish you become a cop, and if you're Italian you get a choice."

That made her laugh, her eyes crinkling up. He stretched his leg out, rubbed at the knee.

"Looking at guys like D'Angelo, it makes you think mob guys are rich. But in the whole family, there's maybe two or three guys making the big money. The rest of 'em, they live like cops. Keep the same hours, eat the bad food, they even talk the same. Hell, a couple years back we busted a guy, he's a rising star in the family. We stop him in his car, open the trunk, he's got a body in there, all shot up. He's taking it to dump it. I'm looking at this corpse, I glance down, he's got a "Support Your Local Police" sticker on his car. I figure it's a joke, you know? The guy's being funny. But he says no, he's all for the cops, wants to see us get tough on the spics and the niggers, keep 'em in their place. He's saying all this while we're putting the cuffs on."

"You hear the same thing on the tapes," Haggerty said. "D'Angelo votes Republican."

"Riccioli know that?"

Haggerty smiled, but she said nothing.

"Anyway," Walsh went on. "In narco, you're out there with the crazies. The Uzi guys. And after a while, you start to realize that half their customers are these white guys in BMWs stopping by on their way home from the office. Who'm I risking my life to protect here?"

"How about the other half?"

"That's why this war on drugs won't ever be more than a publicity stunt. The white guys, they don't want our help. The other half is black kids, got no hope, just enough cash for a piece of the rock. Who cares?"

"I do."

He looked at her, silent. Then he leaned forward, put both hands on her desk, palms down. His voice was tired.

"I did too."

"So what happened?"

He sat back, rubbed at his eyes with the back of his hand.

"You know what happened."

"I heard some vague hints. I checked the files, and that gave me some vague ideas. I'm asking you now, what happened?"

He nodded toward the shelf to her left.

"Coffee's done."

He thought about it while she got the coffee, watching her dump two spoons of Cremora in her cup before she poured.

"How can you stand that stuff?"

"You get used to it, working late. No place to get milk after five."

She handed him a cup, black.

222

"Tell me something," she said as she sat down, stirring with the end of a pencil. "What do you have to lose talking to me?"

"Maybe I've got enough enemies."

"Or maybe just the wrong ones."

He smiled.

"That sounds good," he said. "What's it mean?"

"This thing with D'Angelo was bad luck . . ."

He raised one hand, stopping her.

"No excuses. It was my fuckup."

She paused, nodded.

"Okay. But it started someplace else. If you walk out of this mess, you're just back where you were before the accident. Is that where you want to end up?"

He sipped his coffee, made a face.

"What is this stuff?"

"New Orleans French Roast. Too strong?"

"Bitter."

"It's the chicory. I should've warned you. My boyfriend used to drink it. I got used to it."

"Must've been some boyfriend."

She smiled, shook her head sadly. Then, after a moment:

"You haven't answered my question."

He put the cup down, gazed down at his leg. He took a deep breath, let it out slow.

"Guy that brought me into narco was this lieutenant, Tony Keenan . . ."

As he told her, he could see the rough wood of the bar table, the blue light from the Sam Adams beer sign flashing in his glass. Keenan leaning across the table, asking him if he was happy in Arson, did he like going home with his

clothes stinking of smoke, so his wife wanted to toss 'em out? Had he ever thought he might want to see some more action in the street, get in there where it was flying?

And he had listened, sipping at his beer, thinking about how Anne did hate the smell, but hated the idea of him getting shot even more. Blood, she would say, was harder to wash out than smoke. He tried to imagine himself a few years down the road, still dragging out to fires in the middle of the night, walking around in some dripping ruin in sub-zero cold, wondering what they kept in this warehouse to make it stink so bad, or just sitting at his desk in the squad room with a dictionary, trying to figure out how to spell some of those twelve-syllable chemicals for his reports.

He looked at Keenan, with his expensive suit, the way he had to keep looking around to see who was calling out his name in the crowded bar, raising his hand to wave lazily at some cop who wanted to buy him a beer. He thought about his father, spending twelve years squeezing into his uniform every morning to sit behind a desk, getting fat. Retiring to some little town to run a store. He lifted his glass, watched the blue light fill it. Raising it to his lips, he drank from the light.

The next morning, he applied for a transfer. With Keenan's assent, it went through in a few weeks. That night, lying beside Anne, his voice shook with excitement as he told her.

"This is what I joined the force to do," he said. "Not to walk around a burnt-out building, trying to figure out what happened, but to get right in there and stop it. You go in, catch the guys in the act, send 'em to jail. If they get off, you go catch 'em again. Get right in their faces, show 'em that if they want to screw up the city, they gotta get by you first."

Anne listened in silence, an arm draped across her eyes. It was summer, and she slept in a Police Athletic Association T-shirt she'd found in his closet. He pulled her to him, slipping an arm under the shirt to feel her damp skin. She looked into his eyes.

"You really want to do this, don't you?"

He smiled. He lifted the T-shirt, his mouth finding her breasts.

A week later, he moved his gear down two flights of stairs to an empty locker near the narco squadroom. Keenan pointed him toward a desk.

"There's a supply form in the drawer," he told him. "But don't get too fancy. You won't spend much time here."

The rest of the squad trailed in, heading for the coffee machine before stopping by his desk, shifting the cup to grip his hand. The cups steamed. Their hands were hot.

"So Keenan approached you?"

He paused, looking over at Haggerty. For a moment, he had trouble shaking the feeling of having been woken abruptly from a dream.

"That's right."

"Was that usual?"

"Tony picked his own team. He got away with it because he got results."

Haggerty regarded him. Her fingers toyed with a frayed edge of the blanket on her chair.

"So why you?"

Walsh smiled, shook his head.

"Had you worked together before?"

"We knew each other socially."

"What? You went to bars?"

"Something like that."

"Is that the usual basis for this kind of decision?"

He frowned, shifted in his chair.

"I guess you'd call it a compatibility question. You got to understand, when you're out there on the street, you have to trust your partners all the way. You can't get that from a résumé. So you hang out with a guy, try to get a feel for his character. If he feels right, that's more important than anything you can put on paper. That's how Keenan operated. He hired his buddies."

Haggerty scribbled a note on a legal pad. She glanced up at him, the pen still moving.

"Go on."

For a couple weeks, he'd just watched. Getting a feel for it, Keenan told him. He worked surveillance, sat in a parked car, watching one of the other members of the team make a buy. Got used to the sensation of too much coffee, too many cigarettes, pissing into a Coke bottle, waiting for the buy to go down so you could head back to the squad room, get started on the paperwork. Life through a windshield.

And when he'd just started to think he'd lose his mind to the boredom, wondering if he could still get back into Arson, Keenan handed him over to Jerry Friar, *for refinement*. How to be a junkie, not a cop. How to stop your eyes from scanning the street, concentrate your whole being on the little plastic bag cradled in the dealer's palm. How to dress, where to conceal a wire. How to carry money like it comes easily. The hardest lesson for a cop, Friar told him, grinning.

Walsh paused, thoughtful. Haggerty watched his eyes, knowing he'd come to it, the hidden thing that he would tell

226

her now or evade. He rubbed his eyes hard, making a decision.

How easy, he told her, the money could come.

"We've got a problem."

Riccioli looked up from his computer screen, saw the look on her face as she closed the door, and hit a key to save his memo. He watched her cross the office.

"Where's Walsh?"

"In my office. I gave him some coffee."

"So?"

"He's dirty. The whole squad was. They were skimming the collection plate on the single-unit busts, then splitting the resale."

Riccioli waved her into a chair.

"Are you surprised?"

Haggerty hesitated. She looked tired.

"Yes, I am."

"You like this guy."

"I thought he was straight."

"Did he tell you, or you found out for yourself?"

"He told me."

Riccioli nodded. "That's good." He glanced at his watch, frowned, although he had nothing until three. It was a habit, Haggerty knew, his way of letting you know he was giving you his attention, holding the busy world at arm's length to solve your problem.

"How bad is it?"

"No direct payoffs that he knows of, but a clear pattern of corruption. God knows where that might lead. The unit leader, Lieutenant Keenan, handled the money. He made the deals, took care of his boys. Walsh says no one asked too

many questions. At the end of his first month, they handed him an envelope and that was it. He was on the payroll."

"Interesting." Riccioli leaned back, ran both hands through his thinning hair. "Usual pattern is the low guy handles the nut, takes the biggest risk. If the unit leader's doing it, he might be protecting a connection. Got a friend who only does business with him."

Haggerty watched him work it out, his fingers splayed across the back of his head, thumbs pressed together. He smiled, rocking slightly in his chair. Abruptly, he sat forward, the chair slapping the edge of the desk as he grabbed up a pen, twisted it between his fingers.

"I think we should pursue this."

"In what context?"

He thrust the pen at her.

"Follow your instincts. See what you can get."

"No way!"

Walsh heaved himself out of the chair. Haggerty looked up at him from behind her desk. She could see the anger in his eyes. She felt a twinge of regret, but it was part of the job. She made her voice icy.

"Sit down, Mr. Walsh."

"I've got enough enemies."

"Then I advise you to cooperate with us."

"Not on this."

"You have evidence of an ongoing conspiracy within the Drug Control Unit of the Boston Police Department. I can have a subpoena drawn up in a matter of hours. Or you can agree to confidentiality. Of course, if it goes to trial, you'll be called to testify."

Walsh raised a hand to stop her. His fingers were broad, the nails chewed down to the quick.

"You're not hearing me," he said. "You want to get a subpoena, fine. I'll take the Fifth. I won't testify against cops."

Back down, Haggerty thought. *You're losing him.*

She settled back in her chair, nodded.

"I appreciate your position."

For a moment, Walsh looked down at her. She gestured toward the chair and, slowly, Walsh lowered himself into it.

"I have no desire to pressure you," she began. Walsh cut her off.

"You have nothing to pressure me with. By the time you build a case, I'll be dead."

She shook her head, impatient.

"My instructions are to pursue this matter. That's all, to the word. It could lead to a formal investigation, or we could find that it's only a secondary issue. Do you follow me?"

He considered her for a moment, then nodded slowly.

"You're saying you've got some choice here."

"I'm telling you we have our priorities. Mr. Riccioli has expressed to me a desire that we resolve the current matter before raising new concerns."

He drummed his fingers on the arm of his chair, his brow furrowed.

"So what are we talking about here?"

She spread her hands, smiled.

"Consider my position. What you've told me may break this case open, or it might make any attempt to prosecute D'Angelo on any evidence you provide very messy. If his lawyer gets wind of this, they've got reasonable doubt.

You're a dirty cop, trying to shake down a legitimate businessman. A father grieving for his son. Before you know it, the jury's voting him man of the year. And they're starting to wonder about that accident of yours."

Walsh looked at her steadily, his face very still.

"You got any questions," he said, "better ask 'em now."

She shook her head.

"I tried to put that scenario together at the time. Of course, we didn't have the corruption stuff then, but it didn't fly. Anyway . . ." She found herself looking at the ficus, noticing that it needed water. "I know you now."

He was quiet for a moment, then he nodded.

"All right. You're worried about the jury. Does this put us out of business?"

"No. We just have to be careful to cover all the bases." She looked down at her papers. "A corruption investigation would help. If you gave testimony, we'd have a context for all this. The jury looks at you, they see Al Pacino playing Serpico. A man who has regrets, wants to go back and clean up the department."

He shook his head.

"I'm not sending a cop to jail. I've been there. It's no place for a cop."

She was quiet for a moment.

"You said Keenan handled the money."

"That's right."

"Riccioli thinks that's unusual. Usually, it's the lowest-ranking guy in the outfit."

He shrugged. "That's how it was."

"Maybe he was protecting his contacts."

"I never asked."

"But you had your suspicions."

230

"No."

She paused, took a slim file from an upper drawer of her desk. When she opened it, Walsh saw his photograph—in uniform—clipped to one corner. Below it, a photocopy of his personnel sheet. She flipped through some papers, pulled out a page of handwritten notes.

"Your uncle's a cop."

"He retired last year."

"Worked in the personnel office during the last five years."

"That's right."

"Did a tour in Internal Affairs."

He eyed her, suspiciously.

"What're you getting at?"

"After we talked, I went looking for a copy of your complaint. I checked the index for the three months following Friar's death. It doesn't exist. There's a gap in the document-control numbers on the day your personnel record shows you filed the complaint."

"So they screwed up the paperwork. It happens. I withdrew the complaint anyway."

"But it should have stayed on file. No one in Internal Affairs can remember losing a complaint before."

"Yeah?"

"Your uncle talk to you, Jack?"

"We talked a lot. He had dinner with my dad on Sundays."

She consulted her notes.

"You filed your complaint on Thursday, April twenty-first. You withdrew it Monday, April twenty-fifth."

"If you say so."

"What was in the complaint, Jack?"

* * *

She had him. He could feel it, part of him even admiring the way she led him around the corners, changing direction, until he found himself in a dead end, no place to hide. Walsh had done a lot of interrogations, and he recognized the moment—the suspect going silent, trying to find a way to answer the question. *If it doesn't come quick,* the older detectives had told him, *you got him.* Make them think, make them confess. He'd seen it many times.

He watched her slip the sheet of notes back into the file, straighten the pages. Keeping her hands busy, not looking at him, while she waited for him to answer. Her face was slightly flushed, excited. She knew she'd cornered him, busying herself with the papers to give him a minute. Pushing him hard, then backing away so she didn't lose his trust. Feeling his eyes on her face now, looking up.

"We can't stop now, Jack."

He glanced at the shelf of law books, the stacks of files, the bright colors of the Chagall and the shadows of the ficus swaying on the pale wall.

"Let me try," she offered. "Keenan had a connection that he used to sell whatever you skimmed off the drug seizures, maybe a little information now and then. Possibly an informer who went both ways. . . ."

Walsh shook his head.

"Too risky. Informers are users, very low on the chain. You let one know you're dirty, he'll sell you out for a fix."

"So, it's a dealer."

"Higher. Probably at the top of one of the networks. Figure Tony started with an informer when he was working the streets. The guy sold him out to a big shot, they move up the

ranks together, scratching each other's backs. The informer, he disappears early on."

"All right." Haggerty kept her voice calm. "Then what?"

"Depends. Tony gets to the top of his unit, he becomes a valuable commodity. Hard to keep that a secret on the street. Maybe a bigger fish comes along, claims the prize."

"D'Angelo?"

Walsh laughed.

"Wouldn't that be neat. Keep in mind, Johnny doesn't deal. Never has. Only the bottom feeders in the mob take that risk. There's been a ban on it, ever since the Appalachia conference. Punishable by death."

"We see 'em dealing," Haggerty insisted.

"Top guys?"

"No, but Johnny meets with the importers on a regular basis."

"That's it. He *meets* with them. Guy like Johnny, he sells protection, takes a cut of the profits when some guy deals on his turf. Like the IRS, right?"

Haggerty smiled.

"Johnny's a broker," Walsh said. "You pay, or something gets broke."

"That's an old line."

"All right. But it's true. The dealers, they're just like a guy runs a trucking business, or a construction company. If Johnny doesn't get his piece of the action, they're outta business. Somebody starts hassling their street dealers, or the couriers. Maybe the cops get a couple tips."

"Which brings us back to Keenan."

Walsh was silent for a moment.

"After I joined the unit, we busted a guy up in Charlestown had three keys of coke in a couple suitcases in his

closet. Tony got a tip. The stuff was wrapped in quarter keys. After we make the bust, take the guy down to the car, Tony calls me back. He's got the suitcases up on the bed. He points at these little packages, asks me, 'How many you count?' I say, 'Twelve.' He gives me this look, and he says, 'I only see ten.' Then he walks away. Leaves me there with the stuff. I'm not an idiot, right? He wants me to report ten packs, two and a half keys. It's three in the morning, middle of a project in Charlestown, the whole squad's waiting downstairs. What am I, gonna say no? So I stuff two packs in my coat, close the suitcase, take it down to the car. We get back to the squadroom, Tony calls me into his office. I put the packs on his desk, he drops 'em in a drawer. Then he gives me an envelope, has all this cash in it, almost five thousand. 'Welcome to the team,' he says."

Haggerty kept her eyes on her notes, waiting out the silence.

"After that, I figured I was dirty, but it was part of it, you know? We busted a lot of guys, Jerry and me. And neither of us ever skimmed. Turned in every ounce. Far as I know, the other guys were doing it the same way. I never asked. But every couple weeks, Tony'd hand me this envelope." He looked up at her. "I had kids, a mortgage."

"Wait a minute," Haggerty said. "You're telling me you only skimmed once, but you kept getting paid."

"I did it a couple times. On team busts. It was like a test. Were you with the team. Otherwise, we did the job."

"No quota?"

"Nothing like that."

"You see enough skimming to fill the envelopes?"

"That's the thing. It was never much, even when it happened. After a while, even that stopped."

"When?"

"I'd been with the team about a year. It was a big bust in Southie. You could tell Keenan was nervous. He made this big deal about making Jerry pack up the stuff with everyone there, made us all verify the count."

"An accurate count?"

"Yeah."

"So the skimming stopped then?"

"Far as I know."

"And the money?"

"We still got the money."

She thought about that a while. Then she pulled out his personnel file, consulted her sheet of notes.

"When did your uncle move over to Internal Affairs."

"Forget it."

"What?"

"My uncle's clean."

She looked up at him.

"Did he talk to you about the complaint?"

He hesitated, then nodded.

"But all he said was that I better have some evidence. Told me not to be stupid, he didn't want to see me dead in an alley somewhere. He was right."

"And he pulled the papers."

"He was protecting me."

She started to say something, then let it go. She sat back, her fingers seeking out the fringe on the blanket, twisting it.

"So what spooked Keenan?"

Walsh shrugged. "You hear rumors. Maybe one of the brass looked at him funny in the hall."

"Or maybe the terms of his employment changed. You're

235

saying the skimming stopped, but the money kept flowing. So he wasn't selling a product, but a service."

"Meaning what?"

"Information. Which, as you pointed out, goes both ways. Maybe you tip off a dealer, or else some guy calls you and drops a few hints about the competition."

He nodded, smiling slightly. She blushed, realizing that he was letting her do the talking, amused at her breathless tone.

"You're leading me."

"You would've gotten there without me."

"But this way, you don't have to say it."

"Hey." He raised his hands in protest. "I'm just like you. All I've got is suspicions. If I had evidence, I wouldn't have withdrawn the complaint."

"Even if it meant going to jail?"

"Yeah. I figured I could leave the other guys in the unit out of it, say I hadn't seen anyone else skimming, which was true. I could testify that Keenan approached me on the side, maybe 'cause he figured I had an uncle in Internal Affairs who'd take care of me."

"You really wanted him."

"I could taste it. Jerry was a friend."

"And you're sure it was Keenan who set you up?"

"I'm sure."

"Why?"

He shrugged. "Maybe it was a mistake. Someone got his wires crossed. All I know is my buddy got shot. It could've been me."

"Maybe that was the plan."

"What do you mean?"

"You said Jerry was behind you on the stairs."

"Forget it."

"Whose idea was that?"

"I said, forget it!" His eyes were hard. "Jerry was my friend. I trusted him."

She raised her hands, defensively.

"Okay. Just exploring the possibilities."

"That's not a possibility."

"Fine."

She leafed through her notes, and Walsh thought about Jerry's funeral, a couple hundred officers in dress blues marching up the street to the church, some of 'em stuffed into uniforms three sizes too small, belly hanging over their gun belt. He could see Anne with the wives, crying as Tony carried the folded flag down the steps from the altar to present it to the widow. He stood at attention, his gut churning with rage. Thinking the whole time about proof, the kind you took to court and the other kind, what you needed to be clear in your mind.

His hands gripped the arms of the chair, sweating. Haggerty, bent over her papers, did not seem to notice.

Proof.

24

What could he tell her? How proof can deceive, lead you into darkness? How knowledge can become a quiet hell?

After the funeral, he had packed a small bag, told Anne he was going to ride up to a buddy's fishing camp in Maine for a couple days, let his head clear. She'd nodded, her lips tight. At the highway, he turned south, crossed the Tobin Bridge into Boston, got off the expressway at Savin Hill and headed up into Dorchester. He took a room in a motel that rented by the hour, put a security bar on the wheel of his

car, and walked into the night. He had a name, some contacts, and an evil look in his eye.

Two nights later, he stood in a cold rain in the doorway of a furniture warehouse on Dorchester Avenue, looking up at a figure moving behind the window of a vacant apartment. The building was dark, except for a bare bulb in the entryway. A streetlight flickered next to the window.

He went in through the back, down a narrow alley to a fire door. He popped the lock with a thin strip of plastic, opened the door slowly, the rusted hinges giving only the faintest squeal. Inside, he drew the .38 from the holster at his belt, edged along the dark hall, up two flights of stairs, then left to the street side of the building. There were two apartments overlooking the street. He pressed his ear against a door, heard nothing. He moved to the other, listened, and was rewarded with the faint creak of a floorboard. He moved back to the stairs, descended to the next landing, and settled in the darkness, waiting. An hour passed, then another. At last, he heard a bolt snap back in the hallway above, a door open and close, the sound of a key in a lock. He pushed up into a crouch, his muscles tense, drew the hammer on the gun with both thumbs. He heard footsteps, coming toward the stairs.

The kid was maybe twenty, handsome in a dark way, with his black hair combed back off a high forehead. He came down the stairs in a trot, pulling on his jacket. As he hit the dark landing, he felt a hand close on his throat, shove him back against the steps. His ankle caught the lowest stair, and he fell back. A knee pressed into his chest. He gasped for breath, felt a gun thrust against his teeth. He flinched as

he heard the trigger click, the hammer drop on an empty chamber.

"First one's free," the voice said. "You earn the rest."

He was jerked up by the throat and flung up the stairs. At the top, he tried to get his feet under him. The hand seized him, slammed him off the wall, twice.

"Naughty, naughty."

He felt the gun come up under his chin, pressing his head back. The hand left his throat, patted his pockets. It found the .45 tucked into his pants, pulled it free. His army knife and keys vanished from the pocket of his pants. Then the hand grabbed him by the jacket, spun him around, and shoved him down the hall to the apartment door. The keys clattered onto the floor beside his feet.

"Open it."

He picked up the keys, unlocked the door, thinking about the shotgun leaning against the cabinet in the small kitchen. But as he swung the door open, he felt his feet swept out from under him. A hand caught his hair, dragged him into the apartment, across the living room to a radiator beside the window. His head bounced off the floor, stunning him. He felt his hands yanked up, a pair of handcuffs slipped onto both wrists, tight. He could feel the cold metal of the radiator against the backs of his hands. A foot nudged him over onto his back, so his arms were crossed at the elbow.

A face came into view, pale in the glow of the streetlight beyond the window. The eyes were hard. The man glanced around the empty apartment. Piles of trash littered the floor. A window was broken, and the wind whistled through the room. He rose to his feet, walked down the hall, opening the bedroom doors. He went into the kitchen, emerged with the shotgun. He pumped it, shucking the shells onto the floor,

then tossed it aside. He came back to the window, crouched down beside the kid, smiled.

"Time for a chat."

And then, the question, repeated again and again, no matter what he said. *Who told you?* At first, patiently.

"You a cop? So bust me, save us both time."

The man squatting on his heels, looking down at him, the gun resting on his knee.

Who told you?

"What is this shit? I don't know what you talkin' about. Told me what?"

He saw the hand slip into a pocket, and emerge with his clasp knife. The man dangled the knife over his chest by one finger, swinging it by the small ring at the end. Then, wedging a thumbnail against the blade, he popped the knife open, turned it from side to side so the blade gleamed in the pale light. The knife gave a little flick, and a button popped off the front of his shirt.

Who told you?

"Man, get away from me with that thing!"

Flick, flick. More buttons, then the sleeve, sliced all the way to the elbow. The knife point probed the skin lightly.

Who told you?

The kid tried to jerk away, but the knife pressed harder, breaking the skin, pinning his arm to the floor. Then, suddenly, it was hovering over him, settling again at the base of his throat.

Who told you?

"I don't know! Nobody!"

And the tip of the knife pressed into the skin, drawing blood. The hand drew the knife slowly down the center of

242

his chest and belly—a thin red line. It stopped at the top of his pants, nudged his belt.

You want me to keep going?

The kid screamed as the hand opened the belt, tugged at the zipper. The knife blade slipped under the waistband of his shorts, lifted them away from the skin and sliced through, down the seam to the flap. His hips jerked as the cold blade slipped under his penis. His hands rattled the cuffs against the radiator.

I wouldn't move around too much if I were you, the man said. *My hand might slip.*

So he lay very still. Gritting his teeth as the knife lifted the bit of flesh.

Who told you?

"Take it away, I'll tell you."

The man thought about it, then the knife moved away. There was a faint sound in the hall. As he glanced over his shoulder, the kid grabbed the radiator, swung a foot up, and caught him hard under the chin. His head jerked back, and the kid flipped on his side, kicked him again—an arcing side-kick, like they taught in karate, the heel catching the side of his head, sending him skidding across the floor on his back. He lay still.

The kid glared at him.

"Asshole!"

Then he realized that the key to the cuffs was in the guy's pocket. The knife glittered on the floor, just out of reach.

"Ah, shit."

Walsh woke in the bathroom, draped over the sink, water running across the back of his head. A thin beam of sunlight came through a window in the shower. His jaw throbbed.

He raised his head, the water trailing down his neck and onto his back. He raised a hand to rub at his sore jaw.

Then he saw the blood.

It had dried on his hands, splattered across his forearms and shirt. He looked up at the mirror, saw it on his face.

He took a step back, felt something skid away from his foot. The knife glittered beside the toilet.

He forced himself out of the bathroom, down the hall past the tiny kitchen, into the living room. The kid lay where he'd left him, curled on his side, his hands chained to the radiator. Around him, a slick of blood reflected the light. His shirt was torn away. His chest and belly were slashed and bloody. His head was thrown back, as if with surprise. A trickle of blood leaked from one eye.

For a moment, he thought he might throw up. He slumped against a wall. His body trembled, his hands dark against the pale wall.

"Jack?"

He looked up. Haggerty was watching him, her eyes curious.

"Are you okay?"

He nodded, swallowed twice. He smiled weakly.

"Tired," he said.

"I'm sorry. We should get you set up with a place to stay." She got up. "There's some couches down in the employee lounge, if you need to lie down for a few minutes."

"Thanks. I'm fine."

"You're sure?"

He nodded.

"All right," she said. "I'll go see about the arrangements. It'll just take a minute."

She closed the door behind her, leaving him with the memory of his panic, snatching up the knife, his gun, stepping over the puddle of blood to unlock the cuffs. Wiping down his hands and face with a rag in the bathroom, then zipping his coat up over the stained shirt before slipping out the door.

I did that, he thought, edging down the dark stairs. *I'm capable of that.*

It was a hard thing to live with.

Proof.

25

They put him in a hotel over in Cambridge, a new one over-looking the river near Kenmore Square. It was a fancy place, with cable movies on the television, a complimentary shaving kit on the bathroom counter, and towels so big he could have slept under one. He was grateful for the shaving kit, since he'd packed in a hurry—just a gym bag with some spare clothes and the small metal suitcase that held the Heckler & Koch and a spare clip.

He stood in the shower, letting the water run over him for a long time. Then he pulled the heavy drapes against the afternoon sun, got into bed, and tried to sleep.

It wouldn't come. In his mind, he kept seeing the knife lying there on the bathroom floor. Not the kid; that was the weird part. The knife, stained with blood, beside the toilet. The way it skidded off his foot as he stepped back, like an accusation. His left foot, which meant he'd switched hands, to wipe the blood out of his eyes, maybe. It was this image that used to send him to the bottle, jerk him out of bed while Anne slept to sit in front of the television, glass in hand. Not Jerry's death, like Anne thought, or even the kid. The knife.

He sat up, hit the remote to turn on the television. No whiskey, just the flickering image to clear his mind, ease the pain in his chest. He watched a few minutes of Bruce Willis as a rogue cop, shooting up a skyscraper, then he flipped through the channels. He stopped at a pay-per-view preview, a soft-core movie with two women in a hot tub, then flipped on. A basketball game, and he thought of Danny in the photograph, solemn in his excitement, D'Angelo glaring at the camera.

He shut the television off, got out of bed, and did a hundred sit-ups. As he caught his breath, he laid the metal case on the bed and opened it. Without the stock, the MP5 could be concealed under a heavy coat, hanging by its strap across his back. He smiled, bitterly. *All I need is an empty skyscraper.* He closed the case, shoved it under the bed. Who thinks up that stuff? Bunch of guys shooting machine guns at each other, nobody gets hit. Bruce gets to fling them out the window. No thought, no fear. No guilt.

But what happens if you can't be sure of your hands? If the time comes, you don't know if you can pull the trigger? You put guns in every corner of the house, strain your muscles until they're strong, then you wait, hoping when it happens you see the enemy beyond your gunsights and not the

kid, bleeding, still. You find the waiting your only comfort, not trusting your hands to obey you, to do violence without rage.

He thought of Haggerty, with her pages of notes, her careful analysis. How far does your imagination go, Ms. Haggerty? Are you capable of seeing to the borders, where anger blurs into madness? To an empty apartment, where a killer dies in a way no man deserves? Can you imagine a guilt that is more potent than fear? We learn ourselves, he thought, in our failures of imagination. The hands betray you, and then lay claim to your soul.

I am a killer, he thought. And then, painfully: *Twice.*

He thought about Terry, frightened away by his sudden violence. He had not spoken to her since their walk, unable to think of any words that could ease the image in her mind of him in sudden motion, the cane swinging in his hands. A violent man, she called him. Somehow, he couldn't think of himself that way, even knowing it was true. His hands were broad, rough from years of hard work and bad weather. When he had to fight, they served him well. But he'd never gone looking for a brawl, never taken up a weapon without cause. . . .

He shook his head. How could he claim that? Like his mind wanted to erase the truth that was hostile to its peace. Move it quietly from memory to waking dream, and then on to a distant, uncertain despair, the kind a drunken cop confesses over his beer. It's how you learn to live with it, or around it, to find your way back to yourself as the years pass, as your hands no longer look stained with blood, your eyes no longer watchful and tense. We grow into our sins, he thought.

Or they grow into us.

*   *   *

The next morning, he woke late, put in a call to Haggerty. Her secretary told him she was in a meeting.

"No message."

He had breakfast in a Greek place on Cambridge Street near the courthouse. He sat over his coffee, watching through the window as a pair of lesbians in business suits shared a brief kiss at the bus stop. The bus came, and one got on. The other crossed the street and hurried away, toward Harvard Square.

He caught the Green Line out of Lechmere Station into the city, switched at Park Street, and rode one stop to Government Center, then he walked downstairs to the Blue Line, got a seat out through the tunnel to East Boston. He got off at Maverick, came out of the stairs and turned east, taking his time. It was early still.

He thought about Haggerty, the way her face had changed when he told her about the skimming. Her lips had tightened, her eyes narrowed. For a moment, she seemed to flush. He had paused, thinking she was angry. She took up her pen, bent over her legal pad, making notes. When he finished, she looked up at him, and the betrayal was clear in her eyes.

"Is there anything else I should know?"

He thought about it for a moment, then shook his head. She gave a curt nod, got up.

"I'll have to talk to Riccioli. You want more coffee?"

"I'm fine."

"It'll take me a few minutes. Ask my secretary if you need anything."

She closed the door behind her. He gave her a few minutes before checking the files.

Now, heading down Bremen toward the airport, he carried in his pocket a photocopy of an arrest record, the fruits of his confession. He'd found it near the back of the D'Angelo file, clipped to the surveillance report for the day of Larry's death. Slipping it into his shirt, he left the office, pausing to ask the secretary for directions to the men's room. He got into line at a copy machine, watched a secretary enter a security code on the keypad, then used the same number to run a single copy.

Jimmy Florio. The last entry was an arrest in March of the previous year for assault. In the top left corner was a photograph, a street address just below it. Looking at the picture, Walsh guessed he lived with his mother. She goes to mass, he goes to jail. Got a Bruins poster on his bedroom wall, a bench press at the foot of his bed. *God help me*, he thought. *Another kid.*

The address was a triple-decker in a row of houses not far from the airport. All the houses needed paint, and the roar of the planes taking off rattled the windows. A couple had tiny yards in front, a statue of the Virgin Mary standing on a bed of rocks. The Florio place didn't have a yard, or much else to distinguish it. It had green tile around the windows, a shade darker than the paint, like a Miami Beach hotel. A mailbox next to the door hung askew, and there was a stack of telephone books in yellow plastic on the porch. At the end of the block was a donut place. Walsh got a coffee and sat by the window. It was a little after nine-thirty, too early for a kid like Jimmy Florio, but Walsh wanted to get a feel for the neighborhood. He listened to two men at the next table argue about a story in the *Herald*.

The woman behind the counter had silver hair and a face etched by time. She watched Walsh drink his coffee, and

when he emptied the cup, she was there with a refill before it hit the table.

"You got decaf?" Walsh asked her.

"We got it. You ask me, I'll get it for you. The real stuff's better."

"I'll take the decaf."

She shrugged, went behind the counter, came back with another pot.

"People tell me coffee keeps 'em awake, gives 'em the jitters," she said as she poured. "Me, I drink a cup right before bed. Sleep like a baby."

"You're lucky."

"I'm old, and I'm working in a donut shop. That's lucky?"

"Could be worse."

"I could have the cholera."

"Something like that."

"I should live so long."

She took a rag out of her apron, gave his table a swipe.

"You know a guy named Jimmy Florio, lives up the street?"

She paused, looked down at him.

"Never heard of him."

She stalked back to the counter, gave it a desultory wipe, then leaned on her elbows, looking out the window. Walsh looked too. A tow truck went past, dragging a new Ford van. A few minutes later, it came back, empty. Walsh had passed twelve body shops on his walk from the subway. The van would be chopped down and sold for parts in a few hours. It was a big industry in this part of town, one reason Massachusetts led the country in stolen cars and auto insurance rates. Walsh knew cops who'd spent their entire careers going home every night to a house in Southie with a chop

shop next door. A clean crime, they used to call it. Nobody gets hurt, everybody makes a living. If some guy out in Malden had to pay an extra fifty a year on his insurance, who worried about it? Like a commuter tax—you want to drive to the city, you gotta pay the price.

After a while, Walsh dropped a few bills on the table and left. He walked up the street to have another look at the kid's house, but nothing had changed. In the next block, an old man was sweeping the sidewalk in front of a bar. Walsh crossed the street, watching him stoop to scrape something off the edge of his shoe. As Walsh approached, the old guy straightened, leaned on his broom, watching him.

"How ya doing?"

"I'll live." The man squinted at him. "I know you?"

"Don't think so."

"So whatcha want?"

"I'm looking for a friend of mine, Jimmy Florio. Wondered if you'd seen him around."

The old man leaned to one side, spat into the gutter.

"Lives up the block," Walsh said.

"Yeah? You try knocking on the door?"

Walsh grinned, sheepish.

"Yeah, nobody home."

"So? There's your answer."

"I wondered if he was in town."

The old man squinted at him again, shook his head.

"Good friend, you don't know where he is."

"You know how it is."

"No, can't say as I do."

The old man leaned the broom against the door and went into the bar. Walsh walked up the block. He passed an old woman pulling a small cart full of groceries, but didn't stop.

The last thing he needed was some grandma who'd talk your ear off, grab your sleeve to keep you from walking away. Pretty soon, you know all about her children's kids, the new priest at St. Margaret's, her friend with the aneurysm who needed surgery. He was working the network, the bartenders and waitresses, the people in the neighborhood who know everybody, who hear everything and say nothing, keeping track of what's going on. He didn't expect to learn anything, didn't care really. But they'd pass the word that some guy who looked like a cop was asking about Jimmy. Maybe spook him a little, get him looking over his shoulder.

He could picture Florio, sprawled across his bed, sleeping until noon. He wakes up, goes out for coffee, the waitress says:

"Hey, Jimmy. Some guy in here looking for you."

"What guy?"

"Just a guy. But, Jimmy?"

"Yeah?"

"This guy, he wasn't a friend."

So Jimmy gets nervous, heads up the street for a little courage, and the old man behind the bar tells him:

"Cop in here this morning looking for you. Had a bad leg."

He's sweating now. Thinking about Larry, maybe, or the deputy. Wondering if they traced the car. He panics, calls up his buddy Frankie Defeo, rings the chimes all the way up the line to D'Angelo, sitting in his office down in Southie in an expensive suit. Walsh smiled, imagining Haggerty poring over the surveillance transcripts, pondering the results of his morning's work.

In fact, Walsh didn't care much if Jimmy made the call or

not. He wanted him nervous, but not scared enough to skip town. Get him edgy before dropping the hammer on him. Shake the tree and see what drops. He didn't have a plan, but he figured he could make one up when he knew the score. Until then, he'd follow his instincts, work the streets, knowing that he didn't have much to lose. If you can't wait 'em out, smoke 'em out. When the time came, he'd see what happened. For the moment, it felt good to be back on the streets. He was tired of sitting in a tiny house, brooding on the past, waiting.

He stopped in at a bakery, exchanged a few words with a teenager behind the register at a gas station, then circled back to Florio's block, caught up with the mail carrier, a young woman with a ponytail and a nice walk. He could tell right off that she wasn't from the neighborhood by the way she looked at him, flirting a little, even after he asked his question.

"Jimmy Florio?" She hitched her bag. "Yeah, he's on my route. Cute guy. Always asks me to come in when his mom isn't home, but he's just joking, like."

"That's Jimmy all right."

"Couple days ago I almost said yes."

"I'll tell him to keep trying."

She gave him a coy smile, tugged at her ponytail with one hand.

"You could try, too."

He looked at her young body, her narrow hips and slim legs, and felt flattered. He gave her his best Irish rogue smile, the Jack Kennedy edition.

"Maybe I will," he said. "Tell Jimmy I said hello."

"You got a name?"

"Describe me. Make him guess."

He liked that last bit, imagining as he watched her walk away how Florio would get into it, her little secret, drawing it out to flirt with her as he tried to guess. And when she got around to describing him, the smile fading, fear flickering in his eyes, making her draw back, confused.

He bought a newspaper and headed for the subway, smiling. Probably blow his shot at getting laid, too.

Hello. This is John D'Angelo. I'm away from my desk, but if you leave a message, I'll get back to you.

Johnny hit the flashing button, and the tape rewound.

"I sound like a jerk."

"So you'll do it over."

Maria had the instructions spread out on the desk. She leaned across him and pressed some buttons on the side of the phone. The commands on the little screen at the top of the phone switched to French.

"Look't, you can do all kinda things."

"They got Italian?"

She checked the sheet.

"Nah, they got German, Spanish, and Japanese."

Johnny shook his head.

"I dunno," he said, looking over at his wife. She was by the mirror, fluffing. "I got a phone. It rings, I pick it up. Some people I talk to. It's easy."

"You're a businessman," Angie said, leaning into the mirror. "You go in the offices downtown, they all got these things on their desk."

"The people I deal with, they don't want to get a tape. Christ, I'm telling 'em to *talk* on a tape."

"They don't want to, they don't have to."

256

"It's the idea. These guys, they spend their lives trying not to talk on a tape."

Maria hit some more buttons.

"Here's the auto dial."

She put the speaker on. He could hear the phone dialing, then a click and it was ringing.

"I put in the number for the house."

"Yeah?" Johnny shoved some papers in a drawer. "Anybody answers, you let me know."

"You know what it is," Angie said. "You're telling 'em, I got nothing to hide. I'm a businessman, like everybody else."

Johnny looked at her.

"I'm saying that?"

"It's the nineties, Johnny."

"You see this button," Maria said. "You hit this, it tells you who you called, how long you talked, and how much it cost."

"I know who I called."

"But it keeps a record."

"I don't want a record."

"So don't press that button."

Angie turned to face him. He knew what was coming.

"You hate it."

He sighed, shook his head.

"I don't hate it."

"We shoulda got the briefcase," she said to Maria.

"I like it," Johnny said. "I just gotta get used to it, is all."

She came over to the desk, looked down at it.

"You're sure? 'Cause we could return it."

"I like it."

"What sold me," Angie said, "was the box. You're not

using it, you close the box, you don't have to look at it. That's solid maple."

"It's nice."

"Well, happy birthday, dear."

She leaned in, smeared her lipstick on his cheek.

Walsh read the paper on the Red Line. The governor had vetoed a budget, the state was broke, the Celtics were losing. He got off in Somerville, dropped the paper in a trash can. He took the escalator up two levels to the street, caught his old bus to Medford Square. He gazed out the window at the frat houses as the bus climbed the hill toward the college. A herd of students got off, and the rest of the passengers found seats. When the bus turned north into Medford, Walsh got up, walked to the front. He peered through the windshield as the bus rumbled past his street.

Anne's car was in the drive. Danny's bike lay in the yard. At the end of the block, a Mass Electric van had the street open. Two local cops lounged against their car, watching traffic.

He got off two blocks from the elementary school. For a moment, he thought about walking back to the house, ringing the bell. Then he turned and headed up the street to the school. About twenty kids, younger than Danny, were playing kickball on the concrete playground, supervised by an enormous Hispanic woman, who stood beside the door with her arms crossed. She eyed Walsh suspiciously as he came up the drive, climbed the steps to the door.

"I'm looking for the office."

She jerked a thumb over her shoulder.

"Inside, take your first right."

A black woman sat behind a counter, filling out absence

reports to be sent to parents. She looked up when he came in.

"Can I help you?"

"I need to see Danny Walsh. He's in the second grade."

"Frankie?"

"Yeah?"

"It's Jimmy."

"Hey, Jimmy. How ya doing?"

"We gotta talk, man."

"What's up?"

"You wanna call me back?"

Frankie sighed. The nearest pay phone was three blocks. "Take me a few minutes. I gotta get dressed."

"I'll be here."

Twenty minutes later, the phone next to the men's room in the Doughboy rang twice. There was a pause, then it rang again. Jimmy Florio picked it up.

"Frankie?"

"What's up, my man?"

"There's some guy been hanging around this morning, asking about me. Joey down at the Nightcap says he looks like a cop."

"Yeah? You been a bad boy, stealing from the candy machine?"

"He's got a limp, Frankie."

"Lotta guys got a limp."

"And talk like a cop?"

"If they're cops."

"It's the guy, I'm telling ya."

"How'd he get your name? You drop your wallet in the store?"

"Look, all I know is some guy's spooking my people. The whole neighborhood's lookin' at me funny."

Frankie thought for a moment. Jimmy could hear him whistling softly through his teeth.

"All right," he said at last. "I'll come over there, we'll see what's the story. Hey, if it's our guy, saves us a trip, right?"

"I dunno, Frankie."

"What?"

"This thing is getting kinda close to home. He talked to the girl delivers my mail, for chrissakes."

"We're just gonna see if it's him, okay? You wanna know, don't you?"

"Yeah, I guess."

"So just hang tight. Get me a coffee, I'll be over there in a couple minutes. I gotta move my car by twelve or they tow it."

"I'm not goin' anywhere."

Anne was running late. She had to pick up Danny at school, drop him at her mother's, then get over to the pediatrician for Becky's appointment. She left the car in a bus zone, wrestled Becky out of her car seat. Across the street, children were spilling from the door of the school. A crossing guard herded them through the line of waiting cars onto the sidewalk. She didn't see Danny, hoped he'd remembered to wait for her. If he'd started walking home, she'd lose a half hour looking for him.

She had to push her way into the school against a tide of kids. Danny's room was on the first floor, at the rear of the building. As she passed the office, she heard Mrs. Tillyard, the school secretary, call her name.

Ah, Christ.

A nice woman, but she loved to talk. Not long ago, she'd cornered Anne at a PTA meeting, droning on about her teenage daughter, who had recently fallen for a bus driver on the Lechmere route and now spent hours riding the bus, gazing at the back of his head.

"Girls," she had sighed, looking at Becky. "They're the hardest to raise."

Now she was pushing through the office gate, waving her over. Anne smiled her regrets, pointed toward Danny's classroom, and hurried past. She found him feeding lettuce to a hamster at the back of the classroom, glancing up at her from the corner of his eye, like he had a secret. She waited as he showed her how the animal held the leaf with his tiny feet so he could tear off bits to eat. Then the hamster pooped, and Danny said they could leave.

"He needs privacy," he said. "Like Mommy."

On the way out, Mrs. Tillyard was gone. Anne breathed a sigh of relief. She glanced at her watch. They had twenty minutes to get to the doctor. With a little luck . . .

There was a ticket on her car.

Johnny had a talk with his lawyer, who said he didn't think an answering machine was a good idea. Not a problem really, but just one more thing to go on the subpoena.

"Go tell my wife," Johnny said. "Somebody calls the house, she writes the name on a pad. I tell her, 'You can remember it, right?' But she keeps doing it. I say, 'At least tear the top sheet off the fuckin' pad first, so no one can read it after.' What can I do? She doesn't think that way."

"She's never been on trial."

"Damn right. I protect my family."

The lawyer, a former district attorney named Glasser,

folded his hands on his desk. He wore a Rolex, with a dia-mond-inlaid face, and he enjoyed this gesture, which caused his sleeves to ride up. *Showin' off that watch,* Johnny thought. *Christ, I paid for that fuckin' thing.*

"Would you like me to call her?" Glasser asked. "Explain the situation?"

"Nah. I'll stick the thing in a drawer, pull it out when she comes to the office."

The lawyer glanced at his watch, cleared his throat.

"There's another matter we should discuss, John."

"I'm listening."

"There's been some talk among the uncles about a major push on the RICO charge. I gather we're looking at renewed surveillance."

Johnny shrugged.

"So, what's new?"

"I just thought you should know. We might consider tak-ing a defensive position for the foreseeable future."

"Yeah?"

"Limiting your, ah, new ventures to those that could eas-ily withstand scrutiny. Perhaps a few public relations ges-tures. I hear this late-night basketball league that the Mayor's pushing in Roxbury could use sponsors."

"You're worried about the feds, so I gotta give money to let some niggers play hoop?"

"You might think of it as working on your image."

"We can't find something in my neighborhood?"

"I think that has limited value. The papers play it as a Godfather thing."

Johnny sighed.

"Bastards can twist anything. I ask you, where's the ac-countability?"

Glasser sneaked a look at his watch again, pursed his lips. *Son of a bitch, trying to get rid of me.* Johnny took out a cigar, made a show of peeling back the wrapper, rolling it, sniffing it, digging for his clipper.

"If you feel strongly about it, we could find another charity," the lawyer suggested.

"Nah," Johnny said, lighting the cigar. "You're right. Give it to the niggers."

He puffed, meditatively. Held the cigar up to the light.

"See this," he said. "This is what it's all about. Give me a good cigar, I'm okay."

"You're a lucky man," Glasser said, his voice tight.

Johnny raised an eyebrow.

"Yeah?"

"You have time for the pleasures."

"I make time. If not, what's it all worth? You know what I mean?"

Glasser nodded, glanced at his watch. Johnny puffed, the cloud spreading between them.

"I'm telling ya," he said. "A good cigar. That's all I want."

26

Jimmy Florio sat over his coffee, watching Frankie work his way through a half dozen assorted. He held a napkin under his chin when he bit into a jelly-filled, chewed for a moment, then wiped his mouth on the back of his hand.

"It's the guy," Jimmy told him. "I can feel it."

"So he's got your name. All that says is the cops can't touch you. Otherwise, you'd be sitting up in Suffolk County Jail right now. They figure, let this guy sniff you awhile, get you nervous, maybe you'll do something stupid."

He took a bite of a glazed, caught the waitress's eye and lifted his coffee cup.

"I don't know," Jimmy said.

"He got you spooked, Jimmy?"

"I didn't say that."

" 'Cause if all it takes to spook you is some guy hangin' around, talkin' to the neighbors, we got a problem."

"Frankie, I'm in this thing . . ."

"Yeah, you are."

"I want it done, is all."

Frankie gave him a big smile, clapped him on the shoulder.

"I was hoping you'd say that."

Walsh stopped back at his hotel, checked at the desk for messages. Haggerty had called, wanted to see him. He went up to his room and ordered an early lunch from room service, putting it on the room tab. Nobody had said anything about meals, but he'd guarded witnesses in the past, and he figured the same deal applied.

He watched twenty minutes of CNN until the sandwich came, then brewed a cup of coffee in the little pot that came with the room. It was lousy coffee, Maxwell House in a foil packet, and it came out weak and gray. He poured it into the bathroom sink and tried again, using two packets and half the water. It gave him one drinkable cup, which he took black.

He put in a call to Haggerty, got the secretary again, but she told him that Haggerty could see him in half an hour.

"Take a cab," she said. "We'll reimburse you."

It wasn't a long ride, just over the Longfellow Bridge and down Cambridge Street to the courthouse. The traffic was

light, and the driver, a Haitian with a taste for gospel on the radio, barely slowed as they swerved through a series of yellow lights. At the courthouse, he scrawled a few lines on a receipt, took a five from Walsh, and sped off.

Haggerty was in her office, her jacket off, shifting a dozen bulky files onto a library cart. She waved him into a chair.

"My old cases," she told him. "Riccioli pulled me off about six matters to oversee this operation."

"Is that good?"

"If we pull this off, it's a coup. He's dumping this stuff on some senior attorneys. Everybody wants onto this project."

He smiled.

"Glad to help."

She stuffed some folders onto the cart, looked at him.

"Does that make you angry?"

"Why should it?"

"Maybe you think I see you as a career move."

"No," he said. "You're the only person who came out to see me since I got out of Concord. I could tell you gave it some thought."

"It's true, though. No question this will help me."

He shrugged.

"If it works. Anyway, I was a cop. I know the system. Somebody gets a promotion for doing something, I figure that's progress."

She nodded, leaned against the cart.

"They said at the hotel you were out."

"I had some errands to do."

"I don't think it's such a good idea for you to be running around town."

"It gets kind of quiet in a hotel room."

"And in a grave."

He laughed.

"That's cop talk."

"But it's true."

She moved behind the desk, picked up a sheaf of papers and tossed them across the desk.

"How come you didn't tell me Keenan came to see you?"

"I figured you knew."

"It took us a couple days to trace the car. It was registered to the department, but they didn't have a record of anyone using it."

"Tony likes to bend the rules."

"Clearly." She took up her pen, pulled a pad off a stack of papers. "What did you talk about on your walk?"

"It was a personal matter."

She looked at him.

"I don't buy that."

"You don't have much choice."

"This is not a good time to start holding out on me."

"I told you, it was personal. It's not pertinent."

"Everything is pertinent, Jack. You had an affair, that's personal. As best we can tell, Keenan brought you evidence that the woman you were with on the night of the accident was killed."

Walsh shook his head.

"He brought me a pair of glasses, like the ones she wore. I wouldn't call that evidence, and you wouldn't take it to court. It was a message. For all I know, they went out and bought the glasses. They're not hard to find."

"Tell me what you talked about, Jack."

He shook his head.

"I'm sorry."

She pushed the pad aside.

"All right," she said. "I can't force you. But I hope you know what you're doing."

Me too, he thought. *Me too.*

Russo stuck his head into the office, caught Johnny's eye. Johnny waved him in, the phone pressed to his ear.

"Seven percent," he said into the phone. "That ain't much."

He rolled his eyes, covered the receiver with his hand.

"Fucking accountants."

Then he caught the expression on Russo's face.

"Hang on," he said into the phone. "I got another call."

He punched the hold button, rested the phone on his shoulder.

"What is it?"

"It's Angie. She's locked in her car. . . ."

"She's locked *in* her car?"

"Up at Hanover and Commercial, Johnny. Where Vinnie was killed. She's just sitting there, blocking traffic. A cop was gonna break the window, but some guy from Trio's recognized her. They wanna know what to do."

Johnny sighed, rubbed a hand across his face. He dropped the phone into its cradle, the light still flashing.

"Get the car."

A cop was directing traffic, waving a line of cars past the gray Seville. The drivers slowed as they went past, turning their heads to peer at the woman sitting behind the wheel, motionless, her face a mask. Johnny pointed to an open space at the curb.

"Pull up over there."

He got out, smoothed his tie. Then, calmly, he crossed

through the line of crawling traffic to the car, tapped on the window. Angie stared ahead, as if she hadn't heard it. For a moment, Russo wondered if she was dead. Then she blinked, slowly. He saw tears on her face.

Johnny waved the cop away, dug in his pocket. He produced a ring of keys, unlocked the door. Gently, he eased her over to the passenger side and slid behind the wheel. He lowered the window and spoke to the cop, who nodded, raised a hand to stop the line of passing cars. Johnny made a U-turn across both lanes, pulled up next to Russo. The passenger window slid down, and he leaned across Angie. She had her purse open now, fumbling with a cigarette. Her face was calm, but the tears shone on her cheek. Her hands were shaking.

"I'm gonna go on home," Johnny said. "Something comes up, you call me."

Russo nodded, watched him drive away. Then he swung the car around, headed back to the office.

Christ!

"Riccioli wants to move on this thing. He's looking at Friday night."

"That's quick."

"D'Angelo's holding the rehearsal dinner for his daughter's wedding up in the North End. The wedding's on Sunday. Riccioli thinks we'll catch him off guard."

Walsh laughed.

"What's the plan, I go as the priest?"

She smiled.

"Nothing so imaginative. We figure a tip-off. You're scared, and you've come back to seek conciliation. You'll be meeting with a neutral party in a restaurant near the wharf.

After the meeting, you've got a walk to the car. We figure they'll go for a snatch."

"What's to keep 'em from shooting me, right there?"

"We're putting out word that you have information to trade, but you'll only give it to Johnny."

He shook his head.

"It won't fly. What kind of information could I have to trade?"

She smiled.

"That's Riccioli's trump card."

"I kinda figured he'd have one."

"An informer."

Walsh was silent, looking at her.

"You offer him evidence," she went on, leaning forward. "We'll prepare it. Documents proving to him that there's a government informant in his organization."

He looked out the window, thinking about it.

"How would I get these documents?"

"You're an ex-cop, you've got friends on the force. They want to help you out."

He hesitated.

"These documents, they're good?"

She sat back, gave him a broad smile.

"They're better than good. They're real."

"Yeah?"

"We're pulling them out of our files."

"A real informer."

"For sixteen months now. DEA turned him, but we get copied on the good stuff."

"Won't this put your guy at risk?"

She shook her head.

271

"There's nothing in the documents we'll give you to establish his identity. It's time to reel him in soon, anyway. We leave him in place too long, the information gets too old for the indictment. Hard to confirm. And if Johnny goes down on this score, our boy will just show up at the trial to tap the last nails in his coffin."

He rubbed his face with both hands, a habit that Haggerty was getting to know well. It meant he needed time to clear his head, to get his thoughts straight. He looked up.

"So why do you need me?"

Haggerty leaned back in her chair, smoothed her skirt. "This is a dual-track investigation."

For a moment, Walsh flashed on Riccioli, his broad smile.

"Meaning what?"

"Those guys that shot up your house, they had shotguns, right?"

Walsh met her gaze. "I don't know. I wasn't there."

"From the damage, then."

"Sounds right."

"Why not handguns? Easier to hide."

Walsh shrugged.

"I guess they wanted to be sure."

Haggerty smiled. "Well, there you are. An informant isn't a sure thing. They hide things, they don't tell you everything. If there's something that makes them look bad, they change the story. You put 'em on the witness stand, they get a case of nerves, they start denying everything. You don't hunt bear with a popgun."

"So you need me for insurance."

She shook her head. "You're part of an independent operation. They don't tell me much about the informant. Just

what I pick up from the files. And the guy who's running that show doesn't know much about you. Same target, different game."

Walsh thought about it, nodded. She leaned forward.

"Anyway, your situation puts teeth in the indictment. We can get him on RICO, but this is homicide, maybe kidnapping. Riccioli wants to push the dirty crimes. He thinks the family trials are getting too corporate, almost white-collar. Wants to remind everyone what these guys are."

There was a squeaking from the hall outside, as someone wheeled a cart down the hall. Walsh could hear the hum of the secretary's printer start up, remembering that it was on a table next to the door. Thin walls.

"Who's the neutral party?"

"We thought of Tony Keenan."

He laughed.

"That's a good way to think of Tony," he said. "Neutral."

"Can you swing it?"

"You mean get Tony to set it up?" He shrugged. "I guess we'll find out."

"It needs to be credible," she said. "The documents we can handle. Tony's your job."

"An informer. Tony'll love it." He grinned, shook his head. "Like old times."

"With all the wiretaps and surveillance," she said, "it's still what scares them most."

He was silent for a moment, then he said:

"You know what it tells me, though? If I go down, and the operation burns, you still got him. Somehow, that doesn't make me confident."

"On the contrary. We're handing you some papers that

could put the whole indictment at risk. You think we're not gonna be behind you on this?"

Behind me, he thought.

"Jerry was behind me," he told her. "Look what happened to him."

27

The weather got cold, overnight. The temperature plunged to hover near zero, and the television news showed commuters struggling home, bundled to the eyes against a biting wind. Leaving his hotel, Walsh wished he'd brought a warmer coat, maybe a pair of thermals. It wasn't a day for working the streets.

He didn't have a choice. He had to head down to Washington Street to catch Keenan when he came on duty, then he figured he might swing by Florio's neighborhood, see if he'd stirred up any trouble.

At the Drug Control Unit, the desk sergeant was new. He glanced at Walsh without recognition, went back to his newspaper.

"Keenan around?"

"You're too late. He came in, dropped his stuff off and headed out."

"You know when he might be back?"

The sergeant shrugged.

"Keeps funny hours, you know?"

"You mind giving him a message?"

He sighed, laid the paper aside, and pulled a message pad out of a drawer.

"Tell him Jack was looking for him."

"That's it? Jack?"

"He'll know."

"Lotta Jacks around."

"Just tell him. It's important."

The sergeant shoved the pad back in the drawer.

"Ain't it always."

Coming out of the building, Walsh caught a glimpse of a face in the window opposite. A man was standing with his back to him, looking at the sale placards in the window of a CVS. He had a scarf pulled up high on his neck, but when the morning light caught the glass, Walsh could see it was Brodie. The guy was better on city streets. Probably thrilled to get back, not have to stand around in the trees, freezing his ass off.

He headed for the subway. Give the poor guy a chance to get warmed up.

When Walsh was in his unit, Keenan had been sharing an apartment in a fancy building on Marlborough Street with

his girlfriend, a photographer, but he spent a lot of his time in a splash pad he kept near Chinatown. He'd stop by there a couple times a day, drop something off, or pick something up, change his clothes if they were running a low-end bust on a dirty street.

Walsh came out of the subway on Boylston, walked over to Keenan's old building. He checked to make sure that the name pencilled in below the third floor bell was the same—*T. Cleary, No Soliciting*—then rang the bell. A moment passed, then the door buzzed. He pushed it open, caught a glimpse of Keenan looking down at him from the landing. He was waiting in the door of the apartment, arms folded, when Walsh reached the top of the stairs.

"I'll tell ya, Jack. Couple times when we were running busts, you did things made me wonder if you had a death wish."

He grinned, shook his head.

"Now I know."

"What makes you think he'll buy it."

"I guess it doesn't matter. I don't have a lot of options, do I?"

Keenan was sprawled on the battered couch, one leg draped over the arm. He held a bottle of Sam Adams against his chest. Walsh sat at the Formica table. A shoulder holster hung over the back of the chair next to him, with a black automatic sticking out. Keenan followed his glance.

"You like it? That's my baby." He reached over, slipped the gun out. "SIG Sauer, nine-millimeter. I wanted to, I could go out to Logan, bring down a plane with this thing."

"Get much call for that?"

"Hey, we picked up a load off an Avianca flight out of

Caracas a couple weeks back. They had it sewn into the fabric on the seat backs." He grinned, hefted the gun. "You never know, right?"

"No, I guess not."

Keenan dropped the gun back into the holster.

"You know that holster comes from the same word as hell? Makes sense, don't it? Means a hidden thing, what you hide something under. Like helmet, same word."

"So working undercover . . ."

"You got it. Hell and back." He laughed. "Professor over at Harvard told me that."

"You go back to school?"

"Nah, we busted him during a buy in Brighton."

He took a sip from his beer.

"So you want to talk to Johnny D'Angelo." He shook his head. "Gonna apologize for killing his kid? Maybe reason with him, man to man?"

"My brother's dead, Tony. They shot him in the store."

"Thought he was you?"

"I guess."

"Man, for a serious guy, Johnny hires some clowns. How many times they go after you now?"

"Two, maybe three."

"You feel sorry for the guy, right? Came back here to give him a clean shot."

"I'm sick of living this way."

"Beats the alternative." He nodded at the gun hanging from the chair. "Tell you what, I'll do you both a favor. Whip out my nine, do you right here. Save you some time, spare him a load of mental anguish when his guys fuck it up again. Maybe earn myself some strokes. What'ya think?"

"I'd rather do it my way."

He shrugged.

"Suit yourself."

"You gonna help me, Tony?"

"I don't know. Looks kinda risky to me. They do you, I could come out smelling bad."

"You already smell bad."

Keenan looked at him.

"That a personal remark, Jack?"

"Lady up at the U.S. Attorney's office took a real interest in your little visit to me. Asked some tough questions about the team."

"Yeah? What'd you tell her?"

"I told her I had enough enemies."

Keenan tapped the neck of the bottle with his fingers.

"Well, you're right there."

Walsh picked up the tail again on the way to the subway, caught a glimpse of him as he emerged from an alley beside a Chinese laundry. A thin cloud of steam billowed from a vent near the street. *Stay warm.*

He caught a train over to East Boston, walked over to Florio's neighborhood. The cold had driven everyone inside, and the streets were deserted. Walsh thought about the mail carrier with sympathy. Some days, only hookers, cops, and mailmen are dumb enough to be on the streets. And even the hookers think twice.

Add me to that list, Walsh thought, grimly. *I qualify.*

He stopped in at the Doughboy, took a table by the window. The same waitress was behind the counter. He nodded to her, pointed at the coffee.

"Morning," he said when she came over.

"Whatever."

The coffee raised a cloud above his cup. He slipped his gloves off, rubbed his hands in the steam. The waitress looked down at him.

"You eating?"

"Nah, just waiting for a friend."

"Could be a long wait."

She went back to the counter. Walsh sipped his coffee, looked out the window. A woman dashed from her car to the entrance of a grocery, her head wrapped in a scarf. A row of icicles glinted in the sunlight, still frozen hard.

Walsh got up, went over to the counter, and ordered a large coffee in a paper take-out cup. He snapped a lid on the cup, gathered a couple sugars and a creamer.

"Watch my stuff for a minute?"

The waitress shrugged. He stepped outside, looked down the street to where Brodie stood in the door of a funeral parlor. He walked over, handed him the coffee.

"Too cold for this shit," he said. He stacked the packets of sugar and the cream on top of the cup. "Far as I'm concerned, you could come on inside."

Brodie looked down at the coffee, then met his eyes. He shrugged.

"I get paid for this."

"Not enough."

As he walked away, Brodie called out:

"You gonna be in there long?"

He stopped, spread his hands.

"Long as it takes."

He went back to the restaurant, slapping his arms against his chest. As he came in, the waitress was hanging up the phone. He hunched over his coffee, holding the cup in both hands, close to his face. The waitress came over with the pot.

"Drink it down," she said. "I'll warm it up for you."

"Thanks."

She went back to the counter, leaned on the register. Walsh watched the street. After a few minutes, the door of the Florio house opened. Two men came out. They walked down the block toward him, waited on the opposite corner for the traffic to clear, and crossed over. Walsh felt their eyes on him as they came past the window, pushed through the door.

"Hey, Maxie." Jimmy Florio went over to the counter, slid onto a stool. "You want to set us up here?"

The other man paused in the entryway, looking down at the headline displayed in the window of the *Herald* machine. He dug in his pocket, took out some change, and bought a paper. When he looked up, Walsh met his eyes. The kid grinned at him, held up the paper so Walsh could see the headline: "COP SHOT!"

Defeo. Walsh watched him walk over to the counter, take a stool. He nudged Florio with an elbow, held out the paper.

"You believe this? Cop goes to arrest a guy in the Combat Zone, drops his gun. The guy picks it up, shoots the cop in the foot. Makes the front page."

Florio laughed.

"Bad shot."

Defeo pulled off his jacket. He was small, but there was strength in his arms. Wiry, like one of those Hispanic flyweights who dart around the ring, trading quick jabs. Best kind of fighter to watch, Walsh thought. Easy to underestimate.

Not much chance he'd see this kid go a round. He had the face of a punk, a weak mouth that curled up at one corner when he smiled. The kind of stare a kid learns in the street,

281

practices in front of a mirror until he feels tough enough to pull a gun on a couple walking home from the movies, or go out to the Fens and beat up a queer. No discipline in the eyes, like a fighter gets after years of staring down his own failures of spirit and strength every day in the gym. Just a punk, who can tell you that a gun beats a knife, a knife beats a fist, and the last man standing calls himself tough.

Don't underestimate this one, Walsh thought. He's smart enough to get close to D'Angelo, even win his blessing to marry the daughter. Stay quiet. Let him show you his weakness. He'll lead with it.

The waitress put a box of donuts and two coffees in front of them. Florio poured a half cup of milk into his coffee, then spooned in some sugar. Defeo took it black. He had the paper spread on the counter before him. He laughed.

"Says here the cop disarmed the suspect. You wanna guess what that means?"

"The guy stepped off the curb, got hit by a bus. Dropped the gun, right?"

"I'll buy that."

Defeo swung around on his stool, looked at Walsh.

"So what'ya think, buddy? The bus driver get the collar?"

Walsh shrugged.

"Sounds good."

Defeo nudged Florio, grinned.

"There ya have it. You wanna know something, ask the man."

Florio swung around, gave Walsh a hard stare.

"I know you?"

"Do you?"

He jerked a thumb over his shoulder.

"Maxie here says you been asking questions about me."

Walsh sipped his coffee.

"Man's subtle," Defeo said. "A highly trained professional."

Florio watched the cup settle back on the table. His eyes came back to Walsh's face.

"People round here, we think that's rude. You lookin' for me, I live up the block."

Walsh smiled.

"I'm not looking for you."

"No?"

"Just letting you know I'm here." Walsh shifted his gaze to Defeo, then back. "Thought you could use some help."

They looked at each other, then back at him. Defeo grinned, picked up a donut off the counter, took a bite. He wiped a hand across his mouth.

"Seems to me you're the one needs help, buddy."

"Me?" Walsh raised his cup, looking at them over the rim. "My turn comes, I won't miss."

Defeo's eyes darkened. He put the donut down, wiped his hands on a napkin. He put a hand in his pocket, came out with a roll of bills. He peeled off a few singles, dropped them on the counter.

"Hey, Maxie," he said to the waitress. "Our friend here wants anything, it's on me."

He took a toothpick from a dispenser on the counter, chewed it as he looked at Walsh.

"Don't worry," he said. "Your turn's coming."

Walsh dropped a few coins on the table, reached for his coat. On the sidewalk, Florio was laughing, slapping Defeo on the shoulder.

"Hey," the waitress called after him. She held up Defeo's money. "You're all paid up."

"Keep it," he told her. "You earned it."

He went out the door after them. They turned east, walking past the door where Brodie stood, sipping his coffee, then headed up Meridian. Brodie raised an eyebrow as Walsh came past.

"Sorry. Coffee break's over."

Walsh stayed a half block behind them. They didn't look back, but he could tell by the way they eased along that they knew he was there. At the corner of Decautur, they stopped for a moment, exchanged a few words. Walsh came up on them, but before he reached them, Defeo crossed the street. Florio turned north, heading for the wharves.

Walsh hesitated at the corner. *Set up*, he thought. He watched Defeo turn into a liquor store on Meridian. *Defeo hangs out a few minutes, lets his buddy lead me over to the wharves. Then he comes along, closes the box.*

He turned, saw Brodie watching him from a storefront across the street. He glanced over at the liquor store, then back to Brodie. Brodie lit a cigarette, nodded. He walked up the street to the corner, leaned against a bus shelter. From there, he could look up Meridian to the liquor store, or turn his head and see Florio walking away on Decautur.

Walsh turned, followed Florio toward the docks. Just before the street ended at a chain link fence, he turned off, headed down a narrow street that cut between two warehouses toward the wharves. Walsh glanced back up Decautur, but the street was empty. Up the alley, Florio moved out of sight beyond a loading dock.

Walsh tugged at the hem of his coat, felt the .25 drop into

his palm. A small gun, but it could put a man down. He slipped it into an outer pocket, kept his hand on it.

He started down the alley.

"Hey, Frankie!"

Eddie Fauci grinned at him over a beer display next to the counter—two girls in bathing suits, holding little trays where you stacked six-packs, so the customers can take 'em from a lovely lady.

"How ya doing, Eddie?"

"I figured you'd be in here, get some courage. Whatcha got, two days left?"

"Yeah." Frankie smiled. "Wedding's on Sunday."

"Life sentence, my man."

"Tell me."

Fauci jerked a thumb at the display.

"Like my new ladies? Maybe you wanna take one home. Last chance."

"Quiet type."

"Hey, don't knock it. I been with some girls make this pair look lively."

Frankie leaned against the counter.

"Got a favor to ask."

"Need a place to hide till the wedding's over?"

"You still got that gun I sold ya?"

The smile vanished from Eddie's face.

"Yeah, I got it." He reached under the counter. "You in trouble, Frankie?"

"Nah, just need to make a point."

Eddie laid the gun on the counter.

"Don't go messin' up now. Johnny won't like it, you miss the wedding."

Frankie reached across the counter, took a paper bag from beside the register. He snapped it open with a flick of his wrist, slipped the gun inside.

"I'll get it back today."

Eddie shrugged.

"No hurry."

Brodie leaned against a bus shelter, watching Defeo go into the liquor store. It was a tough call. Let Walsh walk away, or follow the kid. Brodie recognized him from the briefing photos, figured that something was breaking. He wished there was a phone on the corner, so he could call in a backup. For a moment, he thought about walking up to the liquor store, see if they had a pay phone, but just then, Defeo stepped onto the street, paused to slip a paper bag into his coat pocket, then walked away. He was headed back up Meridian, away from the wharves, taking his time.

Brodie glanced up the street toward the docks. He could see Walsh's blue jacket moving out of sight. Walsh was the assignment, but Defeo was turning into a side street now, cutting back toward the wharves. Brodie made a decision, went after him.

He had a hunch they'd all end up at the same place.

Frankie crossed Central Square, turned west on Liverpool and went down a block before turning toward the wharves. He could feel the guy back there, but whenever he sneaked a look, the street was empty. He'd caught a glimpse of him back by the Doughboy, standing in the door of Nardi's Funeral Parlor, saw him again at the bus stop when he came out of the store. He'd been looking for him from the moment they hit the street. He'd never known a cop who wasn't

chickenshit. Wouldn't make a move without someone watching their backs.

He bent to tie his shoe, heard footsteps. Looking back, he caught a glimpse of the guy ducking into a doorway. He smiled. All that training, but if you know cops, you know they're gonna be there. Once you got that figured out, you can spot 'em.

The guy was a problem. If he got too close, he'd mess it up. Frankie looked down at his watch. No time to shake him. He'd have to take him down.

He cut between two houses, then down an alley behind a Chinese restaurant and a hardware store. Just beyond, a door was propped open with a length of pipe. He slipped inside, pulled it closed. He was in a storeroom, huge rolls of carpet leaning against the walls. A-1 Carpets, he remembered, by the docks. His mother used to come here about once a year, trying to get some color in the living room. A stack of pipe leaned against the wall. He picked one, about eighteen inches long, hefted it.

Footsteps in the alley. The guy was moving slow, looking for him. Probably had a gun. He'd be reaching for it about now, getting nervous in that alley. The steps halted near the door, then went past.

Frankie threw the door open, swinging the pipe high and hard. The guy turned, tried to sidestep it, but the pipe caught him on the side of the head, knocking him against the Dumpster. He slid to his knees, blood gushing from his ear. His head sagged against the cold metal.

Frankie looked down at him.

"Sorry," he said. "Private party."

Then he dropped the pipe and walked away.

* * *

287

Walsh came around the corner of the last warehouse, saw Florio standing at the edge of a wharf, smoking a cigarette. He glanced around. Nobody else in sight.

Now what?

He walked over to the wharf. Florio flicked his cigarette into the water.

"Where's your buddy?"

"He'll be along."

He was trying not to look nervous, but his eyes kept shifting over Walsh's shoulder. Further down the wharf, a man came out of a building, got into a truck and drove off.

"Thought we might have a little talk."

"We got nothing to talk about."

"No? Your buddy likes to talk. They got about a dozen tapes over at the federal building. One of 'em, he's showing this guy an ear, got it in a plastic bag. He mentioned your name."

Florio looked at him. Then he leaned over and spat into the water.

"You're fulla shit."

"I heard that tape, I said, 'What a coincidence. I got a brother who's missing an ear.' "

"I don't guess he'll miss it."

Walsh drew his hand out of his pocket, let the gun dangle at his side. Florio glanced down at it, smiled.

"You threatening me?"

Walsh shrugged. He raised the gun and racked the slide, chambering a round. Florio's smile grew thin.

"I didn't kill your brother, man."

"No? Who did?"

Florio shook his head.

"That's not how it works."

"What? You scared?" Walsh put the gun under his chin, pushing his head back. "Someone might hurt you?"

He swallowed, the gun bobbing. His eyes shifted to look over at the alley, then came back to Walsh's face. He smiled.

"Hey, Frankie."

Walsh looked at his eyes. The back of his neck began to itch, but he kept his gaze on the kid's eyes. They flicked over to the alley again, came back. Without looking, Walsh knew they were alone. Then the kid's eyes darkened. He'd made a decision.

The kid stepped back, his hand rising to brush the gun aside. From the corner of his eye, Walsh saw a flash. He grabbed at Florio's other hand as it emerged from his pocket, and the knife slashed his palm. He grunted, twisted away as Florio lunged at him. The blade thrust into his coat below his left arm, and he felt a burning in his ribs. He jerked the gun out of Florio's grip, brought it down against his chest, pulled the trigger.

Florio staggered back, sat down hard. The knife clattered to the ground. There was a hole in his down jacket, and a few feathers drifted into his lap. He leaned back against a piling. He looked up at Walsh, shook his head. Then he winced, closed his eyes, and, slowly, tilted to one side, off the edge of the wharf.

Walsh caught his breath, slipped the gun back into his pocket. He looked down into the filthy water. The body floated, facedown, rocking gently with the waves. He took out his handkerchief, wrapped it around his hand. He could feel blood trickling down his side, and the hand throbbed. The knife at his feet was dark along the blade. For a moment, his mind flashed on another image, a knife skidding away from his shoe across dirty tile.

Then he turned and walked across the wharf, past a loading dock to the street.

"Ah, shit."

Defeo looked down at the body in the water. The waves from a ship passing in the channel tossed it against the piling. A thin layer of scum had formed along the outstretched arms.

He'd heard the shot, coming up the alley. He pulled the paper sack out of his pocket, drew the revolver. But when he reached the wharf, it was empty. Just a clasp knife lying there, the kind Jimmy kept on his dresser. He used to bring it along when they went out, pulling it out in the car, flicking his wrist to make the blade snap into place.

There was blood on the knife.

Defeo shook his head, kicked it into the water.

28

In the drugstore, the pharmacist behind the counter took one look at Walsh and shook his head. The handkerchief around his hand was soaked with blood, and his coat was slashed across the chest.

"You're gonna need more than Band-Aids," he said. "You should get a doctor to glance at that hand. Looks nasty."

Walsh looked down at it. His chest was on fire, but the hand looked worse, a gaping slash across the base of the palm. A little lower, and it would have hit an artery.

"There a walk-in nearby?"

"Health Center over on Gove. Somebody there could sew you up, maybe."

He took the bag out onto the street, unwrapped the gauze and wound it around his hand, over the handkerchief. It didn't do much for the bleeding, but he might get fewer looks on the subway. He unzipped his coat, wincing as he pulled the shirt away from the wound on his chest. It wasn't deep, but he'd need stitches to close it. He unraveled some gauze, pressed it into a flat strip, and laid it over the cut. Then he broke off some surgical tape with his teeth, and fixed it in place. A woman stopped to stare at him. He smiled weakly, zipped up his coat.

He wasn't sure why, but he wanted to get out of East Boston before seeing a doctor. It wasn't likely that anyone at the Health Center would drop a dime on him, but they'd get his name, and you couldn't be sure whose cousin might be working behind the desk. The bandages would hold him for a while, until he made it over to Boston City, or better yet, Cambridge. Less risk dealing with the police, if one of the doctors called it in. Knife wounds, he knew, attract attention.

In the subway, people moved away from him. No doubt the pain showed in his face. He leaned his head against the window and thought about Florio, wondered if he should feel something, if the kid's face, torn between pain and disbelief, would return to haunt his dreams. He hadn't gone there to kill him. Florio had called the play, and he'd been unlucky. A little faster, and the kid would have sunk the knife in his chest.

But he'd moved too slow, and now he was floating in the channel. The body would sink, when the water soaked his coat. If it stayed cold, the channel might freeze. Could be

weeks before he turned up. If not, the homicide boys would have some tough questions for him.

He got off at Harvard Square, walked down to the river. The footbridge was deserted. The wind whipped off the river, and a few drivers on Memorial Drive looked at him like he was crazy. He leaned on the wall, looking toward Boston. He waited for a gap in the traffic, then slipped his hand in the pocket of his coat, palmed the tiny gun, and slid it up his chest. He turned, let his hand dangle over the wall, and dropped it in the river. Then he walked back to the square, caught a bus up Cambridge Street to the hospital.

Anne wrestled the laundry basket up the stairs from the basement, nudging the door closed with her foot. Becky sat in her high chair, banging her plate with a spoon, her face coated with a beard of applesauce.

"More, Mommy!"

"Okay, honey. Let Mommy put the laundry down, all right?"

She carried the basket down the hall, dropped it on her bed. Picking up a pile of Danny's pants, she crossed the hall, pushed his door open with her hip. He was standing on a chair beside his aquarium, his arm in the water up to the elbow.

"Danny!"

He jumped down, the chair toppling. Water dripped onto the carpet from his hand.

"What're you doing?"

He shrugged, his eyes not meeting hers. She dropped the pile of laundry on his bed, and glared at him, hands on her hips.

"Didn't I tell you not to play in the water?"

He nodded.

"Were you chasing the fish?"

"No."

"Then what were you doing?"

He shrugged again, and she felt the exasperation rise within her. She wanted to catch his arm, make him look at her. From the kitchen, she heard Becky start to wail. She threw up her hands.

"Leave the fish alone, Danny. If you torment them, they'll die. Do you understand that?"

He nodded, his gaze fixed on the carpet.

She sighed, turned on her heel. She left him standing there, the water forming a pool next to his foot.

D'Angelo hung up the phone, sat in silence for a long moment. He looked up at Tommy Russo, who shrugged.

"Could be a setup."

Johnny nodded.

"Thursday night. You believe it? We got the fuckin' rehearsal dinner at, what? Seven-thirty?"

"Eight. Angie told me to tell you."

Johnny looked at him.

"She called you, told you to tell me?"

"You were in the john."

"Why do they call it that? I hate that. The john. It's a fuckin' toilet, is what it is."

"All right, so you were in the toilet. She called, told me to tell you."

"Like it matters. We'll still get there a half hour early. Angie'll make me get dressed at five, we'll sit around for two hours, then we'll go. They'll put us in the bar till the table's ready."

"You want me to go over early, make sure it's set up?"

"Nah, you're gonna have to handle this other thing."

Russo looked at him.

"So you want to do it?"

Johnny sat back, smoothed his tie. He flicked a piece of lint off his suit.

"Yeah, Tommy. I wanna do it."

Russo shifted in his chair.

"You buy this story, he wants to talk?"

"I don't have to buy it. He wants to come see me, I'm not gonna stop him."

"And if it's a setup?"

"What's the problem? Some guy wants to see me. Let him walk over to the restaurant, we'll talk. Nothing wrong with that, right?"

"He could be wired."

"Hey, Tommy. I *assume* he's wired. I talk to this guy, I'm talkin' to the judge, okay?"

Russo thought about it, nodded.

"What about the other one, Keenan?"

Johnny smiled.

"Bring him along. I got some ideas."

29

Walsh peeled his shirt off gingerly, tossed it on the table. He saw Haggerty's eyes move across his chest to the bandage. The technician came over to him, ran his fingers across it.

"Cut yourself shaving?"

He took Walsh's hand, turned it over. His finger pressed the strip on his palm lightly.

"These are real, right? Someone pulls these off, they see blood?"

Walsh nodded. The technician pursed his lips.

"Could be a problem. Anybody frisks you, they feel it.

Probably make you open your shirt. Of course, it might distract 'em from the shirt."

Haggerty was looking at him.

"What happened?"

"Ran into an old friend."

The technician laughed.

"What, in a Buick?"

Haggerty gave him a hard stare.

"Wire him up," she said.

The technician shrugged, took a shirt off the worktable, handed it to Walsh.

"The mike's in the collar. Battery pack fits under the knot of your tie. You get about two hours on the charge, from the time you switch it on." He turned to Haggerty. "That enough time?"

"That should be fine."

He nodded, turned back to Walsh.

"It's a portable transmitter, like the old T-4, just a lot smaller."

"Any more reliable?"

"We're up around sixty-five percent with these. They still give out sometimes. The range is still pretty low, so the surveillance team has to stay on you pretty tight. You want to stay out of basements if you can help it."

"What if I can't?"

The technician helped him slip the shirt on.

"Do what you can. It should transmit, unless you get down a few floors. Bottom of a parking garage in one of these downtown buildings, you might have some trouble."

He fumbled with the buttons, wincing as the stitches in his hand pulled. The technician pushed his hands away, buttoned it up. Walsh turned his back on Haggerty, un-

zipped his pants, and tucked the shirt in. The technician adjusted the wiring at his collar.

"You'll have a little bulge, but nothing too bad. You wearing a coat, I guess?"

"Pretty cold out there."

"You'll get the best results indoors, anyway. It picks up some wind noise outside. The coat might muffle it a little, but you can unzip it a couple inches. Don't wear a scarf, though, or we'll end up with a whole tape of your heartbeat."

"I could live with that."

The technician smiled.

"You're all set, then." He put a hand out, smoothed the collar. "I'll tell you what I tell everyone. Best thing is to forget the wire. Don't try to lead the conversation, just act natural. Let the other guy incriminate himself, okay?"

Walsh nodded.

"Good luck to you, then."

He followed Haggerty to the elevator. They rode in silence, got off at her floor. She led him down the hall to her office, closed the door behind him.

"Some cops from Paris Street fished Jimmy Florio out of the harbor this morning."

He settled into the chair beside her desk.

"Yeah? I'm sorry to hear that."

"Did you kill him?"

He looked at her.

"Should I call a lawyer?"

She crossed to her desk, sat down.

"I gather you know we had a tail on you."

"I had some idea, yeah."

"He didn't report in last night. Turned up in an emer-

gency room at Boston City Hospital with a skull fracture. Somebody took a pipe to his head. They found him a couple blocks from where Jimmy Florio floated."

Walsh looked at her.

"You got any coffee?"

She fixed her eyes on her desk.

"There's a limit to what I can overlook, Jack."

"I'm not asking for any favors."

"I need to know what happened yesterday."

He thought about it for a moment. She watched his eyes bear in on a picture on her desk—her mother as a young woman, sitting on a wall at the beach in Miami.

"I wanted some answers," he said. "I never got to ask the questions."

"Did you kill him?"

He shook his head.

"I won't answer that one."

"And the cuts?"

He looked away, watching the sky beyond the window. She frowned, moved some papers around on her desk.

"You having fun, Jack?"

He met her gaze, saw the anger there.

"I'm sorry," he said. "I'm trying to play it straight with you, but I have to protect myself."

She glanced at the bandage on his hand.

"Looks like you're doing a good job."

He smiled.

"A kid with a knife I can handle. It's lawyers scare me."

Her eyes flashed. She started to say something, stopped. She looked away for a moment, then sighed, opened her drawer and took out the coffee.

"You still want this?"

"I'd love some."

She took the pot off the shelf, spooned some coffee into the filter, poured water into the pot from her jug.

"I'm just trying to understand you."

"I want to stay alive."

She looked up at him.

"By tossing Jimmy Florio into the channel?"

"If that's what it takes, yeah."

"You want to explain that?"

He shook his head.

"So we're back to square one."

"I'm afraid so."

She dropped the coffee back in the drawer, reached over to plug in the pot.

"I always feel like I'm pulling teeth with you."

"I've got a lotta bad teeth."

They sat in silence for a while. Walsh looked out the window at the office building across the street. A man was standing at the window, phone pressed to his ear. The man ran his hand over the top of his head, laughed. The coffeepot made a ticking sound as it brewed.

At last, Haggerty took two cups out of her drawer, poured the coffee, passed one of the cups to Walsh. Then she opened a filing cabinet behind her, took out a manila envelope, tossed it across the desk.

"That's for Johnny."

He opened the envelope, glanced at the papers. Transcripts of informant interviews, dated a few months back. The first page was stamped "United States Department of Justice, Organized Crime Task Force, Confidential."

* * *

The phone rang four times, and the machine picked up. He listened to Anne's voice, her cautious greeting, but declined her invitation to leave a message. He waited a moment after the tone, listening to the silence, trying to think of what he might say.

I'm sorry.

He hung up, leaned his head against the pay phone for a moment, his eyes closed. Then he picked up the phone, dialed the number Keenan had given him.

"You know what I could go for tonight?" Keenan grinned at him. "Italian food. How 'bout you?"

The car turned onto Causeway Street, passed the Boston Garden. Walsh thought about Danny, the excitement shining in his face in the photograph. He tried to remember if the Celtics had won the game, hoped for Danny's sake that they'd shaken their mid-season slump for one night. He'd checked the score in the *Globe* at the time, but couldn't remember it.

"The way it's set up, we go to Café Vesuvius, wait for a call." Keenan turned right onto Prince. He slowed, looking for a parking space. "Johnny wants to see you, we walk on over to the restaurant."

"That's good. I could use some coffee."

"Yeah?" Keenan glanced over at him. "You gonna fall asleep on me?"

"I get some coffee, I'll be fine."

"It was me, I'd be climbin' outta my skin."

"Yeah, well. I've had some time to think about it."

Keenan swung the car to the sidewalk next to a hydrant, flipped the visor down to show the Boston Police card. He turned to look at Walsh.

302

"You sure you wanna do this? Not too late to back out."

"Let's go."

They got out, walked down toward Hanover. They passed the restaurant, lit up behind drawn curtains, on the opposite side of the street. Keenan paused, lit a cigarette, glancing over.

"You ever eat there?"

"I took Anne. We had tickets to a show at the Wang."

At Hanover, they crossed the street. Tourists shivered on the sidewalk, looking at the menus posted in front of the restaurants. A crowd of men came out of a sports club, laughing. They shouted to each other in Italian. One of them returned to the door, his face flushed, and made an obscene gesture.

Keenan took Walsh's arm, pulled him past.

"Just what we need," he said. "Get shot on the street before we get there."

Walsh spotted a familiar face on the opposite corner, a female cop who used to work prostitution decoys in the South End. She turned the corner, walked away. Further down the block, a man stepped out of a bakery, came toward them. He passed them without acknowledgment.

Keenan glanced at him.

"That was Sid Billow. You see him?"

Walsh shook his head.

"Well, I saw him. He walked right past me."

He put a hand on Walsh's chest, stopped him.

"What's the story here? This a setup?"

"Tony, there's been surveillance on me from the day I walked out of Concord. You know that. D'Angelo, he knows. Nothing I can do about it."

"That was federal. Billow's local." He glanced around.

"They're running a box, right? Moving the tails around us on the side streets. Shake and bake."

Walsh shrugged.

"Takes a lotta people, Jack. It's a major operation. Means they knew where we were heading tonight."

"It's not hard to figure out. D'Angelo's sitting in a restaurant over on Prince Street. Where else would you run it?"

Keenan shook his head.

"This is stupid, Jack. D'Angelo's guys live around here. I see it, they'll spot it quicker."

"So? Maybe they'll let me walk outta here."

Keenan looked at him. His eyes narrowed.

"You wearing a wire, Jack?"

Walsh spread his hands.

"You want, you can look."

Keenan pushed his hands aside. "Look, I bring you in here with a wire on, they're not gonna like it."

Walsh smiled.

"Since when do you worry what they think, Tony?"

"Don't fuck with me, Jack! This thing's a setup, I wanna know."

"A setup. That's like someone's on the pad and a cop gets killed, right? We could talk about that."

Keenan's hand came up, gripped Walsh's tie. For a moment, they stood there, motionless. Then Keenan smiled. His hand released the tie, smoothed it.

"Fuck do I care, anyway? You're gonna be dead in an hour."

Walsh adjusted the knot of his tie, shifting the battery back into place with the tip of his thumb. Keenan took a dollar from his pocket, stuffed it in Walsh's pocket.

"Get yourself some coffee. I'm outta here."

Then he turned and walked back up Hanover. Walsh watched him until he turned the corner onto Prince, then sighed, crossed the street toward the café. Café Vesuvius was crowded, the windows fogged by the steam from the espresso machines. Walsh got a table after a few minutes, ordered an espresso and a cannoli. *What the hell,* he thought, smiling. *Live dangerously.*

He sipped at his espresso, watched a fashionable couple at the next table. Two men sat by the window, avoiding his gaze. Not cops, he thought. D'Angelo's guys, keeping an eye on him. The cops were outside, watching the café from up the street. He glanced around at the other patrons. A pair of young women caught his eye. They were nicely dressed, talking quietly. But as he watched, he noticed that both kept their handbags on their laps, open. One had moved her chair to face the entrance, and as they talked, their eyes moved over the room.

He ate the cannoli, scraped the plate with the edge of his fork. When his espresso was gone, he ordered a decaf. No sense getting too wound up. He sat over it for a while, then drank it down in a few gulps. When the waitress came by, he waved her over.

"What's the damages?"

"You're all set," she said. She gave the table a quick wipe. "Mr. Russo took care of it."

He looked up. Tommy Russo was leaning on the counter, chatting with the cashier. His face was familiar from Haggerty's file. The *consigliere,* who mediated disputes, arranged bail, conveyed orders.

"I didn't see him come in," he said.

The waitress laughed.

"He came in through the kitchen," she said. "Tommy likes to see what's fresh."

She went back to the counter. As she passed, Russo glanced over. He turned back to the cashier, said something that made her laugh. She looked over at Walsh. Russo straightened, adjusted his tie, came over to the table.

"Mr. Walsh?"

"That's right."

"I understood you'd have company. A mutual friend."

"He had to leave. Something came up."

Russo frowned.

"That's unfortunate." He glanced at his watch. "I'll have to make a call."

"Fine."

"Excuse me."

He walked back to the counter, leaned across and picked up a phone. *Christ,* Walsh thought. *They own the place.* He looked down at his empty cup. His mouth felt dry.

Russo spoke into the phone, listened, then hung up. He came back to the table.

"Let's take a walk."

"We're rolling."

Cardoza watched through the windshield as the two men stepped onto the sidewalk. Two men in leather sport coats followed them onto the street, staying a few paces behind them. They walked up the street toward the corner where the van was parked, passed alongside.

"Walsh and Russo," he whispered into their headset. "Moving west on Hanover, with an escort."

A kid went by on a bike, wearing headphones. Two women came out of the café. Further up the street, a cab

pulled to a stop, the driver peering up at a building, hitting the horn. He waited for a moment, then pulled out, circled the block. At the corner of Prince, a young couple argued volubly. Whispered reports came over Cardoza's headphones as they turned onto Prince, crossing toward the restaurant. The last, from the driver of a tow truck that was hitching up a car parked in a driveway a few doors from the restaurant, came seven minutes after Cardoza's warning.

"They're in."

Cardoza made a note in the log.

"All right, pull back," he said into the headphones. "Perimeter positions."

He turned and looked at a man hunched beneath a pair of headphones, squinting as he listened. Beside him, Haggerty twisted a sheet of paper into a crumpled tube, her face set. The man with the headphones looked up, smiled.

"He switched it on," he whispered. "Nice clear signal."

Cardoza let his breath out. He grinned at Haggerty, but she didn't see him. Her eyes were fixed on the floor, her hands busy twisting the wad of paper.

Walsh stepped into the restaurant foyer, one hand rising to adjust his tie. Ahead was the main dining room, the entrance roped off. Two men stood on either side of the doors, glaring at him. Inside, several dozen people were crowded around a long table. They broke into laughter. Russo took Walsh's arm, steered him to the left, into a narrow bar that ran along one side of the restaurant. Four men sat at the bar, watching him come in. Their sport coats were cheap, cut tight across their broad shoulders.

Russo led him to a small table at the end of the bar, put a hand up to stop him.

307

"Weapons?"

Walsh shook his head.

"I gotta check you out."

Walsh raised his arms, and Russo patted him down. He reached around behind him, ran his hands over the small of his back. Then he bent, ran a hand down each leg, patted his ankles.

"All right," Russo said. "Have a seat. You want a drink?"

"Soda's fine, thanks."

Russo turned to one of the men at the bar.

"Ricky, get the man a Coke."

The man scowled, reached across the bar and drew a Coke. He took a napkin from a pile, came over to the table, set the glass down. Walsh reached into his pocket.

"How much?"

"Forget it."

The man went back to the bar, slid onto a stool. He grinned at the guy next to him, shook his head.

"All right," Russo said. "You're fixed up here. I'm gonna go back in there, finish my dinner. Johnny'll be out when he's ready. You need anything, you tell Ricky."

Walsh nodded, watched Russo walk back to the main dining room. He sipped his Coke, ignoring the stares of the men at the bar. When a few minutes had passed, he wondered if he should turn off the wire, but decided against it. The technician had warned him not to play with it, just turn it on and leave it. He hoped the batteries held up.

After a while, the dinner started to break up. A few couples slipped into the bar for their coats, returned to the dining room for one last stop at the head of the table, then left. Ricky went behind the bar, opened several bottles of red

wine, a few more of brandy, and put them on a tray. He carried it into the dining room, came back to the bar.

"Need some more champagne, Bobby," he said. "Where'd you put it?"

"It's back there." The man jerked a thumb toward a door at the end of the bar. "Got a half a case still."

"Get me a couple bottles, would ya?"

Walsh glanced back as the man passed through the door. It was a storeroom, cases of liquor stacked up. He swallowed, remembering a story he'd once heard about a D'Angelo family soldier, accused of stealing from a dice game, who'd been beaten to death with a whiskey bottle in the back room of a bar. Afterwards, D'Angelo had emerged, opened the bottle, and fixed himself a drink.

A shadow fell across the table. He glanced up, and Johnny D'Angelo looked down at him. He was dressed in a gray silk suit, like an expensive lawyer. His silver hair was swept back, and a diamond sparkled on his little finger. He frowned.

"Walsh?" He pulled out a chair, sat down. "I hear you wanted to talk to me."

Johnny raised a finger to Ricky, at the bar.

"Anisette."

They sat in silence as Ricky poured the liqueur into a tiny glass and carried it over to the table. Russo came in, sat at the bar. Johnny flicked his fingers, and the other men slid off their stools and left the room. Russo remained. Johnny turned to him.

"Where's Frankie?"

"He's talkin' to his mother."

"Get him."

Russo went into the dining room. When he came back, Defeo was behind him, grinning. He leaned over the bar, drew himself a beer. Johnny raised his glass.

"*Salud*," he said. Walsh lifted his Coke. "You're a brave man, Mr. Walsh. Comin' in here."

"I've heard you're a reasonable man."

D'Angelo smiled. He glanced over at Russo.

"Hear that, Tommy. I'm reasonable."

Russo laughed.

"Hey, I always thought so."

Johnny raised the glass to his lips. His eyes appraised Walsh over the rim. He savored the liqueur, taking a small sip, then smiling with pleasure. He nodded at Walsh's glass.

"I heard you were a drinking man."

"Not anymore."

"You go to meetings?"

"Sometimes. Mostly, I just don't drink."

Johnny nodded. "Best way." He smiled. "You go to those meetings, you gotta talk about your sins?"

"That's part of it, yeah."

"Confession is good for the soul, eh?"

"Something like that."

"I believe in confession," D'Angelo said. "I was brought up Catholic. I was an altar boy, even. It stays with you, that stuff, even when the faith is gone. Confession, contrition, penance."

His eyes locked on Walsh's, piercing.

"What do you have to confess, Mr. Walsh?"

Walsh reached for his pocket. Russo slid off the bar stool, caught his hand. Johnny studied Walsh's face, then waved him off. Walsh reached into his pocket, drew out the envelope, laid it on the table.

"I want to live," he said. "Like a man, out in the day-light."

Johnny looked down at the envelope, then back up to Walsh's face. He smiled.

"Don't we all."

Again, they sat in silence. Johnny sipped his drink. He nodded at the envelope.

"Gifts can be dangerous, Mr. Walsh."

"I wanted your attention."

Johnny laughed.

"Oh, you got it. You got my full attention!"

Walsh felt a chill run up his back. His throat felt dry. He pushed the envelope across the table.

"There's a federal informant in your organization. The U.S. Attorney is preparing a grand jury indictment based on his testimony. Word is, you're gonna take a fall this time."

"I've heard that before."

"Maybe you better look at the documents."

Johnny considered him for a moment.

"I'm curious. Why're you telling me? I take a fall, maybe you sleep better at night."

Walsh shook his head.

"That's what the feds tell me. Relax, he's going down. But the way I figure it, you've got friends. They send you away, I'm still watching my back."

Johnny picked up the envelope, looked at it.

"So you bring me this. You figure I'm gonna trade my grief, the memory of my son, for a few pieces of paper."

"I grieve for your son, Mr. D'Angelo. I'll suffer for that night the rest of my life. I'm offering you a warning."

D'Angelo was silent for a moment, then he smiled. He gestured at Defeo, leaning on the bar.

311

"Frankie here, he's gonna be my son in a couple days." He turned to look at him. "What do you think, Frankie? Should I accept this gift?"

Defeo sipped his beer, his eyes fixing on Walsh over the glass. He set the glass on the bar, shook a cigarette out of his pack, nodded at the envelope on the table.

"That don't change nothing," he said. "I say we just do this thing."

D'Angelo shifted his glance to Walsh, smiled.

"The young ones," he said. "You try to teach them patience, show 'em how to take things slow, but . . ." He shrugged. "Honor, that's what matters to the young."

Walsh leaned across the table, tapped the envelope with one finger.

"What's in here could save *your* life."

D'Angelo sipped his drink, considered.

"You want my forgiveness?"

"I want both of us to live without fear."

D'Angelo looked at the envelope. He ran one finger along the seal. Then he put it back on the table.

"You've got a son."

"I never see him."

"I do. Sometimes, I drive out to Medford. I sit there in my car, watching him play in the yard."

Walsh felt himself go pale. He fought the urge to reach out and drag D'Angelo across the table by his hair. He took a deep breath, held his silence.

Johnny watched him, nodded. "You think I'm threatening your kid. Makes you want to rip my arms off, right?"

Walsh hesitated, nodded. Johnny spread his hands.

"So now you know how I feel."

"I know. I had a brother. We weren't close, but he was my

brother. Last week your boys put a bullet through his head. Then they cut off his ear. A trophy."

Johnny frowned.

"I didn't order that," he said, quietly. "I don't know nothing about it."

Walsh looked over at Defeo.

"Ask him, then."

D'Angelo turned, looked at him. Defeo shrugged.

"Hey, Johnny. The guy's fulla shit."

D'Angelo looked back at Walsh. Then he pushed his chair back, stood up.

"Let's go someplace we can talk."

Walsh picked up the envelope, held it out. Johnny shook his head.

"I take that, it's a felony."

"Least of your problems, I'd say."

"Can you give me a name?"

Walsh hesitated, shook his head.

"Then what good is it?"

"I don't know your people. It might give you an idea."

D'Angelo met his eyes.

"And if I figure it out, what do you suggest I do about it?"

Walsh looked at him.

"That's your decision." He held the envelope out. "You want it?"

"Bring it along. We'll talk about it."

Walsh got up, reached for his coat. He paused, glanced down at his empty glass. He pulled a dollar from his pocket, tossed it on the table.

D'Angelo, turning away, stopped. He reached down, picked up the dollar. It was marked in red pen—a row of

lines and boxes across the back of the bill. He looked up at Walsh.

"What's this?"

"A tip."

D'Angelo nodded. He dropped the bill on the table, turned away. As he passed the bar, he draped an arm across Defeo's shoulders.

"C'mon, Frankie," he said. "I want you along on this."

Defeo grinned. Walsh followed, pulling his coat on. He glanced back, saw Russo go over to the table, pick up the bill. Russo sighed, shook his head, slipped it into his pocket.

In the foyer, D'Angelo paused.

"Frankie, get the car." He turned to Walsh. "Wait here."

He crossed the dining room, bending to whisper to a woman at the head of the table. Walsh recognized her from the trial, the way her hand came up to brush her hair back. She listened for a moment, glanced up. Her eyes met his, and she went pale. She gripped her husband's arm, pointed.

"Johnny!"

Walsh felt Russo's hand on his back, shoving him out the door. As the door swung closed behind him, he heard screaming.

30

From the back of the Cadillac, Walsh watched the tourist spots of the North End flash past in a swirl of lights. Defeo drove fast, crossing Hanover, then cutting down a back street toward the docks. Walsh tried to imagine the surveillance team scrambling to keep them in sight, but the thought of the frenzied activity on the streets around them reminded him of his isolation, the car speeding him away. He sat back in the seat, letting the moment carry him along.

Beside him, D'Angelo sat in silence. Russo leaned on the front seat, his eye on Walsh. Defeo whistled quietly between

his teeth. He turned south on Commercial, followed it past the waterfront office buildings to Congress, where he turned east, across the bridge into Southie. He swung down a narrow street near the wharves, past a row of warehouses, and pulled up next to a loading dock. He jumped out, opened the rear door, and dragged Walsh out by the arm.

D'Angelo walked up a ramp to a narrow door, took out a key, and opened it. Inside, he switched on a row of neon lights.

"Time's up," Defeo whispered. He gripped Walsh's shoulder, shoved him up the ramp.

It was cold. Sides of beef hung from hooks in the ceiling, and boxes of meat were stacked on low carts. Johnny led the way down a narrow aisle between the rows of meat. At the back of the building, he stopped at a wide refrigerator door, yanked the handle, stepped back. Defeo shoved Walsh inside.

They stood between racks of meat, their breath coming out in clouds. D'Angelo reached out, straightened Walsh's tie.

"Maybe you're wired," he said. "Tommy says he patted you down. But my lawyer, he tells me they got these remote transmitters, you can hide 'em anywhere." He smiled. "Very nervous guy, my lawyer."

Then he turned, waved a hand around the meat locker. Pigs hung from their ankles. Boxes of steaks lay on stained tables.

"This is good meat, the best. I got an interest in this place. They send me a box of these steaks every week, it'd make you cry to see 'em. You cut into these things, the cow screams. I like to come in here when I got business to dis-

316

cuss, 'cause there's no way to bug this place. All this metal, it blocks the transmission."

He studied Walsh's face, his eyes boring into him.

"Tell me about it," he said.

"What?"

"The night you killed my son."

Walsh felt his stomach seize up. He took a deep breath, let it out. Johnny shoved him back against a table, put his face right up close to him. His voice was a hoarse whisper.

"I want to know."

Walsh swallowed, his throat dry.

"I was with a girl. We went to a motel over in Charlestown, then she was hungry, so I was taking her to eat over on Hanover. We'd been drinking some, and I guess my reactions were slow. We got up by the corner of Hanover, and this guy starts backing into a parking space, so I went to pull around him, and . . ."

He shook his head, his throat tight.

"I didn't even see him. It was like he came outta nowhere. I hit the brakes, I can remember the pedal going all the way to the floor, my leg locking it down just before we hit. It was like there was nothing there, didn't slow us down at all. That's all I remember."

Johnny held him against the table for a moment, his hand on Walsh's chest, right below the microphone. Then he stepped back, tugged at his jacket to smooth it, turned to Defeo.

"Gimme your gun."

Defeo grinned at Walsh, reached under his coat, pulled out a battered .38. He passed it to Johnny.

D'Angelo hefted it, glanced up at Defeo.

"What'd you, buy this off a nigger?"

"Nah."

"You sure it works?"

"Yeah, I'm sure."

Johnny turned back to Walsh, smiled.

"He's sure."

He popped the gun open, spun the chamber, snapped it shut.

"I lost a son," he said to Walsh. "Tomorrow, I'm giving my daughter away. I go home after the wedding, I'm alone with my wife. Empty house, you know?" He gestured to Defeo. "This one, he wants to fill my boy's shoes. He loves my daughter, she loves him. It's an *opportunity*."

"Hey, Johnny." Defeo spread his hands. "It's not like that."

Johnny ignored him, his eyes fixed on Walsh.

"You got kids. Imagine how it feels to have 'em snatched away from you." He shrugged. "I mean, you're gonna say, 'A wedding! It's not like losing a daughter, right? It's gaining a son.' Some shit like that. But I grieve, you know? For my son, for my daughter. For myself, maybe. You spend your life building something up, then . . ." He waved a hand. "It's gone."

He looked down at the gun in his hand.

"Ten years I been climbing outta the gutter. Cleaning up the money, putting it into legitimate investments so my kids . . ." He winced, shook his head. "So my daughter don't hafta get the filth on her hands that I did. Ten years trying to wipe the blood off my hands, and I'm standing here with a gun, I'm gonna blow it. And for what? 'Cause I gotta make a point, show all my people in the street I don't accept an injury?" He shrugged. "To me, this makes no sense. Grief, I can take. It's part of life, right? I got my grief, I

live with it." He looked at Walsh. "I don't forgive. I don't forget. Sometimes, on a good day, I accept."

He gestured to the gun.

"I dream about this. Standing here with a gun in my hand. All I gotta do is raise up, blow a hole in your face. At the trial, sitting there looking at you, thinking 'bout my boy lying there in the ground, I could've killed you with my hands. But I want you to know, I pick up a gun, it's not in anger. I'm protecting my family. You know what I'm saying?"

Walsh hesitated, nodded.

"Good."

Then he raised the gun, shot Defeo in the chest. The sound was deafening in the tiny locker. Defeo stumbled back against a pig hanging from a hook. He grabbed at it, and it came down with a shearing sound, landing on top of him. The pig's eye stared up at them.

D'Angelo snapped the gun open, spilled the bullets onto the floor. He took out his handkerchief, wiped it down, then handed it to Walsh.

"You get a match on this for your brother, I wanna know." He reached over, took the marked dollar from Russo's pocket, tucked it into Walsh's coat.

"Thanks for the tip," he said.

Then he turned and walked out. Russo looked over at Walsh, shrugged.

"Your lucky night."

He followed D'Angelo into the darkness.

31

Riccioli came out of his chair, slammed his fist down on the desk.

"You're telling me you witnessed Johnny D'Angelo commit a homicide, and you let him *hand* you the gun?"

Walsh sat in silence, his face calm. Haggerty noticed that he seemed to have withdrawn into himself, thinking his own thoughts. Riccioli threw up his hands.

"Jesus Christ! You were a cop! You don't have enough sense to preserve the prints?"

"He wiped it down."

"Shit!" Riccioli turned to the window, sighed. "We can't even use your testimony. Your prints are on the gun. A jury'd laugh us out of the courtroom."

He turned on Haggerty.

"What happened to the goddamned surveillance? You were there!"

She shifted in her seat, her face flushed.

"We expected they'd stay within the North End. We had a tracking unit ready, but they were moving pretty fast."

"So you lost them?"

"No. We had them into Southie, and the transmitter was working right up until the end, but in that refrigerator . . ." She shrugged. "Johnny knows the drill."

Riccioli shook his head. He looked over at Walsh, and his eyes darkened. He aimed a finger at him.

"You cut a deal in there, didn't you."

Walsh looked up at him, his eyes calm.

"What kind of deal could I cut?"

Riccioli glowered.

"Defeo takes a bullet, you walk out of there, and we've got no case. That smells like a deal to me."

Walsh shrugged.

"Ask your informant."

Riccioli fixed him with a glare for a moment.

"Get him outta my sight."

Haggerty left him at the elevator.

"I'm sorry," she said. "I'd see you out, but . . ."

"Don't worry about it."

She caught his arm.

"Will you be okay?"

He shrugged.

"I figure I'm safe for now. In a way, he was right. I did cut a deal in there." He smiled as the elevator doors opened. He stepped in, turned to face her. "I just don't know what it was."

Then the doors closed, and he was gone. Haggerty stood there for a moment. Looking up, she caught a glimpse of her reflection in the metal doors. Her eyes looked empty. Like betrayal. She turned and walked back down the hall.

Walsh stopped in a coffee shop down the block from the federal courthouse, checking out the rush-hour crowd. He forced himself to eat a few bites of breakfast. The coffee tasted bitter. He could feel the exhaustion settling in his body.

He'd spent the night giving his account, over and over, to the homicide cops, the federal agents on the Organized Crime Taskforce, the prosecutors. They'd hauled him back to the meat-packing plant in the early morning hours to walk through the scene with a crowd of investigators from the different jurisdictions, each pressing him with questions, probing for inconsistencies. They'd put a typed deposition in front of him, and he'd signed it, initialed each page. His hands were checked with paraffin, the police technician assuring him it was strictly routine in gunshot cases. When it came out negative, he felt the interest in him diminish. He became a witness, whose value lay in the testimony he'd signed. Useful, perhaps, but no longer an object of interest in his own right. If Johnny lets him walk, his stock goes down. Weird.

He raised a finger for the waitress, held up his cup. As she came over with the pot, he got up, went over to the pay phone in the entryway. The number was on an auto dealer's

card in his wallet, stuck in an inner slot, as it had been for almost five years. He dialed it, and a woman answered.

"I want to report a fire," he said. He gave her the number on the phone and hung up.

He bought a *Globe* and a *Herald* from the machines, went back to his table. He put cream in his coffee to make it easier on his stomach and flipped through the papers. He found it on page fourteen of the *Herald*, a body discovered in a meat-packing plant in South Boston, the victim as yet unidenti-fied. So Riccioli had decided to play it down, let it emerge as an unsolved crime, hiding the government's hand. He won-dered when they'd release Defeo's name. Sometime today, probably. The wedding was tomorrow. If they released it in the news cycle—claiming they'd just gotten results on the prints, maybe—they'd get banner headlines in both Sunday papers. He smiled. MAFIA GROOM GUNNED DOWN!

He tried to imagine the scene at D'Angelo's house. Johnny tight-lipped, vowing revenge as the women shrieked. Russo lurking in the background, his face a blank.

The pay phone rang. Walsh slid out of his booth, walked over and picked it up.

"You report a fire?"

"Yeah, Tony. I thought we should have a talk."

The line was silent for a moment. Then Keenan said:

"Jesus, you got more lives than a cat."

"You see the *Herald*?"

"I glanced at it. Who'd they find?"

"Defeo."

Keenan gave a thin whistle.

"You do it?"

"No, Tony. In a way, you did."

"Yeah? How's that?"

"You handed me a dollar before you split."

Keenan laughed.

"You look in his wallet?"

"No, why?"

"You'da found another one just like it. He keeps it folded up in with his credit cards."

Walsh was silent, rubbing at his face with one hand.

"You telling me you set this up?"

"Where you at, Jack?"

"Pay phone."

"Drop a dime. I wanna hear it."

Walsh put a coin in the phone. It gave a short series of clicks.

"Okay."

"You expect 'em to find two bodies, Tony?"

"Hey, don't be cynical. Maybe I was giving you a way out."

"Maybe. Or it could be you figured they'd check my pockets before they dumped the body. Johnny'd see the bill, and you'd get two for the price of one."

"Ah, Jack. Listen to you. What can I say to that?"

"Wouldn't matter much what you said."

"I guess not." Keenan sneezed, twice. "So why'd you call, Jack?"

"Maybe I'm giving you a chance."

Keenan laughed.

"Yeah, we're a couple of gentlemen, all right."

"Any reason I shouldn't take you down?"

"Any way you could, Jack?"

"Yeah, Tony. Last night, I put it all together. You gave me the connection, and I figured out the rest."

"Yeah? What'd you work out?"

"How you and Frankie Defeo were taking down the dealers."

Keenan was silent for a long moment. Then he sighed.

"Listen to you. The way you're talking, I don't have much to lose. Put a guy against a wall, he gets nasty."

"That a threat?"

"Call it what you want."

"I've been threatened a lot lately. It stops scaring you after a while, you know?"

"Jack, the last time you called this number, you were drunk. Sitting in a bar, convinced some guy at the next table was from Internal Affairs. You wanted me to go clean out your house, get rid of anything they could take you on. You remember what I told you then?"

"You said I had nothing to worry about."

"That's right. Well, I'll tell you the same thing now. I've been to your house, and there's nothing in it you should worry about. You get me?"

Walsh took a deep breath.

"Where are they?"

"They're safe."

"What do you want?"

"Give me something to lose, Jack."

32

Keenan nudged the car onto the edge of the sidewalk beside a hydrant, flipped the visor down to show his police I.D. It was late, and the narrow street was empty. Snow had been falling since dusk, the wipers scraping the thick flakes into a ridge at the bottom of the windshield. The children slept in the backseat.

He'd been driving them around for hours, hustling them from the Chinatown apartment twenty minutes after Walsh's call. He'd headed up through the city streets to Revere, where he stopped at a pay phone, made a few calls.

Then down 128 to the Pike, as he quietly assured Anne that he'd get them home quickly, as soon as he got the message that it was safe. They rode out to Worcester, stopped in a diner, the kids fidgeting in the booth as they waited for the food. After five minutes, the baby started to wail. Keenan could feel himself tensing up, wishing he could just tell 'em to shut up, for chrissakes. Smoking one cigarette after another, until he saw Anne glare at him, waving the smoke away from the baby. He stubbed out a half-smoked Marlboro, stalked off to the pay phone. When he got back, the food was there, the kids eating quietly. *If this is what being a father's like,* he thought, *you can have it.*

He killed the engine, but left the heat running.

"Wait here," he told Anne. "I'm gonna take a look around."

She caught his arm.

"You're meeting Jack here?"

"A few blocks." He smiled. "I guess he's making a point."

"What do you mean?"

"I suggested we meet over in Cambridge, but he turned it down. Had to be in the North End."

He got out of the car, walked down the block, pulling his coat tight around his neck. He walked down to Hanover, crossed over, cut through the cobbled square behind the Old North Church, past the statue of Paul Revere, then turned up a side street toward Copp's Hill, watching for parked cars with men sitting in them, couples out for a stroll in the snow, any sign of surveillance. If it was there, he couldn't see it. He climbed the steps to the top of the hill, crossed into the park, and found a bench.

A few minutes passed. In the cemetery, a thick crust of snow was forming on the graves. Someone was buried

there. He tried to remember from when they walked the Freedom Trail in school. A famous guy. But all he could call up was the old story about the Redcoats using the headstones for target practice, getting the locals into an ugly mood before the rebellion broke out. He grinned. Like being a cop.

He heard the crunch of footsteps in the snow behind him. Walsh paused at the top of the steps, his breath clouding in the cold air. He limped across the cobbled park, slumped onto the bench, rubbing his knee.

"I always know when it's gonna snow," he said. "I get this ache in my knee. If it moves up to my hip, means we're getting a couple inches."

Keenan nodded at the cemetery.

"You remember who's buried up here?"

"Cotton Mather."

"Yeah? What'd he do?"

Walsh shrugged.

"I don't know. He was a Puritan or something."

"Puritans." Keenan grinned. "I'll tell you, we've come a long way. You imagine if this guy woke up, saw the two of us sitting here. Not too pure, huh?"

"And we're the good guys."

"So they tell me."

They looked out at the field of graves, the wind blowing the snow into swirling shapes. Walsh looked up into the falling snow. The flakes appeared in the dark sky like the faces in a dream.

"What'ya say we get this over with?"

"You wired, Jack?"

"No."

Keenan glanced around at the empty park, the wind moaning in the trees.

"One thing about this weather, it sure fucks up a surveillance. You remember those busts we tried to run during the blizzard a few years back? I was sitting in a car a half block from the house, I couldn't see shit. All we got on the tapes was wind."

Walsh nodded.

"That was a bitch."

"So you got something for me?"

Walsh got up, put his foot up on the bench and drew a small plastic bag from his boot. Keenan reached for it, but Walsh stepped back. He held it up by one corner, tapped the evidence tag attached at the seal.

"This what Frankie Defeo was looking for in my house, Tony?" He held up the bag, the streetlights glinting on the bullets. "That's what tipped me off. I thought, what's this guy think he's gonna find? I was expecting killers, not a search party. Then it dawned on me." He tapped the bag with one finger. "Three bullets. This one, right here, it's a perfect soft-tissue round. Ballistics guys get limp for a bullet like this. Nice, clean signature—might as well put your phone number on it."

Snow had begun to cling to the bag. He brushed it off.

"Jerry had a buddy in the ballistics lab. Got these rounds out of two floaters they picked up in the harbor a couple weeks before Jerry died. He had this informer, a black kid who sold bottles down in Fields Corner, said a couple of couriers had got off the plane from Bogotá and gone for a swim. Couple days later, the kid's dead, they pull a bullet out of him that could be a brother to these here. Jerry, he's gettin' scared. One night, we go out for a drink, he pulls out

this bag, tells me the whole story. Only problem is, he's not *sure*. He's got some bullets, some street talk, but no proof. Doesn't even want to give me a name. *Somebody's* dirty, he says. Somebody's way outta line. Two days later, we go out on a tip—*your* tip, Tony—and Jerry don't come back. Your basic bullshit raid on some kid working out of a triple-decker, the kind of thing we did every night. Only the kid starts shooting, Jerry catches a bullet. We go in the apartment, you know what we find?"

Keenan shrugged.

"Three keys, still wrapped in newspapers from Bogotá. Stinks like fish. I start thinking about Jerry's informant. I go look in his locker, and there's the bag. Now I got the bullets, the story, but no proof."

"So you filed a complaint."

Walsh smiled.

"You were real subtle, Tony. Even my uncle didn't know who'd put the word out. All he could tell me was that I wasn't gonna testify. He said if I tried, they were gonna find all kinds of nasty stuff with my name on it."

"Nobody's clean, Jack."

Walsh shrugged.

"At the time, that mattered to me. Things change."

The van was hot. Haggerty leaned her face against the fogged window, the headphone pressed to her ear. She strained to hear against the wind, catching a word every few seconds. A moment later, it faded out altogether. She heard wind, then a dull clatter, the muted hum of an engine.

Beside her, Cardoza muttered to himself, adjusted a dial. He picked up a second headset, whispered into the mike.

"Jimmy, you're off 'em again. We got some harbor

sounds, maybe." He listened for a moment. Haggerty caught a snatch of talk, then the wind again.

"Come back on it, Jimmy."

The voices came back, thin behind a roar of static. She thought she heard laughter. Cardoza dropped the headset on the panel, shrugged.

"Best we can do," he told her. "The parabolic only works when the weather's right. The wind screws up the reception, blows it off line a little, you get nothing. We shoulda miked the guy."

Haggerty shook her head.

"He's not part of this operation."

Cardoza looked at her.

"He don't know 'bout this?"

"No."

He shrugged. "Not much we can do. Maybe play with the tape a little, run it through some filters. That's about it."

Haggerty nodded. She pressed the headset against her ear, straining to make out the faint words. Her mind kept drifting to Riccioli, brushing past her in the hall as if she'd had her shot and blown it. He'd spent most of the day closeted with Ken Shaw, his top assistant. Besides Riccioli, only Shaw had a complete file on the D'Angelo matter, including Riccioli's personal notes. It was Shaw, Haggerty knew, who'd been running the other side of the case—the informer.

Sitting in her tiny office, Haggerty had felt the walls closing in. She stared at the Chagall poster, her one touch of color, and the ficus tree in the corner, dropping leaves. Shaw worked out of a corner office, a duplicate of Riccioli's with its paneling and thick carpets. Shaw, the kind of guy who lectured the new assistants on their first day, telling them

how he believed in covering your bases, how his grandpa always wore a belt *and* suspenders, just to be sure. Haggerty smiled bitterly at the thought. *He's sure now, and I'm sitting here with a pair of broken suspenders.* But she'd learned her lesson. She glanced over at her computer. On the screen was the draft of a memo to Riccioli, outlining evidence to support an investigation into corruption within the Drug Control Unit of the Boston Police Department.

Haggerty wiped at the fogged window with her palm. A television gleamed in an apartment window up the street. She rubbed at her temples, pressed the headphones against her ears.

"You see that building?" Keenan pointed across the graveyard to an empty school building, its windows broken and covered with metal grates. A sign warned of attack dogs, and Walsh pictured the dogs crouching in the abandoned halls, prowling through the echoing gym, keeping guard. "Some guy told me that Johnny D'Angelo went to that school when he was a kid. You imagine sitting in the classroom, looking out at all these graves? Christ, they go right up to the doors."

"Scenic."

"They got these little pictures on the headstones, a skull with a pair of wings sticking out of it. Like it's gonna fly away."

"We had that on a patch in the army. Airborne."

"Yeah? You used to jump outta planes?"

"Only when they made me."

"I never knew that." Keenan shook his head. "I come up here, I think about a kid sitting in a classroom, looking out

the window at all those graves. It explains something, you know?"

"What, he learned his lesson?"

Keenan grinned.

"How to make more graves. Maybe they'll put Frankie Defeo up here."

"Funny thing about Defeo," Walsh said. "I kept thinking, 'I know this guy.' His face looked familiar, but I couldn't place him. Then, last night, I'm standing there, looking down at him. He's got this huge pig lying across his chest, and it comes to me where I saw him." He gestured around him. "It was over in Eastie, about four years back. We were running surveillance on a guy who was selling dime bags out of the park over there, trying to get a line on his supplier. One night, this kid comes into the park to make a buy, pulls a gun, and takes the guy down. We got the whole thing on film. I gave you the film, Tony."

"Yeah?"

"Suppose you finish the story."

He shrugged.

"Not much to tell. He was a punk. But he had guts, you know? He used to ride the subway over from East Boston, go down to Dorchester and take down the street dealers. Stick a gun in their face, take all their money. Really pissed 'em off. Some of the gangbangers put a bounty on his head. I heard about it from my informers. When you brought me the film, I figured I'd have a talk with him."

"So you went into business together."

"I gave him a few hints. Maybe pointed him in the right direction a few times. Hey, this kid was doing our job for us. Taking the money and drugs away from the dealers, making 'em nervous. So he didn't read 'em their rights, and maybe

someone got hurt once in a while. You can't tell me you didn't wish for that sometimes. Put some fear into their hearts."

"And the floaters from Bogotá?"

"Very messy. Frankie started getting ambitious, wanted to start hitting the mainline kilo guys. I had to tell him, those guys, you need a tank to get into their houses. For a while, I kept a leash on him. Then one of his buddies who worked out at Logan told him about these Colombian guys who get off the plane every Tuesday, just a gym bag for luggage. Someone meets 'em at the gate, drives 'em away. The next day, they're getting back on the plane to Bogotá. Your basic mule profile. Frankie, he figures all he has to do is wait for these guys one day, tail 'em back to the drop, right? Only he screwed it up, shot 'em both, left their bodies in a bait shop down in Southie. He calls me up in a panic one night, 'cause he knows his prints are all over the place, wants me to go clean it up. Tells me that if he goes down, he'll swing on me, drop the whole thing in my lap. What could I do? We go down there, clean it up, dump the bodies in the harbor."

He spread his hands.

"The rest of it—Jerry's informant, all that—I don't know about. I'm dirty, but not like you think."

Walsh met his eyes, feeling the pressure to buy it, to deny that a cop could have a buddy killed. For a moment, he remembered the stink in the dark stairway, the flash and the sudden smell of cordite, Jerry's blood sticky on his hands.

"So Defeo did it, huh?"

Keenan shrugged.

"What about the night Jerry was killed?"

"Jack, it's tough to let it go when a buddy gets killed. You want to think it out, find the answer, that's natural. And it's

335

worse when it's random, 'cause that means it could happen to you, right? So you go looking for some *reason* for it—the guy made a mistake, or somebody's dirty. If you'd gone to see the counselor, like I told you, he'd have told you that. It happens all the time. Everybody goes through it. Jerry died because some piece of shit didn't want to take the bust. You want a reason? Maybe he was working outside his territory, selling off the books. He gets busted, his friends learn what he's doing, come after him. So it's worth it for him to take a shot at a cop, 'cause if he goes down, he's a dead man."

Walsh thought about it. Keenan leaned forward, his face earnest, pushing it home.

"I'm sorry about Jerry. He was my friend too. But I didn't set him up. That's not the way I do things."

"You set up Defeo."

Keenan laughed.

"Him, I could set up. And look at what happened. You walked outta there. Defeo's dead, you're alive, Johnny's scared—I'd say things worked out right."

Walsh thought about it. He glanced down at the bullets in his hand, reached into his other pocket, drew out a second bag. A single bullet gleamed in the glare of the streetlight.

"You see this?" He held it up in the light. "You wanna guess where I got this?"

Keenan was silent, his eyes fixed on the bullet.

"This one came out of the files," Walsh said. "They pulled it out of a kid you shot five years ago on a bust in Charlestown. The Review Board cleared you on the shooting, and the bullet went into a file, along with a ballistics report on your gun, that Glock you used to carry. What happened to that gun, Tony?"

"It was stolen out of my car. I filed a report."

"That's right. I saw the report in your file. It was stolen the week after Jerry died."

Keenan smiled.

"You've been busy."

"I wanted to be sure." Walsh tapped the second bag. "The funny thing about this bullet? It's a perfect match for the others. A guy in ballistics ran the tests for me this afternoon. A courtroom bullet, he called it. The kind a jury finds real convincing."

Keenan sighed.

"You really want to push me into a corner on this?"

"I wanted to be sure."

"C'mon, Jack. This ballistics guy *claims* it's a match. You know how they can fuck up, especially when they know you want 'em to find something. I mean, you've been holding those bullets for two years. You knew the story didn't hold up. Christ, you even went after the kid who shot Jerry, right?"

Walsh looked at him.

"You knew that?"

"Did I know? They found this kid handcuffed to a radiator in some burnt-out building in Dorchester, stabbed . . . what? Thirty times? Everybody figured you went after him."

Walsh looked down at the bullets in his hand. Then he smiled. He opened the plastic bag, poured the bullets into the snow. Keenan watched him, his eyes narrow. A grin spread slowly across his face.

"What're you doing?"

"I'm setting you free."

"Yeah?"

"Least I can do. You just did the same for me."

Keenan shook his head.

"I don't get you, Jack. You want to explain that?"

Walsh crumpled the plastic bag, stuffed it in his pocket. He met Keenan's eyes.

"That night the kid died? I took the handcuffs with me, Tony. They didn't find him cuffed to the radiator. I took a look at the medical examiner's report after they found the body. All it said was contusions on the upper arms. There was nothing about handcuffs in it."

Keenan's grin faded. Then he shrugged, slipped a hand into his pocket, drew out a pack of cigarettes. He shook one loose, lit it. The grin came back for a moment, but it was weary, forced.

"Stupid mistake. Kinda thing they do in the movies. Columbo, catches a guy on a slip of the tongue."

"I dream about that night," Walsh said. "Wake up with the shakes, thinking I stabbed that kid in a blackout. If I could do something like that, I'd never be able to trust myself, you know?"

Keenan nodded, the cigarette dangled from his lips. He slipped a hand into his pocket, drew out a .38. He laid it on his thigh, nodded at the bullets gleaming in the snow.

"Pick 'em up," he said.

Haggerty looked up at the fogged window.

"What'd he say?"

Cardoza shrugged.

"We'll get it off the tape."

"You gonna shoot me, Tony?"

Keenan glanced down at the gun, shrugged.

"Looks like it."

338

Walsh looked away, shook his head.

"Where's Anne?"

Keenan stared at him for a moment, then he looked away. His shoulders sagged.

"Ah, shit." He nodded at the spire of the Old North, pale in the swirling snow. "They're waiting in the car, down on Salem."

Walsh nodded, tugged his jacket tighter. Then he turned and walked away. As he reached the steps, Keenan called out:

"Jack?"

He paused, one foot on the concrete steps, looked back. Keenan raised the gun, shot him in the chest. The impact spun him around, his foot catching the step and tumbling him back off the steps into the bushes.

Haggerty flinched, jerked the headset from her ear.

"Christ, what was that?"

Cardoza ignored her, snatching up the second headset.

"Jimmy, we got gunshots. Can you see what's happening?"

Haggerty cursed, flung the headset aside. She felt Cardoza grab at her arm as she yanked the door open, stumbled into the cold night.

A light went on in the house next to the park. Keenan knelt in the snow, gathered up the bullets. He rolled them in his palm, surprised at how small they were, hardly worth the trouble. Then, as the yellow light gleamed on one bullet, a thin scratch near the base caught his eye. He looked closer, rubbing the scarred edge with the tip of one finger. His stomach sank.

"Aw, shit."

The bullets were fakes, pried out of their casings with the tip of a knife, flattened with a hammer.

"Shit!"

He slipped them in his pocket, drew the .38 again. He walked over to the steps and glanced into the bushes.

Walsh was gone.

Keenan felt the panic rise within him. He glanced up at the house, saw a curtain fall back. He climbed the steps to the road, trotted away.

Anne had the car running, the heat turned up. She'd opened a suitcase, tucked towels around the children as they slept. She looked up as Keenan got in. Her eyes were tired.

He shook his head, chewing the edge of his lip.

"He wasn't there. I hung around for a while, but he never showed."

"You think something happened?"

"Maybe. Or else he's just being cautious." He wiped the windshield with his forearm, put the car in gear. "All we can do now is take the kids back to your house and wait. If he's okay, he'll show up there."

He eased the car off the sidewalk, taking it slow on the icy cobblestones. Where the street curved, a truck had pulled up in front of a laundry. Keenan tried to squeeze past, pulling up on the sidewalk, but got wedged against a hydrant.

"Shit."

He glanced toward the end of the street, caught a glimpse of a police cruiser pulling across the end of the street, lights off. He threw it in reverse, flung his arm across Anne's seat, backed away from the hydrant. Anne glanced back at the

340

kids, Becky with her head hanging forward, pressed against the strap of the car seat, Danny awake now, his eyes watchful.

"Are we gonna see Daddy?"

"I don't know, honey. Maybe."

His hand slipped under his coat. She caught a glimpse of a small brown box.

"What's that?"

He yanked his coat over it, but not before she'd seen what it was—the plastic treasure chest from his aquarium.

She was starting to ask about it, when she caught a glimpse of movement in the intersection behind them—a man stumbling into the street, bathed in the red glow of the taillights. He was breathing hard. A gun dangled from one hand. A woman emerged from the street behind him, calling to him. He turned, looking up as he heard the car. She gasped, grabbing Keenan's arm.

"Tony! It's Jack!"

Keenan's face tensed. The car jerked as he hit the gas, swerving toward Jack. Anne saw him turn, shove the woman onto the sidewalk, then stumble, his bad leg buckling under him. The car hit him with a sickening thud, and he rolled across the trunk, his hand splaying on the rear window, then slid off one side.

"Jesus Christ!"

The car scraped against the side of a van, throwing sparks. Keenan kept his foot on the gas, fighting the wheel as they started to skid. In the backseat, she saw Danny scrambling after the tiny box, which had slipped from his grasp, scattering tiny pieces of metal that glinted as a streetlight flashed past.

"Tony, stop! You hit him!"

341

He ignored her, cutting the wheel, getting the car into the middle of the street now, picking up speed.

"Tony!"

Her hand found the purse between her feet, shoved the wallet aside, brushed against the cold metal of the gun. She pulled it out, pressed it against his ribs.

"Stop!"

He glanced down at the gun, took his foot off the gas, then stomped the brake. She was thrown back into her seat, felt his hand close on her wrist and push the gun aside. She squeezed the trigger and the gun went off, like an explosion in the closed car. The window next to his face shattered. He looked at her, surprised. The car skidded off a curb, bounced off a parked car, sliding. He leaned across, slapped her, hard. She felt him wrenching the gun from her grip, her finger curling around the trigger. This time, the shot seemed muffled, and the gun tumbled to the floor. He leaned forward to get it, but his hand kept going, skidding off his ankle and coming to rest, like a curled spider, beside his shoe. His head hit the steering wheel, the horn wailing. The car glanced off a light pole, spun, sliding up onto the sidewalk and coming to rest against the front of a store.

The children were screaming.

She saw blood, pouring from the front of Keenan's shirt.

33

The lawyer laid the paper on the bed, leaning forward to tap it with one finger.

"I need your attention here, Jack. What I'm trying to tell you is that the department's liability in this situation is limited, since Lieutenant Keenan was off-duty when the accident occurred. Not operating in his capacity as an officer. You understand?"

The room was hot, and the lawyer's face was bathed in sweat. Walsh lay with his leg hanging from a sling, his ribs wrapped in a thick pad of bandages where the bullet had

whanged off the flak vest. He had one arm draped across his eyes.

The lawyer sighed, looked up at the television flickering over the bed. The sound was off, but the pictures were the same they'd been running all day—Johnny D'Angelo, escorted by two FBI agents, mounting the steps to the federal courthouse, his face emotionless, pausing to smooth his tie before the glass doors. Then a quick sequence of shots: the U.S. Attorney smiling, speaking to a crowd of reporters on the courthouse steps; a young woman at his shoulder, turning away from the camera, her face stony; a car emerging from a basement parking lot, the man identified by the reporter as the government's witness, peering out at the television lights, his face somber as the car sped away.

The lawyer shook his head, settled back in his chair, dabbing at his face with a handkerchief.

"That's some shit, huh? They been after this guy for, what? Twenty years? They finally get him 'cause some guy's tired of being treated like a schmuck? Do this, go there. He gets sick of it, tells the guy, 'Fuck you! I'm gonna talk to the FBI.'" He smirked. "They say the guy's like an accountant, got all the numbers in his head. You imagine? Fuckin' Tommy Russo. Used to drive him around, listening to all his conversations. Now he's spilling it to the feds. He's gonna be famous. The man who got the Godfather. They'll make movies about him, right?"

He glanced at Walsh, motionless on the bed. Was he watching the TV? Maybe he was asleep. Beside him on the bed lay a tiny box. The lawyer glanced at it—a plastic treasure chest, like in an aquarium. He shook his head, picked up his sheaf of papers.

"Listen, Jack. I know you don't want to deal with this

now, but hey, no man is an island. You know what I mean, Jack?"

The toilet flushed, and the wife came out of the bathroom, returned to her seat beside the bed. She ignored the lawyer, glanced up at the television.

Jesus! He wiped his face. *Look at them. Just sitting there, letting him talk on. Not even looking at him. The wife reaching over, lifting the hand off the guy's face, and goddamned if he isn't crying, tears streaming down his cheeks now, the wife leaning over to hold him.*

The lawyer got out of there, fast.